Language, Coffee, and Migration
on an Andean-Amazonian Frontier

LANGUAGE, COFFEE, and MIGRATION

on an Andean-Amazonian Frontier

NICHOLAS Q. EMLEN

THE UNIVERSITY OF
ARIZONA PRESS

TUCSON

The University of Arizona Press
www.uapress.arizona.edu

We respectfully acknowledge the University of Arizona is on the land and territories of Indigenous peoples. Today, Arizona is home to twenty-two federally recognized tribes, with Tucson being home to the O'odham and the Yaqui. The university strives to build sustainable relationships with sovereign Native Nations and Indigenous communities through education offerings, partnerships, and community service.

ISBN-13: 978-0-8165-4070-9 (hardcover)
ISBN-13: 978-0-8165-5716-5 (paperback)
ISBN-13: 978-0-8165-4135-5 (ebook)

Cover design by Leigh McDonald
Cover photo by Nicholas Q. Emlen
Interior design and typesetting by Sara Thaxton
Typeset in Adobe Caslon Pro, Bauer Bodoni Std 2, and Proxima Nova

Publication of this book is made possible in part by the proceeds of a permanent endowment created with the assistance of a Challenge Grant from the National Endowment for the Humanities, a federal agency.

Library of Congress Cataloging-in-Publication Data
Names: Emlen, Nicholas Q., 1980– author.
Title: Language, coffee, and migration on an Andean-Amazonian frontier / Nicholas Q. Emlen.
Description: Tucson, Arizona : University of Arizona Press, 2020. | Includes bibliographical references and index.
Identifiers: LCCN 2019046952 | ISBN 9780816540709 (hardcover)
Subjects: LCSH: Ethnology—Peru—Urubamba River Valley. | Machiguenga Indians—Agriculture—Peru—Urubamba River Valley. | Migrant labor—Peru—Urubamba River Valley.
Classification: LCC F3451.A4 E65 2020 | DDC 985/.44—dc23
LC record available at https://lccn.loc.gov/2019046952

Printed in the United States of America
♾ This paper meets the requirements of ANSI/NISO Z39.48-1992 (Permanence of Paper).

For Sophie and Mae

Contents

Illustrations

Maps

Tables

Acknowledgments

I am grateful to the many friends and colleagues in the Alto Urubamba who have welcomed me into their lives over the last decade. It is only through their goodwill, patience, and generosity that I have been able to conduct this research. In particular, I thank Elvis Nelson Chorobeki Maine, Lucia Maine Palomino, Silverio Maine Capita, Asunción Menkori Korinti, and León Quispe Yapu for their friendship and assistance with my research. Thanks also to the whole community of Yokiri. Of the author's share of the profits from this book, half will be invested in community projects there.

I also thank the Consejo Machiguenga del Río Urubamba (COMARU), who took me in early in my fieldwork and gave me an office and a living space in Quillabamba. Rubén Binari Piñarreal and Plinio Kategari Kashiari have become close friends and colleagues. Thank you to Freddy Hipólito Cusirimay Cusipaucar, Justina Choquehuanca Nuñez, and Claudia Cusirimay Choquehuanca for their great friendship and hospitality in Quillabamba and on the backroads and byways of the coffee frontier. Many speakers of Matsigenka, Quechua, and Spanish spent long hours transcribing and listening to recordings with me, including Julio Korinti Piñarreal, Noemí Gonzales Solís, Gabi Vera, Henry Amador Ríos Tenteyo, Jesús Kategari Kashiari, and Armando Kaybi Álvarez, whose memory will not be forgotten. I benefited from the friendship and hospitality of Manuel Koriki, Susana Binari Piñarreal, Marco Antonio Ccopa, Santiago Vargas Usca and Higidia Ccopa, Omar Santos Pereira, Jesús Santos, and Imelda Chorobeki. I am also grateful to Padre Roberto Ábalos Illa.

I owe this book to the generous mentorship of Bruce Mannheim, Barbra Meek, Sally Thomason, Joyce Marcus, Lev Michael, Conrad Kottak, and Willem Adelaar. I am also grateful to the many friends and colleagues who offered all manner of intellectual, emotional, practical, and institutional support as I wrote various parts of the book, especially Anna Babel, Rodolfo Cerrón-Palomino, Vanessa Díaz, Hussein Fancy, Paja Faudree, Ruth Goldstein, Jane Lynch, Trent MacNamara, Jeremy Mumford, Elana Resnick, David Rosen, Dan Rosengren, Neil Safier, Joshua Shapero, Matthias Urban, Rik van Gijn, and Charles Zuckerman. Thanks also to Allyson Carter and the rest of the University of Arizona Press team for taking interest in my book and helping me improve it. Matt Gleeson's diligent editorial eye greatly improved the book's prose. I am particularly grateful to the three anonymous peer reviewers, as well as Frank Salomon, for their generous and careful attention to the manuscript. Their comments helped me rethink several important aspects of this material as well as the book's broader implications. Parts of this book were written while I was a graduate student at the University of Michigan, Ann Arbor; in residence at Frank Lloyd Wright's Taliesin West in Scottsdale, Arizona; while I was a postdoc at the Leiden University Centre for Linguistics; at Brown University, where I was a fellow at the John Carter Brown Library and Visiting Lecturer in the Department of Anthropology; and during a fellowship at the University of Tübingen in Germany. I am grateful to these institutions for hosting me while I completed the book.

My first trip to the Alto Urubamba was supported by the University of Michigan Department of Anthropology in 2009. The main fieldwork was supported by a Fulbright-Hays Doctoral Dissertation Research Abroad (DDRA) Fellowship and National Science Foundation Doctoral Dissertation Improvement Grant No. 1021842. Any opinions, findings, conclusions, and recommendations expressed in this material are those of the author and do not necessarily reflect the views of the National Science Foundation. During this time I was an affiliated researcher at CISEPA, at the Pontificia Universidad Católica del Perú. Writing was supported by fellowships from the University of Michigan Department of Anthropology in 2012–14. The research leading to these results also received funding from the European Research Council under the European Union's Seventh Framework Programme (FP7/2007–2013) / ERC grant agreement no. 295918. I worked on the manuscript at the John Carter Brown Library while I was a Donald L. Saunders and National Endowment for the Humanities Fellow. At the University of Tübingen, my writing was funded by the

Deutsche Forschungsgemeinschaft (DFG, German Research Foundation)—project number UR 310/1–1. The project also received funding from the European Research Council (ERC) under the European Union's Horizon 2020 research and innovation program (grant agreement no. 818854—SAPPHIRE). All of the photographs in this book were taken by the author, and all of the charts were designed with the help of Sophie Nicolay.

Thanks, finally, to Sophie Nicolay and Mae Emlen, as well as my parents, Julia and Robert Emlen, for their love and support during this project.

Abbreviations

3	3rd person
ABL	Ablative
ALIEN.POSS	Alienable possession
EP	Epenthesis
F	Feminine
M	Masculine
PF	Perfective
PL	Plural
REAL	Realis
REL	Relativizer
RIVER	River
SUBJ.FOC	Subject focus

Language, Coffee, and Migration
on an Andean-Amazonian Frontier

Introduction

One morning in the spring of 2012, I climbed up to a high point of land in the Alto Urubamba Valley of southern Peru to take in the view with an elderly Matsigenka friend named Antonio. Facing south, we looked across the lush, jagged hills at the snowcapped peaks of the Andes looming on the horizon. Turning north, we watched the mist rise above the Amazon plain in the distance. Antonio pointed out some of the landmarks of this perennial Andean-Amazonian crossroads: Here were the overgrown ruins of an ancient settlement built during a prehistoric burst of political expansion from the Andes into Amazonia. There was the trace of a major mule trail used in the early twentieth century to transport rubber collected by enslaved Matsigenka people, including Antonio's own grandfather, during a tremor of violence that shook the region for decades. Here was a hillside where he had grown yuca, hunted monkeys, and collected *katarompanaki* incense as a child, now owned and cleared by an Andean migrant coffee farmer and bisected by a dusty new road. There, beyond, was the broad, densely forested valley that his children had titled through a new Indigenous land law, and where he expected to live out the rest of his days.[1]

For Antonio, the landscape of the Alto Urubamba Valley, the traditional territory of the Indigenous Matsigenka people, is thick with the traces of an intense, multilayered history of interaction between the Andean highlands and the Amazonian lowlands. As endless, varied newcomers have arrived here from the highlands over the centuries—traders, conquerors, refugees, slaves, outlaws, farmers, miners, missionaries, teachers, administrators, engineers, anthropologists, smugglers, politicians, and tourists, to name a few—the region's physical and social landscape has been continually transformed. At some moments, as today, these relationships have solidified into durable interregional social networks, linking people in the valley to others across western South America and beyond. At other moments, newcomers and locals have kept their distance from one another. In all cases, land use activities, linguistic practices, ethnic categories, and political relations have been constantly reshaped.

Highland-lowland interaction in the Alto Urubamba has ebbed and flowed. In the most recent burst of interregional integration, beginning in the 1950s, tens of thousands of Quechua-speaking migrants from the rural Andean highlands (locally known as *colonos*) have made their way to remote parts of the valley in search of land for the cultivation of coffee and other tropical crops (particularly cacao and achiote, whose bright reddish-orange seeds are used to make natural dyes). More recently, migrants have come to work in the sprawling Camisea natural gas project. This extraordinary migratory influx from the Andes has resulted in a burgeoning multiethnic, multilingual frontier society, in which people from various backgrounds have married and formed communities and social networks in which Matsigenka, Quechua, and Spanish are spoken in all combinations. This book is about how this frontier society emerged, and how people from different backgrounds use the three languages in the course of their day-to-day lives as they struggle to make a place for themselves amid great instability and environmental change. The social and economic system that emerged in the forests of the Alto Urubamba since the 1950s was, fundamentally, new to everyone involved—lowland agriculture was unfamiliar to colonos from the highlands, while most Matsigenkas had not participated in commercial agriculture at all until this time. The Alto Urubamba frontier was thus a society of beginners, in which Matsigenkas and Andean colonos worked to make a place for themselves in a social and economic milieu that did not exist before.

This book is based on nineteen months of fieldwork conducted in 2009–12. I remain in close contact with my friends in the region and visit as frequently as possible; the relationships I forged there will last a lifetime. It will be particularly interesting to see how the issues I present in this book evolve in the coming years and decades. In 2009–12, I traveled between dozens of Matsigenka communities and colono settlements, working with farmers in their fields, participating in municipal construction crews, accompanying Andean merchants as they drove through the frontier to buy coffee during the harvest season, attending contentious meetings with local officials, relaxing with friends in their homes, and much else. All the while, I made around 250 hours of audio and video recordings, in all three languages, to understand how people spoke to one another in the many different moments of their social lives as they grappled with the extraordinary transformations around them. I tried hard to pay attention to the lives of both Matsigenka people and Andean migrants—and to the lives of people who navigate an uneasy daily course between those categories—to understand this frontier encounter from as many perspectives as possible. The book is, thus, both an Andeanist and an Amazonianist ethnography.

It is also an ethnography of multilingualism: a holistic account, based on long-term, immersive fieldwork, of how people use various linguistic codes within the social and cultural contexts of their lives, and how societies themselves are built up through those communicative acts. It is about how people on the Alto Urubamba agricultural frontier moved between the three languages as they went about their days, and how their varied linguistic practices were implicated in the changes under way in the valley. By tracing the intricate and varied linguistic contours of everyday life on the multiethnic frontier, I show how Matsigenkas and Andean migrants used language to manage conflicting stances toward the new economic regime overtaking the valley. On the one hand, some interactions were organized around integration into the agrarian society: Matsigenka speakers, for instance, sat alongside Quechua-speaking Andean migrants during state-funded training workshops and used a technical register of Spanish that backgrounded their ethnic differences while foregrounding their common identity as farmers. The interactional dimensions of coffee production thus became points of day-to-day integration within the broader society and a common ground on which the interethnic encounter unfolded. On the other hand, members of Matsigenka communities sometimes donned traditional *cushma* robes during events and spoke forcefully, in Matsigenka, about the need to push back against the very same agrarian society, which threatened to envelop them.

In this way, languages and linguistic features (e.g., words, discourse markers, syntactic constructions, and participant structures) became associated with particular spaces, obligations, and institutions, such that these features could be mobilized relative to particular stances toward the emerging agrarian society.

This process is known among linguistic anthropologists as *enregisterment*: "cultural models of action that link diverse behavioral signs"—for instance, languages, registers, or garments—"to enactable effects, including images of persona, interpersonal relationship, and type of conduct" (Agha 2007, 145; see also Agha 2005; Silverstein 1993, 2003). The effects enacted here included the persona of the farmer, or of the ethnically distinct Matsigenka. These linkages are embedded in *language ideologies*: "cultural conceptions of the nature, form, and purpose of language, and of communicative behavior as an enactment of a collective order" (Gal and Woolard 2001, 1; see also Silverstein 1979; Schieffelin, Woolard, and Kroskrity 1998). In this view, it is not just the case that farmers used a technical agricultural register of Spanish, but also that one could inhabit the socially recognizable persona of a farmer by speaking that way. This persona, in turn, was associated with an integrative stance toward the agrarian economy and society as well as particular ideas about (for instance) how the land should be conceptualized and used. On the other hand, by putting on a traditional cushma garment, standing up in community events, and speaking in Matsigenka, one inhabited a different social persona and invoked a different—and, indeed, opposed—stance toward one's colono neighbors, as well as toward their ways of using and conceptualizing the landscape. Seen this way, language, social organization, and ideas about the land were inseparable.

Crucially, many of the very same people used such enregistered features to embrace the frontier society one moment and oppose it the next. Thus, by switching between languages and registers, speakers effected a pivot between these social personae, sometimes in the same stretch of talk. As I discuss below, this approach to the frontier—treating it as an arena navigated through diverse, interactionally constructed social roles rather than a straightforward clash between opposed groups of people—captures the fluidity of the Alto Urubamba social world as it played out in day-to-day practice.

I first traveled to the Alto Urubamba in 2009 to study multilingualism among Quechua, Matsigenka, and Spanish, because this confluence of languages struck me as an interesting one that upset the familiar binary relationship between a single European colonial language and a single Indigenous American language. What I didn't anticipate was that by paying close attention to how people used those three languages in the course of their day-to-day lives, I would, in fact, also be writing an ethnography about the social dynamics of the emerging coffee industry. It might not at first be obvious why multilingualism and the functioning of the coffee economy would be so closely linked. However, the field of linguistic anthropology shows us that language is not merely a medium for conveying propositions, but also a form of social action that is implicated in nearly every activity we undertake together as humans—including, in this case, coffee cultivation.

Coffee cultivation involves a dizzying array of communicative acts. It is a technically demanding crop, so farmers in the Alto Urubamba had to spend long hours participating in training sessions about fertilizers, seedbeds, fermentation, herbicides, and the like; by participating in such interactions, they *became* farmers, both in terms of technical knowledge and by adopting the corresponding social persona. Meanwhile, at the beginning of every harvest season, farmers and merchants engaged in negotiations in Quechua over crates of beer in roadside homes and bars. These interactions often involved virtuosic displays of language use, and financial success belonged to those who could cajole, flatter, intimidate, deceive, and read between the lines—all discursive skills with devastatingly concrete economic and environmental consequences. These examples show how language is not just an abstract system for exchanging information in speech, but also, in the Alto Urubamba, something implicated in the very emergence of the frontier's social and agricultural system. Speech is not just about the frontier; it *is* the frontier.[2] One implication of this point is that in a society where not everyone has the same linguistic competences and experiences (for instance, in negotiations), interactions themselves could be important sites in the production of socioeconomic inequality.

In this way, as people navigated their way through the countless everyday situations of frontier life, they used Matsigenka, Quechua, and Spanish, which were always embedded in broader ideological associations. As I describe throughout this book, Quechua was associated with rural Andean society and the social dynamics of the agrarian system that has spread throughout the Alto Urubamba. Spanish was used in contexts of public address and debate, particularly in relation to the administrative apparatus of the Peruvian state. The Matsigenka language was connected to Matsigenka ethnicity and to the domestic and kin-based social sphere of its speakers. These three languages were spoken in different combinations from one community to the next, and, in some places, even from one household to the next (as in the community of Yokiri described in chapter 3). Exploring the Alto Urubamba frontier society through its linguistic acts thus shows how Matsigenkas and Andean migrants encountered each other through language and interaction, and how the expansion of the coffee frontier was mediated face-to-face. In this sense, this book offers a microscopic view of the day-to-day emergence of settlement frontiers, in a manner that treats them as a kind of society negotiated among Indigenous people and newcomers rather than as a straightforward clash between opposed groups—a "middle ground," as in Richard White's (1991) ethnohistorical analysis of the Algonquian-European society that formed around the Great Lakes in the seventeenth to nineteenth centuries. This study thus offers insights regarding the functioning of such settlement frontiers to historians examining these questions through the documentary record.[3]

While this book takes language use as its primary empirical focus, it is also an ethnographic look at the day-to-day social dynamics of an ongoing global environmental and humanitarian catastrophe. As the road network works its way ever farther through the remote corners of the Urubamba Valley—opening the way for the eventual colonization of the vast Amazon plain beyond—great expanses of land that were covered in primary forest just a few years ago have now been cleared for agriculture. Deforestation in the Amazon is an urgent concern for the planet: the ability of the Amazon to absorb the planet's carbon output and thus slow down climate change (its function as a "carbon sink") has declined by almost a third over the last decade (Brienen et al. 2015), while at the same time global carbon emissions have increased unchecked. A frightening report from the UN (IPBES 2019) suggests that climate change and environmental destruction have put around a million species around the planet on the brink of extinction, particularly in highly biodiverse places like the Amazon. At least 17 percent of the Amazon forest has already been destroyed (Maretti et al. 2014), and deforestation is approaching a dangerous tipping point that may bring on a widespread and irreversible ecological disaster in which the remaining forest is quickly transformed into savannah (Nobre et al. 2016). Meanwhile, as this book went to press, massive fires raged across the Amazon as farmers cut down vast tracts of forest—often illegally, after trespassing on Indigenous lands—and burned the dried vegetation lying on the land in order to clear it. These farmers were urged on by the anti-conservationist Brazilian president Jair Bolsonaro, who advocates the further dispossession and deforestation of Indigenous lands for agriculture. This is one of the defining emergencies of our time. This book offers an ethnographic perspective on how this crisis plays out at the day-to-day level of interaction, ideology, and social relationships, complementing the kinds of analyses offered by ecologists.

An Integrated Network

The view of Andean-Amazonian interaction that I present in this book is somewhat different from the way in which those regions and their inhabitants are often treated in both scholarly and local discourses. The two regions are generally taken (usually implicitly) to demarcate distinct and self-contained worlds, such that particular languages, cultures, and societies can be sorted into one category or the other. The result of this view is that connections between the two regions are made invisible or interpreted as exceptions to the normal state of affairs. In this book, I argue that this is a misleading view of how the relationships between the two regions actually function, and that much can be learned by tracing the movement of people, goods, and languages between the highlands and the lowlands.

In the Alto Urubamba, the dichotomous view of the highlands and the lowlands is exemplified by the geographer Daniel Gade's observation of a "major cultural-historical cleavage" that has "long divided the Urubamba Valley into sedentary highland people to the south and the semi-nomadic tribes of the tropical forest to the north" (2016, 297). This is a helpful overview of the valley's population geography in its very broadest strokes—Andeans at the top of the valley, Matsigenkas at the bottom—and Gade is to be credited for considering both ends in the same book. However, this characterization of the valley encourages the misleading impression of two distinct groups of people who interact as coherent, separate wholes and who encounter each other only exceptionally.

In this book, I focus instead on the place where the highlands and the lowlands meet in the Alto Urubamba: the agricultural frontier. Here, daily life is not characterized by cleavage, division, separateness, and exceptionality, but rather by connection. Seen from the middle, the valley is *just one world* (a notion I develop in chapter 1) in which the patterns of interaction and kinship among colonos and Matsigenkas are more fluid and integrated than the discourse of Andean-Amazonian division would lead us to expect. When one sets out to understand what actually happens at the interface between those regions, one finds not division but continuity. To be sure, ethnic categories like *Matsigenka* and *colono* are crucial principles of difference in the local social world; they are not, however, empirical and analytical categories that reliably correspond to actual patterns of interaction, behavior, and language, or even to individuals (Brubaker 2004). This distinction is necessary to explain why so many

Matsigenkas and colonos live densely interconnected lives while also managing stark, institutionally codified discourses of ethnic division.

To be clear, the dichotomous view of the valley typified by Gade's description above is correct in the sense that many people in remote Matsigenka communities do not interact regularly with colonos, and that many colonos in the upper reaches of the Alto Urubamba have never encountered a Matsigenka person. This is, in other words, a view from the poles, and those are the parts of the valley that have been described in detail by scholars. However, on the leading edge of the agricultural frontier, where Andean colonos are pushing their way through forests historically inhabited by Matsigenkas, interethnic interaction is a central fact of everyday life. Indeed, the proportion of Matsigenkas in the Alto Urubamba who remain outside of regular contact with Andean colonos at this point is small.[4] As one might expect in such a situation, interactions among Matsigenkas and colonos are frequently characterized by conflict and opposition. However, in many places they have settled into a stable and long-term, if uneasy, coexistence.

To illustrate the nondichotomous nature of the valley, it is helpful to observe that many people on the frontier conduct relationships with their neighbors across ethnolegal boundaries more often than they do with their fellow community members within these boundaries. I was surprised early in my fieldwork when several Matsigenkas in one legally titled *comunidad nativa* (Native Amazonian community) and their colono neighbors—who were linked by ties of *compadrazgo* (ritual co-parenthood)—crossed into each other's communities and reciprocated labor on consecutive days during the busy coffee harvest season. The same Matsigenkas and colonos reciprocated labor less often among members of their own communities, and in fact did not know some of their fellow community members very well. That is, patterns of interaction and obligation in such places were as likely to cross ethnic and legal boundaries as they were to be confined within them, making such boundaries poor predictors of actual social practice. Similarly, Matsigenka children in one comunidad nativa attended a primary school within their community but walked to a nearby colono settlement to attend a secondary school among their neighbors. Bilingual education teachers were allocated according to the ethnolegal status of each community (note that a community can only have one such status), so these children received bilingual Matsigenka-Spanish instruction in primary school and bilingual Quechua-Spanish instruction in secondary school. Of course, this was not a problem as far as their instruction was concerned, since the children were trilingual. In this way, day-to-day interethnic interactions bore an important but problematic relationship to the institutionalized discourses of ethnicity and language in the valley. However, the strength of such discourses (and their incompatibility with a notion like trilingualism) can obscure the dense interconnections among the valley's inhabitants.

Another reason to take interethnic relationships in the Alto Urubamba seriously is that a great number of Matsigenkas and colonos circulate between their homes in the valley and other places across the region for months or years at a time, or move to those other places permanently, creating durable relationships with a broad range of people in the process. Thus the tendency to favor, for instance, legally titled Indigenous Amazonian communities and other protected areas as sites of anthropological and linguistic fieldwork can obscure the dynamics of interactions that take place outside of those places, which in the Alto Urubamba are much more likely to be interethnic and multilingual. As I conducted fieldwork in the frontier settlements and towns of the valley, I came to realize that many of the restaurants, mechanic shops, pharmacies, and municipal construction crews employed Matsigenka people for periods of several months during agricultural off-seasons (for a similar case regarding Ese Eja people in the lowland city of Puerto Maldonado, see Peluso 2015). Some of these young Matsigenkas worked during the day and attended high school at night, and in their free hours they strolled the streets of Quillabamba with their colono boyfriends and girlfriends, eating greasy fried chicken and ice cream on the bleachers by the city's concrete soccer court and dancing in the local *discotecas*. Signs like the one pictured in figure 1, displayed in a store window in Quillabamba, were common: *Necesito 01 joven varón del campo nativo o mestizo. Ayuda: tienda-casa* (I need one *nativo* [i.e., Indigenous Amazonian] or mestizo boy from the country. Help: shop-home). These arrangements were attractive to members of comunidades nativas seeking a foothold in the urban centers, but some employers took advantage of Matsigenkas' relative inexperience with urban life and lack of a local support network to employ them under exploitative conditions.

Urban centers have also seen a rise in prostitution, particularly in frontier towns where large concentrations of young men are employed by the Camisea gas project (Shepard 2012b), the military, or state construction crews. Araujo Salas (2017, 50) reports that the small town of Kiteni (pictured in figure 2 below) was home to twenty bars and three nightclubs that offered prostitution services, while a study by Peru's Environment Ministry found that four hundred women worked in *prostíbares* (brothels) associated with the illegal mining industry in

FIGURE 1 Sign in Quillabamba advertising work in a store and the proprietor's home, 2011. Photograph by the author.

Madre de Dios (MINAM 2013; see also Goldstein 2014, 2015). People in the Alto Urubamba sometimes told me that Matsigenka women had been lured into such employment through false promises of other kinds of work.

Matsigenkas who worked in urban areas often used their earnings to support their families back home, and those earnings played an important part in their communities' economies. Many young Matsigenkas also attended residential schools away from their communities for the better part of each year, where they studied alongside colonos and where many lifelong friendships and romantic relationships were forged. Others attended universities or worked in the highlands, particularly in the nearby city of Cusco (Steele 2015, 2018). Matsigenkas often described their desire to achieve this kind of lifestyle using the Spanish idiom of wanting to *ser algo* (be something)—that is, to establish a professional career and a comfortable urban life, usually through education (Crivello 2011). Thus staying in a remote, forested comunidad nativa and *being something* were considered incompatible. Some of those who sought a middle-class urban life eventually came home, while others did not; returning home was often considered *un paso atrás* ("a step backward" in Spanish) and was a source of some shame for those who reappeared in their communities after a long time away. As one young Matsigenka man told me in Spanish after an unsuccessful attempt to make a life away from his community: "Desgraciadamente, sigo acá" (Unfortunately, I'm still here). People came and went, such that the aggregate of individuals living within a community's legal boundaries could vary dramatically from season to season and from year to year. Through these patterns of mobility, even remote Matsigenka and colono communities were closely integrated with each other and with the regional society. Thus it is more accurate to think of these communities not as tightly delimited, static groups of people, but rather as nodes in a fluid, regional network of migration, interaction, and kinship that cuts across ethnic and linguistic distinctions.

By 2009–12, these patterns of social connection in the valley were accompanied by widespread interethnic marriage. The great majority of the Andean migrants who ventured into the remote corners of the coffee frontier were young men, many of whom caught the attention of Matsigenka women living in nearby comunidades nativas. Such unions were appealing to many Matsigenka women who valued colono men for their integration into the regional economy. (I occasionally heard the statement—considered deeply offensive by the Matsigenkas I know—that the children of Matsigenka-colono unions were *hijos mejorados*, or "improved children," a Spanish idiom used in livestock breeding.)[5] In some comunidades nativas on the frontier, interethnic unions were the rule rather than the exception by the time of my fieldwork. Since most Matsigenka comunidades nativas did not allow colono spouses to live within their boundaries, interethnic couples often ended up dispersed in nearby colono communities, in local towns, or in the migrants' communities or cities of origin in the highlands. Thus interethnic marriage appeared uncommon when one only considered comunidades nativas, simply because interethnic couples were not permitted to stay. These widespread unions between Matsigenka women and colono men made it, in turn, increasingly difficult for Matsigenka men to find wives, sending them downriver to search for romantic partners, and into the more remote tributaries where colonos had not yet arrived. The result has been a gendered system of opposed migratory and linguistic flows—documented in ethnographic examples throughout this book—in which Matsigenka-speaking women moved up the Urubamba Valley toward local towns and into the highlands, while Quechua-speaking men moved downriver and into the more remote tributaries. This is an important link between the dynamics of kinship, gender, migration, economic and landscape change, and the large-scale movement of languages—particularly Quechua—between the Andes and Amazonia (I explore this pattern in more detail in chapter 1). The interregional kinship networks resulting from these patterns often remained tight, and they linked communities and villages in the remote parts of the Urubamba Valley to the towns and cities of the frontier, the highlands, and beyond.

As a result of these intermarriages and patterns of mobility, the question of who "counts" as a Matsigenka or a colono could be quite contingent and contextual. For instance, in the few comunidades nativas where interethnic couples were permitted to live, their children were basically considered colonos, with tenuous claim to Matsigenka identity. This was particularly true in contexts of political representation within comunidades nativas, which are structured according to a law designed to protect Indigenous Amazonian land from colonization (see chapter 5). Having a colono parent often meant that one could not speak with the same authority in community meetings or, in some places, even be selected for positions of leadership. However, when the same people visited colono communities, they were considered Matsigenkas and were thought to be outside the mainstream of the rural agrarian society. In other contexts, such contingencies were elided and a uniform Matsigenka ethnicity was asserted by, and attributed to, everyone in the community—for instance, in census counts, the allocation of bilingual education teachers, and explicit identity performances during anniversaries and protests.

It is important to appreciate just how much Andean-Amazonian fluidity has been generated by the mobility, interethnic marriage, and changing socioeconomic dynamics apparent on the agricultural frontier in the Alto Urubamba. For instance, consider Juan, a Matsigenka man who lived in the early twentieth century and played an important role in mediating between Matsigenkas, Dominicans at the Chirumbia mission, and nearby Quechua-speaking colonos in the valley (Juan's life is described in greater detail in chapter 3; all names used in this book are pseudonyms). Juan spoke Quechua, Matsigenka, and a bit of Spanish, and he recruited Matsigenka laborers to work on colono estates. He also gathered *katarompanaki*, a tree resin used as incense, and brought it to the nearby Dominican mission at Chirumbia for trade. After many years of close interaction with Matsigenkas, Spanish missionaries, and Quechua-speaking colonos, Juan married a monolingual Matsigenka-speaking woman named Eugenia and withdrew from the frontier to work on her father's remote plot of land. Their children grew up as monolingual Matsigenka speakers, far from the influence of Andean colonos. In this complex frontier history, Juan spoke Quechua, Matsigenka, and some Spanish, but his children only spoke Matsigenka.

Compare Juan with his granddaughter Ana María—the daughter of Juan's monolingual Matsigenka-speaking son—who grew up in a comunidad nativa on the coffee frontier in the 1980s. Ana María attended a Quechua-Spanish bilingual secondary school in a neighboring colono community and thus spoke

Matsigenka, Spanish, and some Quechua. Ana María then enrolled in a university in the city of Cusco, where her young daughter now attends a Quechua-Spanish bilingual primary school. Ana María sent me a photograph of her daughter dressed in a traditional highland costume for a celebration with her Quechua-Spanish bilingual classmates: a broad-brimmed hat, a calf-length *pollera* skirt, and a colorful *lliklla* shawl wrapped across the shoulders and pinned at the neck—all signifiers of rural Andean identity, and associated with Quechua language use (Babel 2018). By 2018, Ana María lived with a Quechua-speaking man in the city of Cusco, and her family had essentially integrated into highland society: she spoke Matsigenka, Spanish, and Quechua, and her daughter spoke Quechua and Spanish (though Ana María reported sometimes feeling out of place among her Andean in-laws and friends). Despite the stark discourse of Andean-Amazonian division in the Alto Urubamba, the four generations of this family show just how porous and fluid that boundary can be.

All of this may come as some surprise to those acquainted with the scholarly literature about the Urubamba Valley, in which Matsigenkas appear only fleetingly in research about colonos, and vice versa (note that the same division can be seen up and down the Andean-Amazonian transitional zone). Works written about the valley tend to focus either on remote Matsigenka comunidades nativas and other protected areas far beyond the agricultural frontier, or on colono communities farther up the valley where Matsigenkas have not lived in substantial numbers for more than a century. I do not wish to suggest that these differences in focus represent a shortcoming on the part of these works—many descriptions of Matsigenkas (e.g., Rosengren 1987; A. W. Johnson 2003) and of Andean colonos (e.g., Fioravanti 1974; Gade 2016) in separate parts of the Alto Urubamba are of the very highest quality and offer rigorous and sensitive accounts of each part of the society. It is, furthermore, quite possible to spend time in Matsigenka and colono communities at either end of the valley and never witness an interethnic encounter. My point is, rather, that the field, in aggregate, is subject to a sampling bias, whereby those parts of Matsigenka and colono societies that are most removed from one another are taken to be representative of the wholes. This in turn encourages a particular interpretation of what happens in the middle—a boundary, a clash, an exception, an encounter between irreconcilable others—even though the reality of the frontier encounter is quite different.

Another point I wish to make in this book is that recognizing the interconnectedness of Andeans and Amazonians in the Alto Urubamba is not just an academic matter; it also holds important political significance. First, a view of Matsigenkas and Quechua-speaking migrants working together as coffee farmers in the tropical lowlands—linked in tight networks of kinship and interaction—draws attention to a range of social worlds beyond the familiar images of Indigenous Andeans as rural highland agropastoralists and Amazonians as remote lowland hunter-horticulturalists. To borrow Philip Deloria's phrase (2004), the appearance of Indigenous people and languages "in unexpected places"—particularly in places so firmly embedded in the global economy—contributes to a diverse and humanizing representation of contemporary Indigenous life in South America.

Second, the circumstances that have brought Matsigenkas and colonos together in the valley today include the global coffee industry (and its attendant deforestation), destructive natural gas extraction, and the bloody and lawless cocaine trade—each providing commodities, it must be noted, that are consumed mostly by inhabitants of the industrialized global North rather than by Matsigenkas or colonos themselves. These burgeoning industries, operating in a local context of weak regulatory enforcement, lack of genuine political will to protect the region's most vulnerable people, and a truly awe-inspiring influx of cash, have created a situation of pervasive corruption and violence. Similar situations can be found up and down the long expanse of western South America, where some of the most volatile geopolitical flash points have emerged at the Andean-Amazonian interface, disproportionately affecting the region's most vulnerable people. Conflicts and issues include the struggles of Indigenous Amazonians to protect their land (Brown 2014), sex trafficking (Goldstein 2014), deforestation (Alvarez and Naughton-Treves 2003), reckless oil drilling (Sawyer 2004; Cepek 2018), cocaine production and smuggling (Kernaghan 2009), and destructive mining practices (Swenson et al. 2011), to name just a few. To the extent that some of these problems are a result of western Amazonia's integration into the Andean sphere, overlooking the actual social dynamics of that integration risks allowing these problems, too, to remain invisible.

Languages, Groups, and Publics

The foregoing introduction to the Alto Urubamba's changing social and economic landscape raises some basic questions regarding the region's multilingualism. How do we approach language in such porous and flexible societies—

particularly when that very porousness runs counter to the discourses of ostensibly straightforward ethnic division in the society? How can we study objects like languages and societies at the same time that we try to deconstruct those very objects? And how can we understand multilingual interactions as implicated in—rather than merely reflective of—the sociopolitical and environmental transformations under way in the valley?

These are some of the questions that I wrestle with as I describe the social and linguistic panorama of the Alto Urubamba throughout this book. To begin with, I attempt to move beyond the notion of the *ethnolinguistic group* as an analytical concept for understanding language and social relations in the valley. This language ideology, which has long had a firm grip on the way in which Indigenous South Americans are described, posits a natural, one-to-one relationship between a language and an aggregate of people who are clearly delimitable by ethnicity (and, often, also by territory). This creates "a model of the world," Eric Wolf writes, "as a global pool hall in which the entities spin off each other like so many hard and round billiard balls" (1982, 6). Such a vision of language and social relations is ill-suited to the Alto Urubamba, which is characterized by interethnic marriage, trilingualism, and a deterritorialized pattern of language organization generated by the constant circulation of people across a wide range of places and circumstances.

Note, however, that while the ethnolinguistic group is inadequate to describe the facts of language use in the Alto Urubamba, as a concept—the social imaginary of the "language community" (Silverstein 1998)—it plays a central organizing role for people in the valley. It underlies all manner of institutions that mark and reproduce ethnolinguistic categories, including the sharp legal boundaries that demarcate the territories of Matsigenka and colono communities, as well as the allocation of Quechua and Matsigenka bilingual education teachers, which is done in a way that presupposes a straightforward relationship between ethnicity, territory, and "mother tongue" (note the assumption that students can only have one). It is a testament to the durability and pervasiveness of this conceptual division that it is difficult to even discuss the region except in the language of twoness (Matsigenkas and colonos, highlands and lowlands, etc.).

Linguistic anthropologists and sociolinguists have long acknowledged the problems that arise from assuming natural correspondences between bounded social groupings and unitary linguistic codes (Weinreich, Labov, and Herzog 1968), and from using folk concepts like the ethnolinguistic group, or the "tribe," as objects of linguistic analysis (Hymes 1968). A helpful alternative has been the *speech community*, which John Gumperz defined as "a field of action where the distribution of linguistic variants is a reflection of the social facts" (1968, 383; see Irvine 2006 for a review)—for instance, a village in India where four languages were distributed among a multilingual population (Gumperz and Wilson 1971), or New York City, where linguistic variants are socially patterned across a vast urban population (Labov 1966). Focusing on the facts of interaction allows us to move past the strictures of ethnic group–ness described above. More recently, linguistic anthropologists have pointed out that membership in such communities, beyond the facts of interaction, is also a matter of sharing common ideas about how languages are used in a society—a "mutually intelligible symbolic and ideological communicative system," as Marcyliena Morgan writes (2014, 1). In fact, the regular use of languages may not even be the foremost fact in the constitution of such communities, as in situations of language endangerment and revitalization where affiliation to a code can be a more relevant factor— what Netta Avineri calls a "metalinguistic community" (2012; see also Avineri and Kroskrity 2014; Shulist 2016).

The classic definition of the speech community, which locates the human aggregate in the heterogenous facts of interaction, is helpful in places like the Alto Urubamba agricultural frontier, where people interact in three languages across territorial boundaries and ethnic categories as a matter of course. The kinds of contemporary work on the topic mentioned above are also illuminating for this case in their embrace of the language-ideological dimensions of identity and ethnicity—a broader theme that has been explored in several excellent recent ethnographies by linguistic anthropologists of Latin America (e.g., Babel 2018; Faudree 2013; Shulist 2018; French 2010). This book takes a somewhat different focus than those works do, in that it is less about national, macropolitical, and institutional questions of language and identity (though such things are certainly relevant). Instead, this book is more about the day-to-day experience of farmers and merchants, whose engagement with those kinds of discourses in 2009–12 was more indirect, as they transformed the forest into farmland.

To understand the linguistic dynamics of the Alto Urubamba, we also have to ask how linguistic variation and multilingualism are socially structured with respect to particular domains of activity. Here, the notion of *communities of practice* is helpful: "aggregate[s] of people who come together around mutual engagement in an endeavor" (Eckert and McConnell-Ginet 1992, 464). Here, the countless activities of everyday life put one into contact with different constellations of people, and these activities are connected to different linguistic codes (e.g., languages, registers, and discourse genres), spaces, and social values. On the Alto Urubamba coffee frontier, the members of a multiethnic frontier community might participate in several communities of practice over the course of a day: a coffee cultivation workshop in a municipal building, in Spanish, with farmers from across the region; a beer-fueled Quechua gossip session about local merchants, held on a roadside, with neighbors; and a relaxed evening of story-telling, in Matsigenka, with family members at home. Each of these practices is conducted among different aggregates of people—in some cases, across ethnic categories and legal boundaries—and each is connected to particular linguistic codes, spaces, and social values. Importantly, the concept of the community of practice also helps us understand inequality, since these communities are often organized along principles of difference like gender (Bucholtz 1999). People in the Alto Urubamba might not possess the necessary linguistic competence or social authority (based on gender, age, or ethnicity, for example) to participate in some of the practices mentioned above—for instance, Quechua gossip sessions about merchants, where much crucial economic information is disseminated. This allows us to see how inequality and exclusion play out in interactions.

A final observation from the field of linguistic anthropology that will be helpful in conceptualizing the relationship between language and social relations throughout this book has to do with how people produce particular social identities in interaction (see, for example, Bucholtz and Hall 2005), and how the kinds of enregistered linguistic and cultural practices described above are involved in that process. To begin with a simple example, consider what it means for a first-language Matsigenka speaker who grew up beyond the frontier to sit with Quechua-speaking colono friends on the roadside after a long day of coffee cultivation, pass around a bottle of beer and a small plastic cup, and joke in Quechua while listening to Andean *huayno* music over a portable radio. These enregistered interactional behaviors are indexically linked to the social persona of the rural Andean farmer, and by participating in them, a Mat-sigenka person also asserts their belonging in the broader agrarian society—which includes hundreds of thousands of other rural Andean farmers across southern Peru. (However, whether a Matsigenka person comes to be accepted as a legitimate member of that society is another question, as we will see in chapter 4.) This is an "imagined" social grouping, in the sense in which Ander-son ([1983] 1991) uses the word, rather than one based on the empirical facts of interaction: those hundreds of thousands of farmers do not know each other, but they have an awareness of their shared membership in a virtual social aggregate that is mediated, in part, through indexical associations with shared cultural phenomena like music, drinking, and language. Linguistic anthropologists have come to use the term *publics* to refer to such imagined social aggregates (Gal and Woolard 2001). We might refer to the imagined social aggregate invoked through the practices mentioned above as an *agrarian public*, or perhaps also an *Andean public*, since Andean ethnicity is associated with the agrarian world taking root in the Alto Urubamba.

One advantage of the notion of publics is that they are virtual and imagined, and thus negotiable and contextual. For instance, when our Matsigenka farmer bids farewell to her colono friends on the roadside, in Quechua, to participate in the anniversary celebration of a comunidad nativa in Matsigenka, she moves away from the social field of the *agrarian public* into the social field of the ethnically defined *Matsigenka public*. The relevant indexes here include the traditional cushma garment, Matsigenka songs, and use of the Matsigenka language. A different virtual human aggregate is projected here, as well as a different set of cultural expectations and commitments and a different stance toward the encroaching agrarian economy.

In this manner, it is possible to conceptualize the experience of daily life on the coffee frontier, at least in part, as movement between different imagined social groupings and their indexically associated linguistic and cultural forms. This is a semiotic approach to the multiethnic frontier encounter. However, we can go further and point out that the two publics described in this example—the agrarian public and the Matsigenka public—are also defined in opposition to one another. They emerge through a process of semiotic differentiation (Irvine and Gal 2000): according to the local conceptualization of the social world, Matsigenkas and Quechua-speaking colonos are mutually exclusive categories, and the bundles of indexes associated with each one are carefully distinguished. This is why one does not hear Quechua in official invocations of Matsigenka ethnicity, or Matsigenka in contexts of Andean ethnicity, even though a great many people speak both of those languages and participate in both social domains.

In this way, I focus on language and interaction in this book as an alternative to the folk concept of an encounter between distinct ethnolinguistic groups, which is inadequate to capture the fluid and porous social categories of the Alto Urubamba frontier. Instead, I shift my focus away from groups and toward situations and interactions in which people navigate different social identities through the use of enregistered linguistic and cultural practices.

Speaking the Frontier

In the end, most speech on the Alto Urubamba agricultural frontier is implicated, more or less directly, in the consolidation of a new regime of economic activity and land use in the Amazon rain forest. It may seem that multilingual discourse and the economic dynamics of frontier expansion are connected only indirectly; indeed, these topics are studied by distinct groups of scholars and are rarely brought together. However, language exists in the real world of human affairs—"situations" are speech's "natural home," as Erving Goffman writes (1964, 135)—so the social nature of language can only be understood within a holistic view of the situations that humans encounter in the course of their day-to-day lives. During my fieldwork in the Alto Urubamba, most situations involved coffee production in one way or another. Conversely, since most of what we do as humans—economically, politically, etc.—is accomplished through social relationships, interactions, and situations (Goffman 1983), then language use itself is an important dimension of matters like the local dynamics of frontier expansion and deforestation.

I came upon the coffee industry accidentally, when it became clear early in my fieldwork that it was impossible to understand multilingualism in the Alto Urubamba without also understanding what people actually do with language in their day-to-day lives—namely, attend to the countless daily tasks of producing coffee. Thus I only address coffee farming to the extent that it becomes relevant to understanding the linguistic situation, and I do not intend this book as an exhaustive economic analysis of the industry. Anthropologists have written a great deal about the global coffee trade—notably S. Lyon (2010) and West (2012)—and I refer readers to those works for sophisticated ethnographic accounts of coffee production.

Instead, I wish to make the simple observation that, insofar as coffee production is embedded in a social world, it is also embedded in a linguistic world. As Judith Irvine argues (1989), the common idealist conceptualization of language as a mere conduit for information obscures the fact that linguistic acts can have substantial value within an economic system. For instance, the price of a particular piece of metal increases dramatically if an authorized expert commits the linguistic act of authenticating it as gold. Even more directly, Wolof-speaking griots in Senegal make a living by exchanging praise songs for cash. Negotiations and bargaining sessions are another salient example of the linguistic and interactional mediation of economic exchange, as in Brigittine

French's study of Guatemalan market encounters (2000) and Richard Bauman's analysis of the poetics of selling in a Mexican market (2001; see also Keane 2008). Meanwhile, on the Alto Urubamba agricultural frontier, people spend their days managing, through all manner of linguistic interactions, the practical aspects of transforming the rain forest into cash-generating farmland. Every tense roadside negotiation, every petition for the use of a municipal front-end loader, and every impassioned public speech advocating the construction of a road to this or that patch of forest is implicated in the creation and expansion of the Alto Urubamba agricultural economy. In other words, multilingual practice (what people say) and socioeconomic behavior (what people do) are inseparable, bringing language use and economic change—and ultimately the destruction of the Amazon rain forest itself—into the same analytical frame.

This argument has an important implication: if becoming a coffee farmer requires speaking in certain ways, and not everyone on the frontier has the same kinds of linguistic and communicative competences (Hymes 1972), then interaction itself can be a site where socioeconomic inequality is created and reproduced. For instance, many Quechua and Matsigenka speakers were unfamiliar with the technical Spanish discourse of coffee production—fermentation, degrees of humidity, quantity of nitrogen in the soil—that was essential to success in the competitive coffee market. Similarly, first-language Quechua speakers who mastered the complex tactics of Quechua negotiations had an upper hand vis-à-vis their Matsigenka-speaking neighbors and trading partners who were joining the commercial economy for the first time and might not speak Quechua as confidently. These disparities had real implications for economic participation—as Judith Irvine writes, "Verbal skills and performances are among the resources and activities forming a socioeconomic system; and the relevant knowledge, talents, and use-rights are not evenly, randomly, or fortuitously distributed in a community" (1989, 255). My Matsigenka friends who struggle to find their way in the labyrinthine Alto Urubamba coffee economy would certainly recognize something of their own lives in that observation. Furthermore, beyond the issue of communicative competence per se, not all people are considered equally legitimate participants in particular kinds of discourse. For instance, Quechua-speaking colonos and Matsigenka people might both find their own voices silenced in meetings with local government officials in which their own knowledge and agency are marginalized (Albó 1973; Huayhua 2013; Mannheim 2018c). It is here that language ideologies are connected to the substantial power asymmetries that affect both

Matsigenkas and Andean colonos in the precarious world of the agricultural frontier.

The Andes and Amazonia

The nation of Peru is often conceptualized as comprising three parallel geographical regions: the *costa* (coast), *sierra* (Andean highlands), and *selva* (Amazonian lowlands).[6] This division guides much official and popular discourse about Peru (Santos-Granero 2002; Orlove 1993), and the distinction between the Andes and Amazonia in particular has provided a principle of division for much ethnographic and linguistic research in the region. Peru's tripartite geographical scheme is also the basis of a system of racial categorization that posits types of people corresponding to the three geographical/ecological areas: those of European descent on the costa (as well as Afro-Peruvians [Greene 2007]), Andean *campesinos* (peasants or farmers; formerly called *indios*, or "Indians") in the sierra, and *nativos* (Indigenous Amazonians) in the selva (Greene 2007, 2009; Steele and Zanotti 2014). Radcliffe and Westwood describe such demarcations in terms of "racialized imaginative geographies" (1996, 118), in which categories of people are associated with particular geographical regions, and vice versa. In Peru, these geographical-racial categories are also connected to economic activities (capitalist wage labor, agropastoralism, and hunting-horticulture, respectively) and are consequently ideologized in a hierarchy in which "the sequence of coast, highlands, and jungle is the story of national progress, an undertaking that had nearly been completed on the coast, that was underway in the highlands, and that had scarcely begun in the jungle" (Orlove 1993, 328; see also Whitten 2011).

But, keeping in mind the power of this racial discourse, what does it mean to say, as an analytical matter, that some societies and languages in the region are "Andean," and that others are "Amazonian"? On the one hand, these labels have a certain intuitive appeal. The geographic division between the Andean highlands and the Amazonian lowlands is indeed dramatic, and some languages and societies are located mostly or entirely on one side or the other. Furthermore, the kinds of lifestyles that come to mind when we think of people in one or the other macroregion tend to be quite different. However, when we move beyond the task of simply locating speakers of particular languages and societies in the geographic space of South America (and in the relevant sections of the library shelving system), the discourse of Andean-Amazonian division can obscure as much as it illuminates.

First, the discourse of Andean-Amazonian division invites us to treat each macroregion as an internally coherent and undifferentiated mass, and as partaking of a common underlying essence that makes Andean and Amazonian people each "of a kind." In this view, for instance, Matsigenkas and other Indigenous Amazonians thousands of kilometers away in eastern Brazil, through the invocation of "Indigenous Amazonia," are attributed an essential likeness—one that is not shared with the Andean migrants whom many Matsigenkas interact with every day and even count as their own kin. While few would explicitly endorse such an essentializing notion, it joins the background of implicit presuppositions that lend intelligibility to questions like "What do Andeans believe?" or "How do Amazonians use the land?" or "What kind of Spanish do Andeans speak?" or "What do Andeans and Amazonians think about each other?" As such discourses presuppose a common experience or essence among Andeans or Amazonians, they elide the substantial cultural and linguistic variation within each macroregion. They also make invisible, for instance, the non-Indigenous people who in fact make up the majority of Amazonia's population (Nugent and Harris 2004; Vadjunec, Schmink, and Greiner 2011). These include colonists (Campbell 2015), cattle ranchers (Hoelle 2015), cocaine producers (Kernaghan 2009), quilombòlas (the descendants of escaped slaves in Brazil; Leite 2000), and many others. Given that only 8.1 percent of the population of the Peruvian Amazon lived in comunidades nativas according to the 2007 census (INEI 2007)—a rough but helpful proxy for the proportion of people who would characterize themselves as Indigenous Amazonians—this homogenizing discourse is misleading indeed.

The second problem with the (again, usually implicit) discourse of the Andean-Amazonian geographic division as a meaningful predictor of social phenomena is that it encourages us to think of each macroregion as bounded and separate, and thus to mistakenly consider the connections between them to be trivial or exceptional to some natural state of affairs. In relation to this point, we need only consider one of the major observations of Andean ethnohistory over the last fifty years: that people in the Andean region have tended to arrange themselves across—rather than within—elevational zones, which has frequently brought them into parts of Amazonia inhabited by Indigenous people.

Agropastoralists have long diversified their subsistence activities by practicing pastoralism in the high grasslands, cultivating potatoes below, growing maize in the lower intermontane valleys, and farming tropical crops such as coca and fruit in the Amazonian foothills and plain. Accordingly, social networks have been distributed across discontinuous land holdings in these ecological zones—often at substantial distances—forming so-called "vertical archipelagos" through which diverse products are exchanged (Murra 1972, 1984). This was an important feature of Inka state organization, and, despite the profound disruptions and transformations of vertical archipelago arrangements since the colonial period (Mumford 2012), aspects of the system have remained an important part of life in the region through the present day (for twentieth-century iterations, see Nuñez del Prado 1969; Harris 1978; Collins 1985; Fioravanti-Molinié 1975). Indeed, as Eric Hirsch points out regarding mobility in the Colca Valley of Peru in the early 2000s, much of the experience of day-to-day Andean life is rooted in the "historically persistent vertical orientation of Andean motion" (2018, 194)—perhaps now more than ever, since modern infrastructural investment in the Andes has made it easier than ever before to make a life across elevations. When we read John Murra's observation about the contemporary Andes that "it is common to find households whose members are familiar with environments radically different from their native homes" (1984, 123–24), it is important to recall that in some cases those environments are also the homes of Indigenous Amazonians, as in the Alto Urubamba. It is this very traditional aspect of Andean motion—east/west movement across elevations as much as north/south movement within elevations—that makes the Andean-Amazonian geographic division a poor predictor of social phenomena in western South America.

An important iteration of this interregional pattern is the current burst of migration from the Andes to Amazonia, which picked up speed across South America in the twentieth century. In chapter 1, I describe how tens of thousands of people have made their way from the rural Andes of southern Peru to even more sparsely populated corners of the Alto Urubamba frontier, in a process that I call *rural-to-remote* migration. Another recent ethnography that describes a comparable process of Andean-Amazonian migration is Anna Babel's *Between the Andes and the Amazon: Language and Social Meaning in Bolivia* (2018). This book is about a Bolivian town called Saipina, located halfway between the highland city of Cochabamba and the lowland city of Santa Cruz, where people negotiate social identities based on a host of overlapping binary distinctions: Andean versus Amazonian identities, styles of dress, political parties, ways of speaking Spanish (i.e., with greater or lesser degrees of Quechua influence), and much else. People in Saipina have staked out an intermediate *valluno* (valley-dweller) social identity in which, for instance, women wear knee-length skirts instead of the long pollera skirts of the highlands or the short skirts of Santa Cruz, and the local variety of Spanish exhibits a moderate degree of influence from Quechua. The sense of ethnic *between*ness that Babel describes in Saipina is similar in some respects to the *just one world* notion that I describe in the Alto Urubamba, but among the many distinctions between that book's scholarly contribution and my own, one might say that I focus more on the *across*ness of Andean and Amazonian social relations in the Alto Urubamba—that is, the day-to-day integration of those geographical regions rather than the emergence of a distinct, intermediate form at their intersection. Babel's study also represents an interesting contrast with Andean-Amazonian relations in the Alto Urubamba: in Bolivia, the Amazonian city of Santa Cruz is associated with the Spanish language, modernity, and European heritage, set in contrast to the Quechua-speaking, traditional, Indigenous heritage associated with the highlands. Indigenous Amazonian languages are not relevant in this case. Thus the geographical configurations of language and Indigeneity in our studies are quite different, and the comparison illustrates the diversity of Andean-Amazonian transitional zones.

A critical view of the discourse of Andean-Amazonian division—of two geographically demarcated, internally coherent, minimally interacting wholes—recognizes it as a historically constructed discourse rather than an empirical fact. Indeed, there is little evidence that such a totalizing racial geography existed in anything like its current form before the nineteenth century (Emlen 2017a, 559–61). This is not to say, of course, that the Inkas and early Spaniards did not perceive people in Amazonia to be different from people in the Andes, as we can see, for instance, in the famous illustrations of exoticized lowland people in Guaman Poma de Ayala's *Nueva corónica y buen gobierno* (1615/1616). I simply mean to say that, as far as I can tell, the institutionalized, mutually exclusive, and geographically defined modern racial categories of "Indigenous Amazonian" and "Indigenous Andean" do not have reliable counterparts early in the historical record.

Certainly, large-scale pre-Columbian Andean sociopolitical formations shifted focus from localized, interregional east-west relations to a pan-Andean north-south axis (Whitten and Whitten 2008, 231–32), which constructed the lowlands as peripheral to the Andes (Santos-Granero 2002, 546–47), even while extensive interregional trade persisted between the highlands and the lowlands. An Andean-Amazonian distinction was amplified during the colonial period, when eastern populations that served as intermediaries between the highlands and the lowlands disappeared or were incorporated into one or the other region, with Christianization serving as a diagnostic in some cases (Barclay 2001; Santos-Granero 1985; Dudley 2011; Oberem 1970; Whitten 2011; Uzendoski 2004; A. C. Taylor 1988). The "Andeanization" of some intermediate people and spaces (Santos-Granero 1985, 34–35) across the eastern slopes coincided with European diseases that decimated populations in the lowlands and the cloud forests (Raymond 1985, 49; Loughlin et al. 2018), breaking formerly continuous interregional ties and making the Andean-Amazonian boundary even starker (Hornborg and Hill 2011, 13; Barclay 2001; Saignes 1985). These historical processes severed Amazonia from the Andes and constructed the lowlands as a place of alterity to be explored, conquered, incorporated, and consumed (Santos-Granero 2002). Later scholars would interpret this division between the Andes and Amazonia not as a contingency of history, but rather as a reflection of a putative incompatibility of cultural systems adapted to different ecological contexts—as in Julian Steward's claim that "the extraordinarily limited influence of the Highland on the Montaña is intelligible mainly in terms of unlike environmental conditioning of the cultures" (Steward 1948, 508; cited in Adelaar and Muysken 2004, 499). The attendant notion of the Andean-Amazonian transitional zone as a "geographic barrier" echoes throughout modern writing about South America—quite contrary to the cross-elevational logic of Andean social organization. However, in the last decade or two, scholars have come to recognize the importance of Andean-Amazonian connections (Babel 2018; Santos-Granero 2002; Pearce, Beresford-Jones, and Heggarty, forthcoming; A. C. Taylor 1999).

These patterns of interelevational social organization and landholding have important implications for understanding the region's sociolinguistic ecology. Because social networks have often been arranged discontinuously across ecological zones—rather than in blocks in the landscape—so too have languages, creating a tangle of interspersed languages and pervasive multilingualism (Mannheim 1991). This is the case with the people in this book, who speak Matsigenka, Quechua, and Spanish in all combinations and make their lives between far-flung communities, settlements, towns, and cities ranging from the Andean highlands to the Amazonian lowlands and beyond.

There is evidence that such interelevational linguistic patterns go back quite far in the region's history: for instance, the early ancestor languages of both the Quechuan and Aymaran families, some 2,500 years ago, each had separate, highly developed vocabularies for crops, products, domesticated animals, and sophisticated agricultural techniques at a wide range of ecological zones, suggesting that the speakers of both ancient languages were thoroughly engaged in subsistence activities in those zones (Emlen and Adelaar 2017). Such patterns of discontinuous, interelevational language distribution help explain the profound contact influences that have emerged among the region's languages at various times, as well as the continuities among neighboring dialects and languages that confound attempts to demarcate them with clear boundaries (as in the case of both the Quechuan and Aymaran languages). It is for this reason that "Andean" is an unsatisfying label for Quechua's diverse social and geographic distribution: while Quechua is, of course, widely spoken in some parts of the Andean highlands, the very nature of Andean social organization has pushed it westward to the coast and eastward throughout the adjacent Amazonian lowlands, creating an unbroken zone of Quechua language use running clear from the Pacific Ocean to the Brazilian border (Emlen, forthcoming).

Another prominent case concerns Yanesha' (alt. Amuesha), an Arawak language of central Peru, which exhibits a great deal of lexical and morphosyntactic influence from the neighboring, nonhegemonic variety of Yaru Quechua (Wise 1976; Adelaar 2006). The pervasive borrowing of Quechua suffixes and lexical items, including for terms of emotion and sensation, suggests a close, cross-elevational relationship based in kinship among neighbors rather than dominance by conquerors of the type that occurred later during the Inka period (C. Barbieri et al. 2014). Cholón and Hibito, spoken in the Alto Huallaga Valley of northern Peru, also exhibit considerable historical influence from Quechua (Tessmann 1930; Adelaar and Muysken 2004, 460–75), and Quechuan varieties that have extended into the lowlands of northern Peru show influence from lowland languages, including Lamas Quechua (Adelaar 2008, 266) and Chachapoyas Quechua (Valqui and ZieMendorff 2016). A contemporary situation similar to the multilingualism of the Alto Urubamba involves Asháninka-Quechua-Spanish trilingualism in the department of Ayacucho (see, e.g., Díaz Martínez 1969). Notably, these cases of multilingualism are not based solely in top-down, hegemonic power relations between a colonial language and Indigenous languages—the type of relation that has been a prominent focus in Andean linguistics. Paying attention to small-scale multilingualism among neighbors who speak Indigenous South American languages affords a more varied view of sociolinguistic relations in the region (e.g., Narayanan 2018; Mannheim 2018b), including between the Andes and Amazonia.

One of the contributions that I hope to make with this book is to offer a focused ethnographic case study that helps explain some of the regional linguistic patterns recently identified among South American languages. Since 2014 I have been working with an interdisciplinary team of researchers at Leiden University and the University of Tübingen to learn more about the linguistic prehistory of South America, and I have become interested in how these patterns in the Alto Urubamba might inform this effort. In particular, there is a growing consensus among linguists that the Andean-Amazonian geographic boundary is not a helpful predictor of linguistic typological phenomena (for instance, the features of sound systems and grammatical structures). In fact, such typological features tend to transition gradually from the highlands to the lowlands (Michael, Chang, and Stark 2014; van Gijn and Muysken, forthcoming; van Gijn 2014), and they appear to be more consistent with a broad division between eastern and western South America than between the Andes and Amazonia per se (Krasnoukhova 2012; Birchall 2014; Epps and Michael 2017). Indeed, macroregional designations such as the Central Andes may not be predictive of typological patterns in the first place (see Urban 2019). It is more productive to conceptualize much of the Andean-Amazonian region in terms of a gradual typological cline, likely arising from multilingual networks that spanned elevational and ecological zones.

While such patterns can be detected at the level of the continent, identifying the specific historical sociolinguistic relationships that led to those patterns is another matter. Thus I seek to complement this kind of historical-typological linguistic work by offering an in-depth ethnographic case study to show how one such regional network is organized and how it came about historically. This is the focus of chapter 2, which gives a detailed historical presentation of highland-lowland linguistic dynamics in the Alto Urubamba. By combining broad, continent-level analyses of large data sets with focused ethnographic and historical case studies, we can move forward with our understanding of how multilingualism and language contact have unfolded in South America throughout the millennia (see also Beier, Michael, and Sherzer 2002).

Fieldwork

Conducting research at the Andean-Amazonian interface presents a number of interpretive and practical challenges. To begin with, the powerful folk and scholarly ideology of Andean-Amazonian division casts the in-between space as something of a no-man's-land. I often heard from people in the region that "real" Quechua-speaking Andeans live at the top of the valley adjacent to the highlands, above two to three thousand meters, while "real" Matsigenkas live below one thousand meters or far up the valley's remote tributaries. I also heard from Amazonianists that Quillabamba (~1,000 meters) was a highland city, while Andeanists considered it to be in Amazonia; in effect, it was off the map for each group of scholars. The area in between—where trilingualism abounds and ethnic categories are fluid and contextual—is thought to be unrepresentative of anything at all.

For this reason, when I began my fieldwork in the valley, many people were surprised that I would want to spend my time in multiethnic and multilingual frontier communities. If my goal was to study Quechua, why didn't I head back up into the mountains? Or if I was interested in Matsigenka, wouldn't I do better to travel downriver and up one of the distant tributaries to a protected comunidad nativa where Quechua speakers hadn't yet arrived? Implicit (and in some cases explicit) in such objections was a normative vision of unmixed, monolingual societies. Thus I had to resist being pushed, under the sheer weight of the categories, upriver or downriver—both in my fieldwork and in writing this book. Keeping in mind the goal of writing an ethnography that was at once Andean and Amazonian, I tried to camp out, stubbornly, in the most thoroughly in-between places I could find, awkward though it so often was.

A second, related challenge of my fieldwork was managing the everyday politics of boundary-straddling. As I discussed earlier, the Andean-Amazonian interface is laden with an ongoing history of conflict: the arrival of mostly poor Andean farmers seeking land in traditional Matsigenka territory has set off bitter confrontations over boundaries, resource use, and political representation. For this reason, the in-between-ness of my fieldwork sometimes prompted suspicions about the nature of my loyalties. When I traveled from one Matsigenka community to visit a neighboring Andean migrant man, he asked me in Spanish, with a degree of candor that is unusual in such conversations: "¿Estás con ellos, o estás con nosotros?" (Are you with them [i.e., the Matsigenkas], or are you with us?). In other cases, Matsigenka friends also became concerned about the version of events I would hear when I went to listen to the story of an Andean migrant who had settled nearby.

Such us-or-them questions were not easy to answer. My position, then and now, has been that it is my professional responsibility to understand all sides of the issue and to hear all versions of the events, and that attempting to understand and hear them all does not constitute an endorsement of any one. I feel strongly that any book about an interethnic encounter like this one cannot be based on the perspective of only one side.

I resolved this tension, to the extent that I could, by making it my explicit policy to approach all parties from a position of maximum empathy and openheartedness. Occasionally this position brought me into frank discussions with both colonos and Matsigenkas, which usually converged on a common recognition: that both parties—the vulnerable highland farmers and climate refugees who are racialized and disdained at the margins of Peruvian society and have come to seek a better life in Amazonia, and the Indigenous Amazonians struggling to protect their land—have legitimate grievances. Furthermore, since they are now, for better or worse, stuck with each other, the more pertinent question is how to coexist peacefully. However, despite this diplomatic position, I always kept sight of the fact that there is real violence and abuse on the coffee frontier which must be brought to light. As a disciplinary matter, I believe that anthropologists must not shy away from such uncomfortable situations, lest the field prove irrelevant to the real problems of the world (for a similar sentiment, see Bourgois 1995). For these reasons, my fieldwork has been a constant diplomatic tightrope, as I have tried to acknowledge that conflicts on the frontier are the product of systemic problems in the region, without turning away from acts of abuse, exploitation, and cruelty. In line with my personal convictions, ethical research approval, and agreements with the communities, I have been careful to omit information when people crossed legal or ethical lines, which was nearly constant in the unregulated and chaotic social world of the agricultural frontier. However, despite the negative picture that might emerge from this description of the agricultural frontier, I wish to emphasize—and I hope it will be clear throughout the book—that the great majority of the people whom I have come to know in the valley maintain peaceful, cordial, and respectful relations with all of their neighbors.

Finally, the fieldwork that led to this book was difficult simply because a small minority of the valley's inhabitants have made the agricultural frontier a dangerous and volatile place. For one, as I discuss in chapter 1, relatively few people on the coffee frontier have a long-term investment in the valley: many are interested in attaining a cheap plot of land, cutting and burning off the vegetation to develop it into farmland, and selling it at a profit to finance a commercial operation elsewhere. Paired with a lack of regulation and oversight, this short-term interest has resulted in staggering social and environmental abuses (see, for instance, the fires that raged across the Amazon in 2019, which were set by agricultural colonists to clear the foliage they had cut). In addition, the remote and treacherous eastern Andean slopes are a magnet for illegal activity. The region is remote enough to harbor all manner of illicit economies beyond the reach of the state, but close enough to both the highlands and the greater Amazonian river network to be a convenient outlet for such economies. Thus, the region's day-to-day stability, at least on the frontier, was held in place more by powerful economic interests and other nonstate power brokers than by the state apparatus.

This stability has always been precarious. For instance, during my fieldwork, large portions of the valley were known locally as *zonas rojas* (red zones), controlled by cocaine-smuggling narco-terrorists and off-limits to everyone, including the police and the military.[7] This is because 13 percent of the coca leaf grown in Peru comes from La Convención (which includes the Alto Urubamba) and the adjacent Lares Valley (UNODC 2018). Some of this coca leaf is cultivated for legal, traditional consumption, but much also finds its way into the illegal cocaine trade. A system of institutionalized corruption has allowed the cocaine trade to persist undisturbed at the margins, as long as it remains contained and does not threaten the region's broader stability. However, this balance was upset in April 2012 when a group of heavily armed cocaine smugglers abducted around thirty-six gas company workers in the town of Kepashiato and marched them into a remote corner of the Matsigenka community of Inkaare (an incident I discuss in the conclusion of this book). After the hostages were freed several days later, a violent confrontation broke out between the smugglers and the Peruvian military inside Inkaare, killing people on each side and displacing the approximately 125 Matsigenka residents of Inkaare (who all survived) to a makeshift refugee camp at the COMARU headquarters in the provincial capital of Quillabamba. I had a small room and office at the headquarters, and the people of Inkaare with whom I spoke revealed great trauma and fear about returning to their community. Thankfully, the Matsigenka and colono people I lived with during that time knew that they would not be targeted by the narco-terrorists as long as they kept out of their way—though the collateral damage could be substantial, as in Inkaare. However, as the military operations of April 2012 scattered the narco-terrorists throughout the frontier, I was advised to leave the area, and I cut my fieldwork short by a month. During the several intervening days that it took to find a ride out of the frontier, I slept with a machete under my pillow, amid rumors of dangerous narco-terrorists moving through the nearby forests. This made the end of my fieldwork a harrowing experience, but also a genuine education in the dangers and instabilities that the valley's inhabitants face every day.

Research Sites

Over the course of nineteen months in 2009 and from 2010 to 2012, I conducted fieldwork in many kinds of places in the Alto Urubamba. As I mentioned, my intention was to understand this interethnic encounter from all sides, so I divided my time among remote communities of Matsigenka speakers far beyond the agricultural frontier; Quechua-speaking migrant communities higher up the valley, where the only evidence of Matsigenka people was through distant memories and place names on the landscape; migrants' home communities in the highlands; and, most of all, the communities, frontier settlements, and river ports at the leading edge of frontier expansion, where the forest meets the farmland in any given year and where the business of interethnic relations plays out in daily interactions among neighbors, kin, and trading partners. I also spent time driving around the frontier with Quechua-speaking merchants, who buy coffee from colono and Matsigenka coffee farmers and serve as their primary link to the regional agricultural economy. Many of these trips were hypnotic all-night hauls featuring sparse and intimate conversations among a handful of merchants while the headlights illuminated just a few yards of the dusty, forest-shrouded road ahead. Over two months I was embedded with a group of *lancheros* (boat pilots)—both Matsigenka and colono—who lived in the frontier river port of Ivochote and were responsible for steering goods on long wooden boats between the highlands and the Amazon plain through the treacherous Pongo de Mainique ravine (Ivochote is pictured in figure 8 below). These young men drank beer in the town's sawdust-floor cantinas, joked in all three languages, and spent their free hours sitting on tattered folding chairs on a bank overlooking the Urubamba River. They also worried about how they would support themselves in the coming years once the point of river access had moved downstream to the next port. In all of these places, I joined and recorded every meeting, construction crew, negotiation, river journey, legal proceeding, TV broadcast, harvest, road trip, funeral, hunting expedition, archaeological excavation, wedding, baptism, and birthday party that would have me (and more).

The Matsigenka Council of the Urubamba River (COMARU) also gave me a room in their headquarters and boarding house in the provincial capital of Quillabamba, where I got to know Matsigenkas from around the valley who were visiting the capital for one bureaucratic reason or another. From this base in Quillabamba, I conducted extensive interviews with NGO workers, Indigenous representatives, taxi drivers, journalists, activists, businesspeople, and municipal officials; I also learned about the urban lives of Matsigenka people making a burdened living among the restaurants and mechanic shops of Quillabamba, as well as newly arrived Andean migrants suffering alongside them in the unfamiliar tropical climate. I am very grateful to Rubén Binari Piñarreal and Plinio Kategari Kashiari for welcoming me at the COMARU headquarters in Quillabamba. I also visited the Las Malvinas natural gas plant, a center of the region's extractivist economy and a hub of interethnic interaction, in 2011.

Places in the Alto Urubamba where I conducted fieldwork are indicated on map 1 (note that I also carried out research in the Bajo Urubamba and in the nearby highlands, but those field sites are not indicated on this map). Legally titled comunidades nativas and protected areas are shaded, and comunidades nativas where I conducted fieldwork are shaded darkly and labeled with capitalized text. Andean migrant settlements where I carried out research are indicated with dots and labeled in plain text. Note that these are legal and landholding categories and, as I discuss throughout this book, do not necessarily correspond to language and ethnicity.

After around eight months of broad, multi-sited fieldwork in various parts of the Alto Urubamba, I sought out a multiethnic community in which to conduct a more focused linguistic and ethnographic study. I was invited to stay in the comunidad nativa of Yokiri for about eleven months, where I also made frequent visits to the nearby colono settlements of Huillcapampa, Nueva Luz, Otingamía, Palma Real, Quellouno, Chapo Boyero, and Estrella. This was an ideal place to carry out research on interethnic interaction: Yokiri was formed between the 1970s and early 2000s by a range of Matsigenka families who had been affected by Andean colonization in different ways, together with a family of Andean migrants. When I spent time there in 2009–12, the area including Yokiri was at the very edge of frontier expansion in the region. It had just been connected to the road network, and the people who lived there were actively engaged in transforming the region from an isolated patch of mountainous forest inhabited only by a few Matsigenka families into an expanse of thriving farmland, home to thousands of newly arrived Andean migrants. This was the

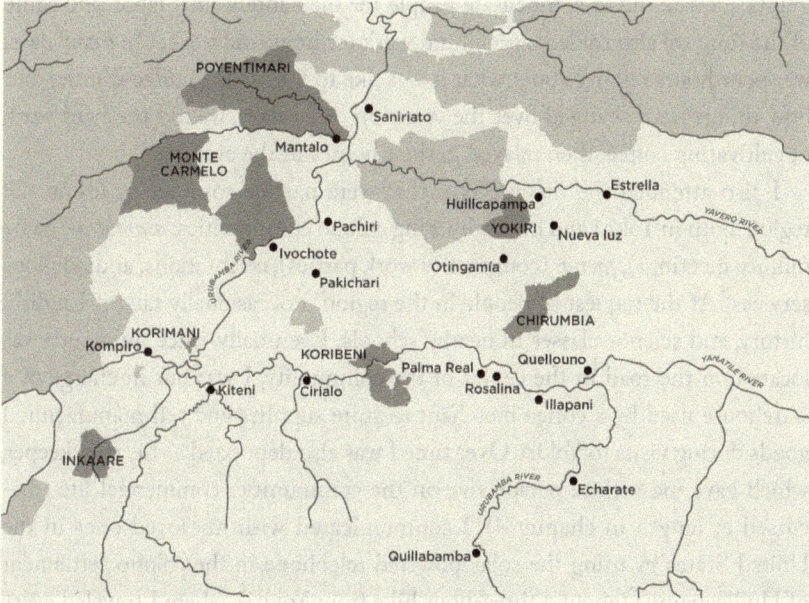

MAP 1 Field sites in the Alto Urubamba. Map designed by the author in QGIS. GIS data from Instituto del Bien Común. IBC-SICNA. Enero 2017, incluye información levantada en gabinete, AIDESEP-CIPTA, GEF PNUD, GOREL y PFS. Author's GPS data also used. Rivers and labels added by the author.

most thoroughly trilingual place I had visited in my fieldwork, and it was caught up in a dramatic burst of frontier expansion and environmental devastation.

The people of Yokiri graciously welcomed me into their lives, and I formed close relationships with them and their neighbors that will last a lifetime. When I first arrived, the nineteen male heads of household and I spent two days building a small house for me to live in near the primary school (this central area of the community is described in chapter 3 and pictured in figure 12). This generosity indebted me to each of these men, and I spent the next several weeks visiting each house to reciprocate their labor by working in their coffee fields. This gave me the opportunity to spend time with most of the community's families. They lived widely dispersed across the landscape—most of the community's nineteen houses were between a one- and three-hour walk from my own—so I often stayed for several nights in their homes. After that, I continued hiking out to the community members' houses to work with them in their coffee plantations and learn about the languages in their lives. My research grants allowed me to compensate people for their intellectual labor, and some of the time we also traded agricultural work for linguistic work. On many days, we spent hours talking about what it was like to live on the coffee frontier and how things have changed over the years; on other days, we did the hard work of cultivating coffee, then relaxed in their homes in the evening.

I also attended the many events that were part of community life in the region, both in Yokiri and in neighboring colono communities: *asambleas* (community meetings), *faenas* (community work parties), celebrations, and religious services. At the request of people in the region, I occasionally taught English, history, and science classes in nearby schools. Eventually, since my house was located on the road in the center of the community, I was put in charge of a warehouse used by a coffee merchant to store supplies and sell manufactured goods during visits to Yokiri. Over time I was also deputized as his storekeeper, which gave me a close perspective on the community's commercial life (discussed at length in chapter 4). I communicated with my loved ones in the United States by using the solar-powered telephone in the colono settlement of Huillcapampa (about a three-hour hike from Yokiri), where I traveled every few weeks to buy food and supplies.

In Yokiri, and in all of the communities, towns, and roadsides where I conducted my fieldwork, I made audio and video recordings of linguistic interactions. Many of these come from Yokiri, where my long residence allowed me to work with most of the hundred or so community members, speaking each of their languages. However, my corpus of data comes from a broader range of places and circumstances in the region and includes the voices of over 160 individuals. The whole corpus comprises around 250 hours of audio and video recordings, and I employed five Quechua- and Matsigenka-speaking research assistants to help transcribe and interpret these recordings, as well as to make recordings of their own. Like many linguistic anthropologists, I was only able to use a relatively small portion of these recordings as I wrote this book.

Given the rapid pace of change in the Alto Urubamba, I discuss events specific to my fieldwork in the past tense throughout this book. In doing so, I hope to emphasize that my fieldwork in 2009 through 2012—as is true for all fieldwork, everywhere—took place at a particular historical moment. By the time this book is published, much of what I describe will be outdated; indeed, some of it was outdated before I even left the field. Thus I intend this book as a time capsule, so that future readers will know how the Alto Urubamba came to be the way it is.

Structure of the Book

This book comprises two parts, containing three chapters each, followed by a brief conclusion. The first part explores the linguistic and social dynamics of the coffee frontier at the level of the region (chapter 1), throughout history (chapter 2), and at the micro level of a single multiethnic community (chapter 3). I use these perspectives to propose a vision of the region in which Matsigenkas and colonos are closely linked in a multiethnic, trilingual social network spanning the Andean highlands and the Amazonian lowlands. Chapter 1 begins with a broad introduction to colonos and Matsigenkas, and to the Matsigenka, Quechua, and Spanish languages. Using census data and personal histories, I explore how and why tens of thousands of mostly male Andean farmers have come to make their lives in the heart of traditional Matsigenka territory, focusing on the little-described process of *rural-to-remote migration*. I then show how this migratory influx has led to widespread interethnic marriage, and how these marriage patterns are linked to the Quechua language moving downriver with men and the Matsigenka language moving upriver with women. I conclude that the Alto Urubamba is best understood not in terms of distinct Andean and Amazonian spheres, but as *just one world*.

In chapter 2, I step back from the present day and survey the historical context of highland-lowland interaction and multilingualism in the Alto Urubamba. I have chosen to include this chapter in hopes of contributing to ongoing research on the linguistic prehistory of South America, which has emerged as an exciting new field in recent years. The valley has probably been inhabited by humans for more than 10,000 years, but all three languages currently spoken in the valley appear to have arrived relatively recently. A clear pattern emerges from a close look at the social, economic, and linguistic history of the valley: throughout the centuries, the Alto Urubamba's agricultural potential has outpaced the available labor. For this reason, people have migrated there—or been brought there by force—from a wide variety of circumstances. These people include laborers resettled by the Inkas from modern-day northern Peru and Ecuador, African slaves in the colonial period, neighboring Andean agropastoralists throughout the last millennium (and surely before), and countless others. At the same time, the paradoxical combination of the valley's close proximity to the Andean heartland and its geographic inaccessibility have made it a destination for all manner of people seeking refuge at the margins of Andean society—for instance, the Inka nobility in exile, farmers fleeing oppressive labor obligations, and today's cocaine smugglers. In all cases, people from a wide array of circumstances have come into contact with the valley's local populations to various extents, creating multilingual frontier societies that have echoes in today's situation. However, it is impossible to say anything concrete about the valley's languages and socio-linguistic dynamics before just a few centuries ago.

In chapter 3, "A Community Forms," I offer an in-depth ethnographic look at the small multiethnic frontier community of Yokiri, where I spent about eleven months in 2011–12. Yokiri's population (less than a hundred people at the time) came from a wide variety of circumstances across the region: remote areas far beyond the frontier, a nearby Dominican mission, coffee plantations in the Yavero Valley that used enslaved Matsigenkas as laborers, and a rural part of the Andean highlands. Each of these places was home to different lan-guages, cultural practices, and economic activities, and as those people married together to form the community of Yokiri, they created households that each had their own sociolinguistic histories. Yokiri is something of a microcosm of the coffee frontier, and a close look at the community and its history shows how the dynamics of multilingualism and frontier expansion play out among families and neighbors.

In the second part of the book, I build on the sociolinguistic and historical presentation in part 1 by exploring some of the contexts of speaking that were particularly relevant to the day-to-day experience of frontier life in 2009–12. In chapter 4, I begin by describing the linguistic life of coffee production on the Alto Urubamba frontier. Here I argue that becoming a successful farmer is as much a process of adopting culturally specific interactional practices as it is a technical process of learning agricultural methods. Furthermore, these linguistic and interactional practices become the common ground on which Matsigenkas encounter their Andean migrant neighbors and join the surrounding agrarian society. Of the countless linguistic interactions that are involved in coffee pro-duction, I focus on four: participating in agricultural training workshops, in Spanish; negotiating for a good price with the merchants who drive through the frontier during the harvest season, often in Quechua; using the provin-cial radio station to coordinate the movement of coffee and shame delinquent debtors, in Quechua and Spanish; and exchanging coffee for money on market day, the moment when farmers and merchants actually come together to make a sale. These types of interaction involve different languages and different cul-tural expectations about how the languages should be used. In this way, I show how the agricultural economy is linguistically mediated, how it is embedded in broader ideologies of language and ethnicity in the valley, and how socioeconomic inequalities can arise as a result of varying communicative competences.

In chapter 5, I describe how people in comunidades nativas on the coffee frontier began to engage in a new type of interactional context—the *asamblea* (community meeting)—in which the novel political subject of the *comunero* (community member) was constructed. This mode of social organization emerged through use of the "public speech" discourse genre and through the almost exclusive use of Spanish, which was considered to be an ethnically neutral language vis-à-vis Matsigenka and Quechua, and thus the most acceptable language for public, official speech in multiethnic communities. The domain of political action that was constituted through these interactions was the central means by which members of comunidades nativas on the Alto Urubamba fought to establish a space of autonomy and self-determination in the tumultuous emerging frontier society. In this way, interactions related to participation in the agrarian society presented in chapter 4—mostly in Quechua—and asamblea interactions oriented toward differentiation from that society—mostly in Spanish—represented opposed domains of morality and political action.

Chapter 6 explores the discourses that people drew on as they talked about the landscape of the Alto Urubamba in different contexts. As a case study, I present how people from different backgrounds interpreted the mysterious etymology of the toponym Yokiri, and how these interpretations were embedded in broader conceptualizations of the landscape, its history, and even the kinds of beings that were thought to inhabit it. Some Matsigenka speakers invoked a particular mythic view of history in their etymologies through use of the myth narration discourse genre, in which the landscape is inhabited by spirits that kill humans who venture into their territory. However, during an asamblea the very same places were described, in the Spanish discourse genre of "official talk," as a potential site for road construction and agricultural development. This chapter explores how such different—and apparently contradictory—discourses could coexist in Yokiri's culture of interaction. The chapter concludes that as the landscape of the Alto Urubamba is transformed, so too are the ways in which people speak about the landscape—and vice versa, since so much of the process of becoming a farmer involves learning to navigate the interactional world of coffee farming (as I argue in chapter 4).

The book ends with a 2012 incident that unfolded in the Matsigenka community of Inkaare, where a battle broke out between the Peruvian military and a group of heavily armed cocaine smugglers. I chose to conclude with this incident to draw attention once again to the high stakes of frontier expansion in the Alto Urubamba. Significantly, this battle took place just a few kilometers from where the Inkas operated a capital-in-exile for almost four decades after the European invasion in the sixteenth century. These incidents demonstrate the perennial nature of global geopolitical incursions into the forests of the Alto Urubamba, and they show how Matsigenkas and Andean migrants have fought to find a place for themselves within the tumultuous and ever-changing social world of the valley.

PART I

An Interregional Society

Chapter 1

People and Languages on the Coffee Frontier

O n the banks of the Yavero River, about thirty kilometers from its confluence with the Urubamba River, there is a colono settlement called Huillcapampa (see map 1). In 2009–12, it consisted of a wide, grassy central square hemmed in by a single row of wooden buildings, which—though undifferentiated from the outside—housed an assortment of homes, dirt-floored bars, general stores, and warehouses, as well as a small secondary boarding school. The sheer hills that loomed above Huillcapampa were covered in a patchwork of riotous forest, neat cow pastures, and tangled coffee plantations.

To walk through Huillcapampa in 2009–12 was to be immersed in the multilingual and multiethnic social milieu of the coffee frontier. Quechua-speaking migrant women in long polleras (traditional Andean skirts) sat on wide, rough-hewn benches in front of their stores, offering a basic meal of eggs and rice to laborers at the end of a long day of work in the coffee fields. Matsigenka families from the nearby comunidades nativas of Yokiri and Matoriato strolled through town, speaking Matsigenka. Some wore traditional woven cushma gowns, but most preferred polyester soccer jerseys emblazoned with the names of regional coffee distributors and hardware stores. Andean colonos and Matsigenkas sat side by side on stools drinking beer and Inca Kola, joking in Quechua or Spanish, and opining about the concerns of the day: which farmers' coffee was especially high in quality; where the municipal road crews were planning to make improvements in the coming months; how to fix a coffee pulper with a stiff crank; and who stole the wheelbarrow that had been left overnight by the construction team building the new health post. Matsigenka parents turned away from these Quechua and Spanish conversations to scold their children in Matsigenka. Meanwhile, teenagers from the secondary boarding school—around a third from Matsigenka comunidades nativas and two thirds from colono migrant communities, during my fieldwork—chased each other around the grass, bought candy from Quechua-speaking store owners lounging in front of their wares, and took turns jumping off a low, muddy cliff into the Yavero River below, a welcome relief from the oppressive heat of the valley bottom.

In the 1950s, this region of the Yavero Valley had been dense rain forest, inhabited only by a sparse network of Matsigenka families. The nearest Andean settlement was still more than thirty kilometers upriver. Georg von Hassel, a German civil engineer, described this area's potential for Andean colonization during an early expedition there in 1904: "In all of the plains that are formed in the bends and turns of the hills and the river, there are magnificent fields for all kind of crops; the ancient [Inka] terraces are only covered by grass, so they don't present serious difficulty for establishing plantations; the many waterfalls that offer their strong driving power [for mills] and a beautiful and healthy environment, qualify this valley for colonization; it is an enchanted paradise" (Hassel 1907, 372; my translation). Matsigenka people are occasionally mentioned in von Hassel's description, but his account emphasizes the lower Yavero Valley's openness and potential for colonization. By the 1950s, once a terrible malaria epidemic that had peaked in the 1930s was brought under control, thousands of Andean colonos began working their way down the Yavero Valley in pursuit of von Hassel's dream.

Since Indigenous Amazonians did not have a legal structure through which to title their land until the 1970s, the Matsigenkas who lived in the stretch of the Yavero Valley that was colonized before that time were either displaced farther into the Yavero Valley and its tributaries or incorporated into the rural agricultural society that had come to surround them (see map 1). Those who joined the agricultural society learned Quechua and worked in the coffee fields of the migrants who had occupied their land. Many Matsigenka people also had children with colonos during this time (mostly Matsigenka women and colono men), creating a kinship network that spanned both sides of the frontier. One Matsigenka couple named Ángel and Cristina, who were young children when colonos first arrived in the 1950s, described to me what this experience was like one day when I visited their home (transcript 1). In this conversation they referred to Quechua-speaking Andean colonos as *gente blanca* (white people), a common term among Matsigenkas that invokes the Andean migrants' status as colonists rather than their skin color (which is often darker than that of Matsigenkas). Both Cristina and Ángel speak Matsigenka, Quechua, and some Spanish; in this transcript, Ángel speaks Spanish, and Cristina speaks Quechua, marked in underlined text. Note that Ángel's Spanish is heavily influenced by both Quechua and Matsigenka, and may be unfamiliar to some Spanish-speaking readers. Similarly, Cristina's Quechua is influenced by Matsigenka.

Transcript 1

ÁNGEL: Mi papá tenía un terreno grande. Cuando ha venido gente blanca, todo ha quitado pe. Ha venido, entra y hace roce y lo que allí es, "¡A trabajar pe!" Trae ropa, es engaño ya. Trabajando tranquilo mientras, ¡azo! dueño es él pe, gente blanca. Así era pues. Ahora es dueño ellos ahora pe ooh, caramba. . . . Por eso gente blanca ha venido, si no tiene papeles—ellos han hecho papel, todo ya está.

CRISTINA: Mana título mana papel kanchu, nada. Anchhay gente blancokuna hamunku hunt'arapunku hunt'arapunku chayman.

ÁNGEL: Todo ha llenado.

ÁNGEL: My father had a big piece of land. When the white people [i.e., colonos] came, they took it all away. They came and cleared [the forest], and everyone who [was] there [i.e., the Matsigenkas], it's, "Get to work!" They brought clothing [as gifts], that's a trick. Working normally, while damn! while he's the owner, the white person. That's how it was. Now they're the owners, damn. . . . That's why the white people came, if you don't have papers—they made papers, and that was that.

CRISTINA: If you don't have a title or papers, nothing. That's how the white people came and filled up and filled up [the valley] there.

ÁNGEL: They filled it all up.

When the Peruvian comunidades nativas law took effect in the mid-1970s, Matsigenkas living immediately beyond Huillcapampa formalized their claim to the communities of Yokiri to the southwest and Matoriato to the west (see maps 1 and 4). This blocked further colono settlement in these parts of the Yavero

Valley, though it was too late for the many families upriver from Huillcapampa to recover their land. In this way, Huillcapampa—surrounded by Matsigenka communities on two sides and created through an encounter between colonos and Matsigenkas like Ángel and Cristina in the mid-twentieth century—came to be a center of the multiethnic frontier by the time of my fieldwork in 2009–12. Some of Ángel and Cristina's siblings and children married colonos, while others married Matsigenkas; all of these people and their children passed through Huillcapampa frequently as they visited their kin and carried on the countless daily interactions, in all three languages, that made up the social life of the coffee frontier. Whether particular members of this sprawling multi-ethnic and multilingual kinship network "counted" as Matsigenkas or colonos depended very much on one's perspective, and on the context of interaction.

With the goal of introducing the linguistic, ethnic, and economic panorama of places like Huillcapampa, this chapter gives a general overview of the Alto Urubamba agricultural frontier in 2009–12. I begin with a general description of the frontier society, and then I give an introduction to Matsigenka society and language. This is followed by a description of Andean society and the Quechua language, and their projection into the lowlands through the process of rural-to-remote migration. Finally, I discuss interethnic marriage and offer a vision of the Alto Urubamba as *just one world*, rather than distinct Andean and Matsigenka worlds.

The Agricultural Frontier, 2009–2012

There is a paradox at the heart of the Alto Urubamba. On the one hand, its jagged, densely forested hills make it one of the most impenetrable landscapes on Earth. For this reason, it has long served as a refuge for the Indigenous Matsigenka people, as well as for countless others seeking protection in its forests (including, most famously, the Inkas, who operated a capital-in-exile in those forests for decades after the Spanish conquest). On the other hand, the proximity of the valley to the vast agricultural heartland of the southern Peruvian Andes has also made it a conduit of interregional trade and a target of agricultural colonization.

Much of the valley's history has unfolded through the interplay of these contradictory characteristics. In fact, paradoxically, at some moments it has been the valley's very isolation that has pushed it into the center of global affairs. The density of its forests, combined with the valley's proximity to the highlands, is what made it a viable base of operations for the Inkas in exile—inaccessible enough to let them hide from the Spanish for decades, while close enough to allow periodic assaults on the nearby city of Cusco (see chapter 2). Today's cocaine producers operate with impunity in the same secluded forests (as I describe in the conclusion of this book), but also run a sprawling distribution network afforded by the valley's position at the junction of the Andean road network and the Amazonian river system.

This combination—inaccessibility paired with close physical proximity to the Andean heartland—has presented a special kind of economic opportunity for highland farmers today: land in the Alto Urubamba is bountiful and cheap, given its isolation, but also close enough to the highlands to allow for profitable commercial agriculture. The only missing piece in this equation is aggressive road construction to link the expansive tracts of undeveloped tropical forest to the nearby highland economic sphere. The agricultural economy and, later, revenues from the massive Camisea natural gas project have spurred this investment in construction and created a labyrinthine road network extending from the Andes to the remotest corners of the valley.[1] This confluence of factors—inexpensive land, proximity to the highlands, and frenzied infrastructural spending—has transformed the Alto Urubamba into a burgeoning agricultural frontier and brought tens of thousands of highland migrants into the lives of Matsigenka people like Ángel and Cristina.

I have defined the term *agricultural frontier* elsewhere as "a zone of rapid economic and demographic transformation resulting from the incorporation of landscapes with no major commercial agricultural activity and relatively low population densities into a regionally or globally linked capitalist agricultural system, often through colonization at the expense of indigenous people, and almost always resulting in ecological devastation" (Emlen 2017a, 563). I find this to be a useful and suitably narrow definition that captures the economic and environmental context of the Alto Urubamba and situates the colono-Matsigenka encounter. Parts of the valley that were heavily forested just a decade or two ago are now productive farmland; meanwhile, frontier outposts like Huillcapampa that were carved out of the forest a few decades ago now have health posts, schools, modern sanitation systems, and electricity (which arrived in Huillcapampa during my fieldwork in 2012). Some even had Internet cafés where local farmers and Matsigenka people sat side by side using Facebook, as well as bars equipped with flat-screen televisions and satellite cable for watching soccer games, *telenovelas* (soap operas) from Lima and other Latin American countries, and John Wayne Westerns dubbed in Spanish, in which some frontier migrants found echoes of their own lives. (In some frontier bars, paying colono customers sat inside, while Matsigenkas who couldn't afford to buy drinks stood in the dirt behind the building and watched the television over a chest-high wall. I often wondered what they thought of the frontier dramas depicted in the John Wayne Westerns.) Meanwhile, the provincial capital of Quillabamba—a sleepy crossroads just a few decades ago—is now home to a thriving middle class with multistory homes and disposable income to spend at the many dance clubs and fried chicken restaurants that have appeared across the city.

Much of the Alto Urubamba's newfound prosperity is due to recent dramatic investment in transportation infrastructure. Whereas just a few decades ago it took days to travel between the cities of Cusco and Quillabamba, by the early 2000s the trip could be made in just a half day's drive, mostly along paved roads. The trip is by now so easy that some highland residents travel to Quillabamba—recently branded *la ciudad del eterno verano* (the city of eternal summer)—to enjoy a weekend in the tropical climate. This unprecedented level of highland-lowland connection has stimulated the tropical fruit, cacao, and coffee industries, and tropical products are now distributed cheaply to markets across the highlands and beyond. Meanwhile, the huge Camisea project, operated by a consortium of multinational energy companies, exploits the largest natural gas reserve in South America, which sits squarely underneath the territory of Matsigenkas and other nearby Indigenous people. This project is a centerpiece of the Peruvian economy, and it supplies much of the country's energy. It has brought tens of thousands of labor migrants to the most remote parts of the valley, and royalties from the project have made the district government of Echarate—where many Matsigenkas live—one of the most well-funded in Peru. Cocaine production has also brought wealth into towns and cities around the valley, though this activity remains mostly at the margins and its economic effects are difficult to assess. Investment in transportation infrastructure has linked the region to the broader lowland river network as well: one can now drive from Quillabamba nearly to the Pongo de Mainique (the gateway to the Amazon plain) in less than a day, and from there board a boat bound for the Ucayali River ports of Sepahua, Atalaya, and Pucallpa (and the Amazon River beyond).

The Andean expansion down the Urubamba Valley over the twentieth and twenty-first centuries has taken place through a steady succession of river ports.

Drivers and traders from the Andes make their way downriver to the terminus of the road network, where they meet boat pilots who move their wares into the Amazon plain and supply them with tropical goods for distribution in the highlands. Road travel is cheaper, faster, and safer than river travel, so highland merchants prefer to travel by road as far as they can. In the late nineteenth and early twentieth centuries, the junction between the road and river transportation networks was the Rosalina hacienda (see map 1); by the early 1970s the Urubamba River port had moved to the town of Kiteni (Rosengren 1987, 19), which is pictured in figure 2. In the 1980s and 1990s it had progressed as far as Tintinikiato and Ivochote, pictured in figure 8. During my fieldwork in 2009–12, I spent two months embedded with an association of boat pilots in Ivochote as they worked to reestablish the river port in the new town of Saniriato. Saniriato is at the boundary of the Santuario Nacional Megantoni, where road construction is not permitted—at least not yet. Note that this form of connection between the Andes and the lowland river network has a long history: for instance, in 1835 the point of contact was El Encuentro, a sandy beach at the confluence of the Yanatile and Urubamba Rivers (near the town of Quellouno),

FIGURE 2 The frontier settlement of Kiteni, 2011. Photograph by the author.

where two to three hundred Piros and Matsigenkas met highlanders and traded forest products for manufactured goods (Miller 1836; see map 1). The junction was farther upriver in earlier decades and centuries.

The rapid integration of the Alto Urubamba into the agrarian heartland of the Cusco highlands over the twentieth century is reflected in the transformation of the landscape. As patches of forest in the valley are claimed and prepared for agriculture, roads are eventually built to connect them with the highlands; these roads then provide access to develop the next patches of forest beyond. The result is a relentless march down the Urubamba River and up its tributaries of highland migrants and the frontier economy and society they bring with them. Whereas a few decades ago most of the region was blanketed in continuous cloud forest, now it is a patchwork of farmland, islands of titled Matsigenka land, and protected reserves. If agricultural development continues at its current frenzied pace, nearly every bit of land not protected in a reserve or a comunidad nativa will soon become farmland.

The day-to-day experience of deforestation in the Alto Urubamba is one of constant struggle against the unstable and volatile landscape. Cutting and burning the forest makes the environment drier and more prone to wildfires, of the kind that had engulfed the Brazilian Amazon as this book went to press in 2019. It also removes the root structures that hold the muddy soil together, leading to terrible erosion and mudslides. One afternoon in the rainy season of 2011, while I was staying in a small colono frontier hamlet, a mudslide nearby blocked the course of a small, knee-deep river (such a blockage is known in Spanish as a *represa*, or "dam"). The people of the valley knew that the ominous halt in the flow of the river meant that the water was building up on the other side of the represa, and that it would soon burst forth, possibly sending water careening into the town itself. The panicked residents ran to the represa with shovels to clear the blockage, shouting to each other in Quechua over the roar of the accumulating water. When it broke, a deafening wall of water rushed down the riverbed. A man with two cows had been standing near the bank waiting to cross, and the torrent carried one of the cows downstream, where within seconds it had disappeared below the surface, never to be seen again. Thankfully, the town was safe and no people were hurt; however, the same river was blocked by a mudslide again in 2014, this time sending the deluge of water careening into the town. The flood destroyed buildings and buried a children's playground, but this happened in the middle of the night, so nobody was hurt (RPP Noticias 2014). In 1998, a much larger represa led to the tragic Aobamba flood, which destroyed the town of Santa Teresa. Remarkably, only seventeen people were killed—the population scrambled to a high point of land when they saw the rapidly declining water level, saving hundreds of lives. The erosion caused by deforestation has made experiences like this an omnipresent fact of life in the valley. This is the daily experience of living in a landscape in crisis.

Andean migrants and Matsigenka people, however, have tended not to use the landscape in the same ways. Matsigenkas living in titled comunidades nativas have cleared the forest more slowly than their colono neighbors, while areas protected by the state have, so far, proven to be an effective bulwark against deforestation. Map 2 shows forest cover loss from 2000 to 2018 in the Alto Urubamba (data from Hansen et al. 2013). Far more forest has been lost in the colonization zones outside of the comunidades nativas (Yokiri, Matoriato, and Poyentimari) than within them—though land has also been cleared in the comunidades nativas as their residents have adopted the commercial agricultural

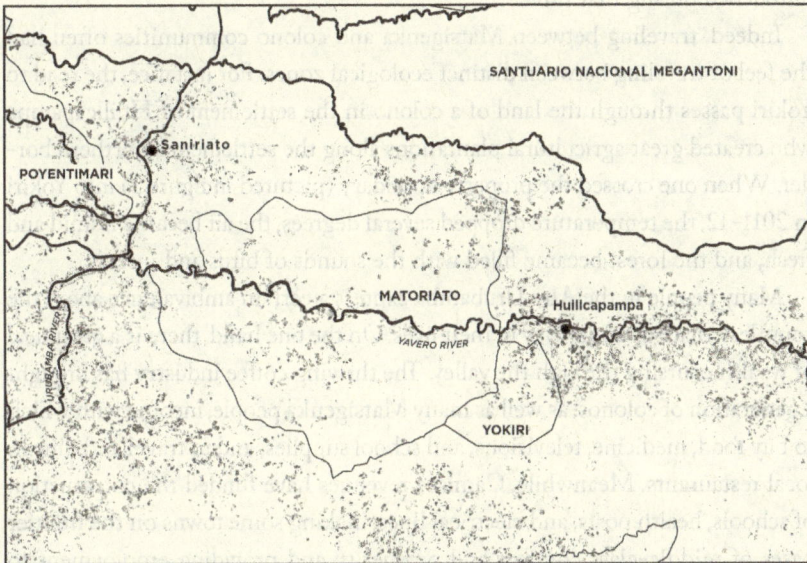

MAP 2 Loss of forest cover in the lower Yavero Valley, 2000–2018. Map designed by the author in QGIS. GIS data from Hansen/UMD/Google/USGS/NASA; Instituto del Bien Común. IBC-SICNA. Enero 2017, incluye información levantada en gabinete, AIDESEP-CIPTA, GEF PNUD, GOREL y PFS. Author's GPS data also used. Rivers and labels added by the author.

FIGURE 3 The property boundary between Huillcapampa (left) and Yokiri (right) is also an ecological boundary (2011). Photograph by the author.

practices of their colono neighbors. Meanwhile, the forest of the Santuario Nacional Megantoni protected area, at the top of the map, has been virtually untouched during that time.

Indeed, traveling between Matsigenka and colono communities often had the feel of traveling between distinct ecological zones. For instance, the road to Yokiri passes through the land of a colono in the settlement of Huillcapampa who created great agricultural plantations along the settlement's northern border. When one crossed the property boundary (pictured in figure 3) into Yokiri in 2011–12, the temperature dropped several degrees, the air became humid and fresh, and the forest became filled with the sounds of birds and insects.

Many people in the Alto Urubamba express a certain ambivalence about the countless changes under way in their lives. On the one hand, there is a great deal of wealth coursing through the valley. The thriving coffee industry has brought a generation of colonos, as well as many Matsigenka people, income with which to buy food, medicine, televisions, and school supplies, and to travel and dine in local restaurants. Meanwhile, Camisea revenues have funded the construction of schools, health posts, and electrical lines, making some towns on the frontier oases of middle-class comfort and prosperity and providing employment to virtually anyone who wants it. Infant mortality is down; life expectancy is up; schoolchildren look to the future with hope.

On the other hand, life on the coffee frontier is exceedingly difficult for a great many people, and fraught with the uncertainty and anxiety that are inherent to a society undergoing chaotic and destructive change. Matsigenka people who lived by fishing just a couple of decades ago find the streams choked with mud from erosion and empty of life (a problem faced by Indigenous Amazonians all across the Andean frontier; Tallman 2019). The dozensfold increase in population density, the omnipresent grinding of diesel engines, the periodic roar of dynamite across the hills, and the constant threat of land invasion add a degree of claustrophobia and psychological strain to the background of everyday life. The cocaine trade has raised fears of violent strangers traveling through remote parts of Matsigenka communities at night; people look over their shoulders more than they used to. Matsigenkas find that their waking hours have been reallocated to the unceasing feedback loop of clearing land, growing coffee, and spending their earnings on food that they once acquired from the landscape. Many must work harder and harder just to keep up, and fear that the frontier society is spinning out of control—that the bewildering changes all around them will one day swallow them up and leave them with nothing at all. Many colonos express the same anxieties, particularly those who come from difficult circumstances in the highlands and now find themselves alone and overwhelmed in a remote, unfamiliar environment, far from their loved ones and the relative comforts of community living. Everyone is trying to find their footing on this shifting ground. Though data are not collected on such matters, depression is certainly up too, as well as alcoholism.

There was a Spanish turn of phrase—*dejar algo*, "to leave something behind"— that I heard over and over when people, both Matsigenkas and colonos, reflected on their lives and their hopes for the future. *Sólo quiero dejar algo para mis hijos* (I just want to leave something behind for my children) was the refrain, with the goal that the next generation might one day leave the frontier and become comfortable, city-dwelling professionals. Amid the upheavals of frontier expansion, one's modest daily toil was redeemed by a better life for the generations to come. This sentiment is at once hopeful, melancholic, and a touch fatalistic—it expresses a belief that upward mobility is attainable, but also that it is already too late for one's own life. These emotional burdens are central to the experience of day-to-day life in places like the Alto Urubamba, for Matsigenkas and colonos alike.

However, I do not wish to suggest that all is suffering and dread on the coffee frontier: there are as many moments of joy and fulfillment as there are of anxiety and alienation. A good laugh is easy to find. In this book, I try to present as full an emotional range of frontier experiences as possible, by seeking out the good and not turning away from the bad (for reflections on balancing the realism of a "dark anthropology" with the optimism of an "anthropology of the good," see Ortner 2016; Robbins 2013).

Matsigenkas and the Matsigenka Language in the Alto Urubamba

The best place to begin a description of the Alto Urubamba's social and linguistic fabric is with the Matsigenka people. Since the time of the earliest records, Matsigenkas have lived along the Urubamba River and its remote tributaries, as well as in the adjacent watershed of the Manu River (see chapter 2 for a historical overview). Traditionally, Matsigenkas have subsisted on hunting, fishing, gathering, and horticulture (A. W. Johnson 1983), though commercial agricultural and wage labor have become increasingly important parts of daily economic activity in recent decades. Matsigenka society has been described in terms of "family-level" social organization (A. W. Johnson 2003), a typological classification introduced by Julian Steward to describe Great Basin Shoshonean society: "a family, alone and unaided, could obtain virtually all the food it consumed; manufacture all its clothing, household goods, and other articles; rear and train its children without assistance; take care of its sick except in time of crisis; be self-sufficient in its religious activities; and, except on special occasions, manage its own recreation" (1955, 103; see also Rosengren 1987). Consistent with this kind of social organization, many Matsigenka families have tended to live in small hamlets dispersed widely across the landscape, a pattern of social organization and settlement layout that is common among other Indigenous peoples of the Andean-Amazonian foothills, including Asháninkas (Varese 2002, 25) and Ashéninkas (Hvalkof and Veber 2005; Killick 2007). The kinship system attributed to Matsigenka people in the anthropological literature is based on a distinction between parallel cousins (the children of same-sex siblings) and cross-cousins (the children of opposite-sex siblings); the latter are considered ideal marriage partners (A. W. Johnson 2003, 159–68; O. Johnson 1978; Rosengren 2017). One benefit of this practice is that it allows people to find spouses within their own communities and thus avoid either bringing outsiders into their land or losing population and creating obligations to people in other places.

The Matsigenka language is a member of the sprawling Arawak family, which comprises dozens of languages scattered throughout Amazonia and the

Caribbean (Aikhenvald 1999). The Kampan subgroup of the Arawak family, which includes Matsigenka, is concentrated in the eastern Andean foothills and the adjacent Amazon plain (Michael 2008, 212–19). However, some Matsigenka communities in the Alto Urubamba also include territory in the northern slopes of the towering Vilcabamba Range, up to four thousand meters in elevation, raising the question of how meaningful it is to characterize Matsigenka as an "Amazonian language." Several thousand people speak the three varieties of Matsigenka—Alto Urubamba, Bajo Urubamba, and Manu—which, along with Nanti, form a dialect continuum in that order (Michael 2008, 218). Nanti and the three varieties of Matsigenka are more or less mutually intelligible, even at the extremes of the continuum, which suggests a relatively recent arrival in the Urubamba Valley (see chapter 2). For more about the Matsigenka language, see Snell (2011) and Vargas Pereira and Vargas Pereira (2013).

Matsigenka people have always lived in a wider variety of circumstances than the dispersed, decentralized communities described above, but their modes of living are especially diverse today. On the agricultural frontier, where they are joining the rural agrarian society of the Andes, many Matsigenka communities have become more nucleated; this tendency is particularly strong in communities founded by Dominican missionaries in the early twentieth century and by Evangelical missionaries in the mid-twentieth century. The last century of missionary influence has also generated a degree of social stratification among Matsigenkas: those who grew up in Dominican missions or Evangelical communities are more likely than others to work and study in local urban centers, speak Spanish, marry colonos, and occupy positions of leadership in the Indigenous organizations. Some Matsigenkas—particularly from Dominican and Evangelical communities—have also migrated permanently to towns and cities in the region, and some attend universities in the city of Cusco, where they may receive scholarships from the Camisea gas consortium to pursue professional degrees (Steele 2015, 2018).

Matsigenkas from all backgrounds are subject to substantial discrimination and marginalization within Peruvian society. National discourses of race treat Indigenous Amazonians as being outside of the country's civic and economic life and incapable of social advancement; at best this attitude has led to a paternalistic stance among policy makers and fellow citizens, and at worst it has made them subject to all manner of abuse, exploitation, and neglect. The latter tendency can be seen particularly clearly, for instance, in Matsigenkas' dealings with the Camisea natural gas project, the geopolitical juggernaut that looms over much of life in the Alto Urubamba (Smith 2005). The periodic spills that have plagued the project have disproportionately affected Matsigenka people, since the drilling sites and gas pipeline are mostly in areas that are—ostensibly—set aside for Matsigenkas. At the same time, even though Matsigenka communities have borne the steepest costs of gas drilling, they have not seen many of the benefits: despite the deluge of money that pours through the valley, only a pittance is invested in those communities (D. Hill 2016; Shepard and Oyola 2017). In 2011 I attended a meeting in a Matsigenka community where a gas pipeline had recently been built through the forest. The leaders there criticized the local government for also clearing land to build medium-tension electrical lines linking two neighboring colono communities to the electrical grid without also providing access lines for the Matsigenka community itself.

As the rural agrarian society of the Andes has come to surround them, many Matsigenka speakers have begun to shift to Spanish and, to a lesser extent, Quechua. This shift has accelerated as increasing numbers of Matsigenkas marry colonos and move to urban centers near and far. However, there are still enough monolinguals and stable Matsigenka-Spanish bilinguals, even among the youngest generations, that the language is not perilously endangered at the moment (it would probably be considered "threatened" on the scale proposed by *Ethnologue*; see Simons and Fennig 2018). There are limited attempts to institutionalize language revitalization programs, but most Matsigenka speakers I know do not find this to be an urgent priority, nor has the discourse of language endangerment been widely adopted. Matsigenkas speak the variety of Spanish that is widespread among rural highlanders—the distinctive *Andean Spanish*—which is quite different from other varieties of Spanish around the world. Andean Spanish has emerged as Quechua speakers adopted Spanish as a second language and imported various aspects of Quechua grammar (see, e.g., Sánchez 2003) and phonology (see, e.g., Pérez Silva, Acurio Palma, and Bendezú Araujo 2008; Babel 2018; Cerrón-Palomino 1975; Huayhua 2013) into it—a process that linguists call *substrate influence*. This Quechua-influenced variety is the kind of Spanish that Matsigenka speakers are exposed to, and they also apply their own features from Matsigenka. This complex trilingual product exemplifies the tangled history of multilingualism and migration between the Andes and Amazonia (for more about the Spanish spoken in the Alto Urubamba, see Emlen, forthcoming).

As I discuss throughout this book, many Matsigenka speakers on the coffee frontier manage complex bilingual or trilingual lives. Conversations among family members in the home generally take place in Matsigenka, while interactions with colono neighbors are generally conducted in Quechua or in Spanish, depending on the Matsigenkas' familiarity with those languages. Meanwhile, engagements with state actors occur almost exclusively in Spanish. This language ideology—which posits an indexical association between Spanish and Peruvian institutional life on the one hand, and between Quechua and the rural agrarian society on the other—is imported from the highlands, and it plays an important role in the organization of multilingual discourse on the frontier (see chapters 4 and 5). However, some parts of the state apparatus have come to be conducted in Matsigenka—most notably the EIB (Bilingual and Intercultural Education program), discussed further in chapter 3, which offers limited Matsigenka language curriculum in comunidades nativas. The state has also begun training Matsigenka and Quechua interpreters to mediate in prior consultation meetings (de Pedro Ricoy, Howard, and Andrade Ciudad 2018). During my fieldwork, the local radio station Radio Quillabamba also broadcast a popular hour-long weekly radio program in Matsigenka called *Iriniane Mavaintini*, squeezed in among the Spanish and Quechua programming.

Ethnic consciousness is a complex issue among Matsigenkas in the Alto Urubamba, but in my experience, most do not feel a strong sense of belonging to such a grouping (see also Rosengren 2003; A. W. Johnson 2003). During my fieldwork, Matsigenka ethnicity mostly became relevant during explicit contexts of identity-based political action, like protests against the Camisea gas companies and meetings with COMARU (Consejo Machiguenga del Río Urubamba, one of the Indigenous organizations that represents Matsigenka people). These were the only times that many Matsigenkas wore traditional cushma gowns and employed other material signifiers of ethnic identity. Some public displays of the Matsigenka language were implicated in the creation of an ethnic public—for instance, Matsigenkas who listened to the weekly *Iriniane Mavaintini* radio program were acutely aware of a Matsigenka ethnic identity, if only during that moment. This was especially true since they knew that their language was being broadcast into the homes of thousands of colono families across the valley, which served as a potent political statement.

The principle of ethnic difference was certainly an important element of interactions between Matsigenkas and colonos (as I discuss throughout this book), but not necessarily in reference to Matsigenkas as part of a bounded ethnolinguistic group. This is because, despite the long history of discrimination that has defined Matsigenka entanglements with broader Peruvian society, the notion of a Matsigenka ethnolinguistic group itself emerged only within twentieth-century ethnopolitical discourses and has still not been widely taken up on the ground. Indeed, there is little tradition of formal leadership in Matsigenka society (Rosengren 1987), and the traditional family-level social commitments and dispersed settlement pattern have not been conducive to the emergence of a broad and enduring ethnic consciousness. Before the late nineteenth century, the ancestors of today's Matsigenka people were simply called *campas*, along with other speakers of Arawak languages on the eastern Andean slopes; the term *Matsigenka* (which means "person") was first introduced as an ethnonym by Dominican missionaries in the late nineteenth and early twentieth centuries as they sought to distinguish their apostolic prefecture from that of the Franciscans, who continued to use the term *campa* (Rosengren 2004, 11–12; 1987, 37). This grouping also corresponded to a linguistic distinction between Matsigenka and the other Kampan Arawak languages farther north, which are notably different. The label *Matsigenka* was not adopted by Matsigenka people themselves until the 1960s. However, as the demographic and economic circumstances of the valley have brought new challenges—Andean colonization, natural gas extraction, and cocaine smuggling, to name a few—Indigenous mobilization through the discourse of ethnicity has become increasingly important in their lives. The institutional codification of ethnicity through state entities like the bilingual education program and legal categories for land titling has made ethnicity a more salient social category among Matsigenkas today, though only in particular contexts, particularly those involving the state (and opposition to it). The formation of ethnicity through interaction with the state is a familiar process in South America (Jackson 1995).

Colonos use several words for Matsigenkas, most of which are considered offensive and derogatory. The most common Spanish terms are the very offensive *chuncho* ("savage" or "wild Indian," from the Quechua *ch'unchu*, of the same meaning), *nativo/a* (native), and *salvaje* (meaning "savage," mostly archaic). The specific ethnonym *Matsigenka* and its Hispanicized spelling *Machiguenga* are often used, as well as *Machiganga* (mostly among older colonos in Quillabamba and in published texts from the early twentieth century). Some of these labels are also suffixed with the Spanish diminutive *-ito/-ita* (e.g., *chunchito/a* [little savage], *nativito/a* [little native]), which makes the terms particularly offensive and patronizing. However, the offensiveness of these terms is not always recognized in Peruvian society at large, and it is still possible to hear policy makers using them in official discourse.

Interestingly, *chuncho* is also related to the Matsigenka term *chonchoite* (note the suffix *-ite*, meaning "spirit"), which refers to a semihuman "cannibalistic savage" figure lurking at the periphery of Matsigenka society. Note the portability and recursivity of this concept (Irvine and Gal 2000): colonos use the label to position Matsigenkas beyond the periphery of their society, while Matsigenkas use it to invoke the same peripheral status of semihumans beyond their own social boundary.

Andeans and the Quechua Language in the Alto Urubamba

Given the remote and isolated context in which many Matsigenka speakers in the Alto Urubamba have lived over the centuries, it is no small irony that some of those communities are just a few tens of kilometers, as the crow flies, from the rural agricultural heartland of the southern Peruvian Andes. These places are so close that several of the snowcapped peaks that figure prominently in the day-to-day consciousness of many Quechua speakers in the highlands (e.g., the towering Salkantay; Boelens 2014) are also visible, from the other side, from Matsigenka communities. As a result, when modern, state-funded infrastructural development finally managed to clear a path through the valley's vertiginous topography and thick vegetation beginning in the mid-twentieth century, the short stretch of hills between the highlands and the Amazon plain was colonized by Andean farmers at an extraordinary pace.

Most of the migrants on the agricultural frontier of the Alto Urubamba come from the adjacent rural Cusco highlands—particularly the provinces of Calca, Urubamba, Anta, Canchis, Quispicanchi, Paruro, Chumbivilcas, and Paucartambo—and many of them visit and maintain close connections to their communities back home. The predominant mode of subsistence in these highland communities is agropastoralism, which combines the shepherding of camelids and sheep on the high grasslands with the cultivation of tubers, corn, and other crops at a variety of elevations. Many excellent ethnographic works have been written about these places in the rural Cusco highlands, notably Catherine Allen's (1988) description of the community of Sonqo in the nearby province of Paucartambo.

Most people in the rural Cusco highlands speak Southern Peruvian Quechua (Cusihuamán Gutiérrez 1976a, 1976b; Mannheim 1991), a member of the

Quechuan language family. The Quechuan family is spread across thousands of kilometers of western South America from southern Colombia in the north to Argentina in the south. It appears to have originated in central Peru, where it underwent intense contact with the ancient ancestor language of today's Aymara varieties and then radiated both northward and southward some two thousand years ago (for more about the history and structure of the Quechuan language family and its early contact with Aymaran languages, see Adelaar and Muysken 2004; Cerrón-Palomino 1987, 2000; Emlen 2017b; Emlen and Adelaar 2017; Emlen and Dellert, forthcoming; Heggarty and Beresford-Jones 2012; Mannheim 1991; Parker 1963; Torero 1964). Southern Peruvian Quechua is spoken by one to two million people today—a huge number, by the standards of an Indigenous American language—though it remains a politically marginalized and racially stigmatized language (Huayhua 2013).

As I mentioned earlier, most colonos in the Alto Urubamba speak the distinctive Andean variety of Spanish, which developed as Andeans imported Quechua grammatical features, phonological patterns, and vocabulary during the process of language acquisition. Andean Spanish, like Quechua, is associated with pernicious racial stereotypes in the Andes. In the highlands, Spanish and Quechua are each associated with a broader semiotic division that runs through the middle of many aspects of daily life. For instance, Anna Babel (2018) shows that the Spanish/Quechua dichotomy is mapped onto other distinctions, including pants / traditional pollera skirts, urban/rural, lowland/highland (in the case she examines, with reference to the urban center of Santa Cruz in the lowlands), and distinct political parties. It is interesting to note how such a principle of sociolinguistic division is refracted in the Alto Urubamba, where the presence of three languages complicates the kind of binary distinction found back in the highlands. For Matsigenka speakers, Quechua is associated with getting ahead in the rural agrarian society that has come to surround them, while Spanish is connected to Peruvian institutions, some of which—notably, the comunidad nativa legal structure—are designed to protect their land from the encroachments of the rural agrarian society.

Andean migrants in the Alto Urubamba usually call themselves by the Spanish terms *andino* (Andean), *colono* (settler), or *campesino* ("peasant," a term that carries racial as well as socioeconomic meaning). Less often, they use the Quechua term *runa* (Quechua-speaking person) (Allen 1988). The Spanish term *mestizo*, which is heard throughout Peru and refers to mixed European and Indigenous Andean heritage, is less common in the valley. The history of the

Alto Urubamba—the frontier, at least—is conceptualized locally in terms of an encounter between Indigenous Amazonians and Andeans, such that the European/Indigenous, coast/highland, urban/rural dichotomies invoked by the term *mestizo* are not understood to be the most relevant historical framework (for more about this term, see de la Cadena 2000, 2005). Matsigenkas in the Alto Urubamba have their own suite of labels for Andean colonos, most of which are considered offensive. The most common Matsigenka terms are *ponyarona* (or "highlander," from the Quechua *puna runa*, "highland person") and *virakocha* (or "white person," from the Quechua *wiraqucha*). The latter can refer to people with lighter skin but is also used more or less interchangeably with *ponyarona*. This term is intriguing: the Quechua term from which it comes, *wiraqucha*, refers to fair-skinned people of European descent, but Matsigenka speakers have borrowed it to refer to Quechua speakers themselves—whom they also call *gente blanca*, "white people" in Spanish, as in transcript 1 above.[2] This is another example of the recursive nature of racial terms in the Alto Urubamba. The Matsigenka use of both of these terms invokes the Andeans' status as colonizers of the valley rather than European descent or skin color—Andeans tend to have darker skin than Matsigenkas, and pale-skinned people from Europe, North America, the Peruvian coast, and some other Latin American countries like Argentina are sometimes called *gringos* (Santos-Granero 1991, 88). Another common Matsigenka term for colonos is *tovaiganankitsirira*, a construction best translated as "the ones who are becoming many," in reference to the rapid Andean influx into the Urubamba Valley.[3] Matsigenkas also refer to Andean migrants with the Spanish labels *colono* (colonist), *colonizador* (colonizer), and *campesino* ("peasant," the most neutral and respectful term).

Rural-to-Remote Migration

Scholars of Andean society have come to focus in recent decades on migration and mobility—in particular, the movement of people between rural highland communities and urban centers in the highlands and the coast (Lloyd 1980). For instance, Paerregaard (1997) describes migration from the rural community of Tapay in the Colca Canyon to the cities of Arequipa and Lima, drawing attention to the interconnectedness of those rural and urban spaces (see also Ødegaard 2010; Seligmann 1995; Altamirano 1984; Matos Mar 1986). Scholars have also noted that these migratory processes do not always end in the coastal cities—a recent study by Ulla Berg (2017) describes people from rural communities in the Mantaro Valley of central Peru who migrate to cities on the Peruvian coast, and from there to the United States. International Peruvian migrants often remit money to care for their children and families back home (Leinaweaver 2010). These studies have been accompanied by an increasing recognition of Indigenous-language speakers in the urban spaces of Peru and the ongoing shift they are making to Spanish (Klee and Caravedo 2006; S. Myers 1973; Marr 1998).

However, despite this emerging scholarly focus on mobility and migration in the Andes, less attention has been paid to a different, but important, demographic trend: the movement of people from the rural Andean highlands not to cities but to the remote Amazonian lowlands. I mean the term *rural-to-remote migration* to refer to the movement of people from nonurban agricultural areas to places that are even more sparsely populated and further removed from the agricultural economy. Consider figure 4, which shows population growth between the 1961 and 2007 censuses in (1) the rural highland provinces of Cusco; (2) the city of Cusco; and (3) the adjacent Amazonian lowlands (defined

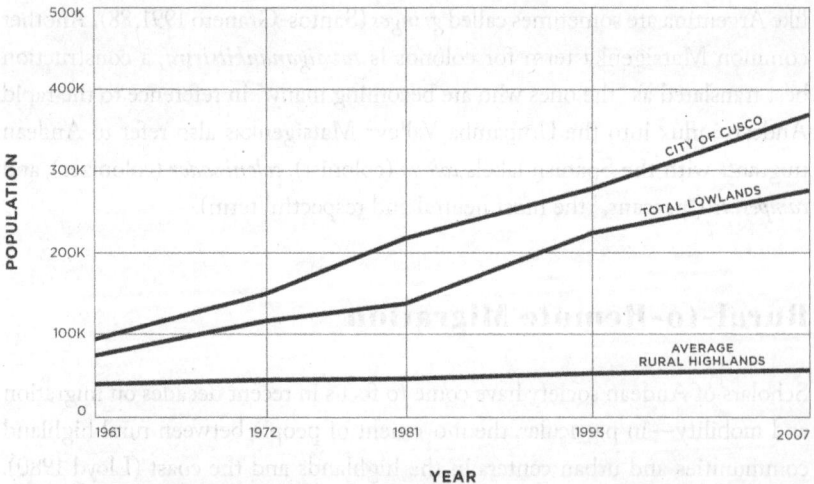

FIGURE 4 The population of the eastern lowlands is growing almost as quickly as that of the city of Cusco. Population growth in the city of Cusco, the lowlands east of the department of Cusco (La Convención and Madre de Dios), and the rural highland provinces of the department of Cusco, 1961–2007. Data source: INEI (1961, 1972, 1981, 1993, 2007). Graph designed by the author.

here as the combined populations of the province of La Convención and the department of Madre de Dios).[4] The populations of the rural highland provinces have stagnated or even decreased during that time, while the population of the city of Cusco increased by 287 percent and the population of the eastern lowlands increased by 260 percent.

To explore this phenomenon in greater depth, we can ask where Andean migrants in the province of La Convención have settled. For instance, have they joined the thriving urban center of Quillabamba, making this simply another kind of urban migration, or have they instead sought out more remote patches of forest? To answer this question, figure 5 presents district-level census data from the province of La Convención from 1981 to 2007. I divide these data into three categories: (1) the urban center of Quillabamba; (2) the upper valley (the rural districts of the Alto Urubamba above Quillabamba that have been

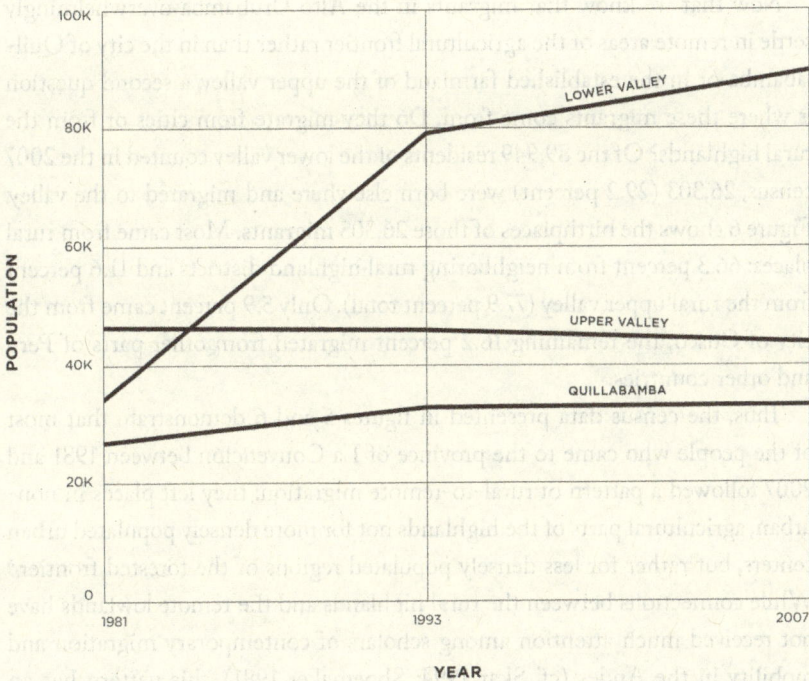

FIGURE 5 The lower valley is the primary target of migration in La Convención. Population growth in the city of Quillabamba, the upper valley of La Convención (the pre-twentieth-century frontier), and the lower valley of La Convención (the contemporary frontier). Graph designed by the author.

integrated into the adjacent highland sphere since at least the nineteenth century); and (3) the lower valley (the districts of the Alto and Bajo Urubamba
downriver from Quillabamba, which include the current agricultural frontier
and the forests beyond).[5]

These data show that the lower valley, which includes the agricultural frontier, has grown rapidly—nearly tripling in population between 1981 and 2007—
while the city of Quillabamba has grown more slowly (its population increasing
by just 24.5 percent during that time). Meanwhile, the population of the upper
valley decreased by 5.4 percent, consistent with the trend of demographic stag-
nation in the rural Andean provinces themselves (see figure 4). In other words,
the rapid population growth in the lowlands of La Convención from 1981 to
2007 was due almost entirely to people moving to the most remote parts of
the valley, rather than to the city of Quillabamba or the more settled parts
of the valley.

Now that we know that migrants in the Alto Urubamba overwhelmingly
settle in remote areas of the agricultural frontier rather than in the city of Quillabamba or in the established farmland of the upper valley, a second question
is where these migrants come from. Do they migrate from cities or from the
rural highlands? Of the 89,949 residents of the lower valley counted in the 2007
census, 26,303 (29.2 percent) were born elsewhere and migrated to the valley.
Figure 6 shows the birthplaces of those 26,303 migrants. Most came from rural
places: 66.3 percent from neighboring rural highland districts and 11.6 percent
from the rural upper valley (77.9 percent total). Only 5.9 percent came from the
city of Cusco; the remaining 16.2 percent migrated from other parts of Peru
and other countries.

Thus, the census data presented in figures 5 and 6 demonstrate that most
of the people who came to the province of La Convención between 1981 and
2007 followed a pattern of rural-to-remote migration: they left places in nonurban, agricultural parts of the highlands not for more densely populated urban
centers, but rather for less densely populated regions of the forested frontier.[6]
While connections between the rural highlands and the remote lowlands have
not received much attention among scholars of contemporary migration and
mobility in the Andes (cf. Skar 1994; Shoemaker 1981), this pattern has an
important precedent in the so-called "vertical archipelago" system of landholding described in the introductory chapter of this book, in which Andeans have
controlled land at multiple elevations and in multiple ecological niches to diver-
sify their economic activities.

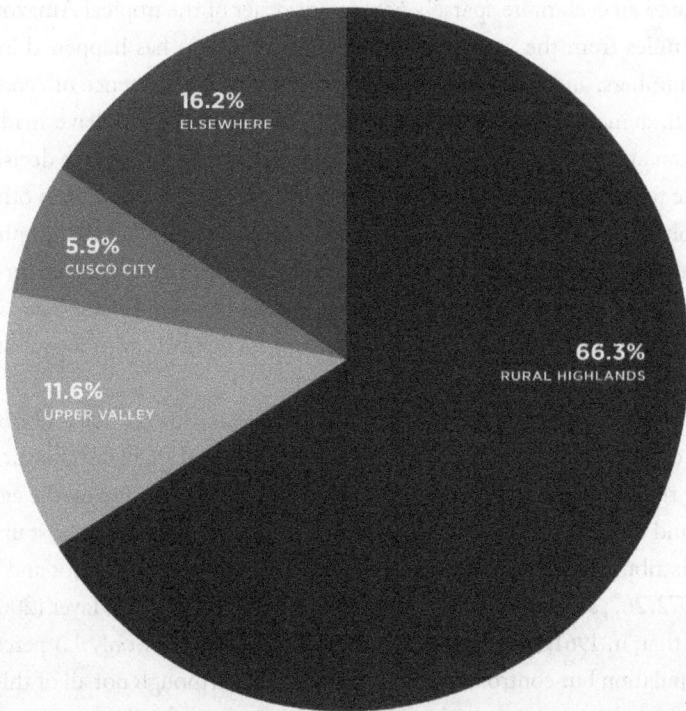

FIGURE 6 Migrants in the lower valley come from the rural Andes. Birthplaces of lower valley migrants (INEI 2007). Graph designed by the author.

Making a Home in the Forest

So it is that tens of thousands of Quechua- and Spanish-speaking farmers from the Andean highlands have come to make their homes on vast tracts of remote, undeveloped land in the heart of traditional Matsigenka territory. This migratory wave has been so intense that by the early 1960s only a third of the residents of La Convención had been born there (Fioravanti 1974, 59; Craig 1969, 282). This demographic transformation was by no means unique to this part of Amazonia: the population of the Peruvian lowlands as a whole multiplied roughly eightfold between 1940 and 2007, about twice the national average rate (INEI 1940, 2007).

What explains this dramatic Andean exodus into the tropical lowlands? It is noteworthy that a person from the frigid, rural Andean highlands would migrate to an even more sparsely populated corner of the tropical Amazon rain forest, miles from the nearest road; that this migration has happened in such great numbers, and so quickly, is truly remarkable. A confluence of economic, political, demographic, and, more recently, ecological factors have made this choice an attractive one for many rural Andeans. In some cases, the decision to migrate to the lowlands is born of desperate conditions back home; in others, it is simply a way to improve one's lot, or to experience a new social and physical environment. In general, however, the decision comes down to a desire for social mobility: to *superar* ("improve oneself" or "overcome"; see Leinaweaver 2008) or *ser algo* (be something)—that is, to become an urbanite with a professional career rather than a rural agriculturalist.

One reason that highland farmers have migrated to the Alto Urubamba has to do with the difficulties of life in the nearby rural highlands, particularly during the 1950s and 1960s. Population growth had put pressure on the agricultural land base at a time when, as measured in 1961, Peru had the most unequal land distribution among fifty-one countries surveyed by C. L. Taylor and Hudson (1972, 267; see also McClintock 1981, 64). In fact, Enrique Mayer (2009, 14) shows that, in 1961, large haciendas (estates) accounted for only 1.3 percent of the population but controlled 75 percent of the land (though not all of this land was arable). Meanwhile, nearly 600,000 poor Andean families were squeezed onto about 4.7 percent of the land. As a result of this crushing inequality, many Andean families had barely enough land to support themselves. This situation eventually set the stage for the peasant uprisings and subsequent land reforms of the 1960s and 1970s (see Blanco Galdós 1972; Fioravanti 1974; Hobsbawm 1969). At the same time, it also sent unprecedented numbers of Andean campesinos into the eastern lowlands in search of new land. The Alto Urubamba—with its bountiful land a stone's throw from the highlands—served as a sort of pressure release valve for poor Andean farmers (though the rights of the Indigenous Amazonian people already living there were generally not considered). Then, as the agrarian reform expropriated the hacendados' land in the province of La Convención itself, beginning in the 1960s, thousands of Andean campesinos were freed from their labor obligations to take up residence in local towns and cities like Quillabamba, move back to the highlands, or venture farther down the Urubamba Valley into the agricultural frontier in search of new land. As the precariousness of life in the rural Andes becomes further exacerbated by climate change in the coming decades (Perez et al. 2010; Urrutia and Vuille 2009), this eastward migratory wave does not appear likely to abate any time soon.

A second factor stimulating lowland migration was that, while these pressures were building in the rural highlands, the expanding road network was opening up new parts of the Alto Urubamba to colonization and making agriculture there more profitable. At the same time, a terrible malaria epidemic that ravaged the valley in the 1930s finally ended in the 1940s (see chapter 2), allowing the repopulation of the Alto Urubamba beginning in the 1950s. The agricultural colonization of the eastern lowlands was promoted by the government of Fernando Belaúnde Terry in the 1960s—what he called "Peru's own conquest" (1965)—as one solution to the "man-land" imbalance mentioned above (Grillo Arbulú and Sharon 2012, 118). All of this coincided with an increase in coffee prices (Craig 1969, 283), which made coffee cultivation an attractive economic opportunity for families struggling to provide for themselves in the rural highlands. Since the Indigenous people of the lowlands were not considered to have legitimate claim to the lands they inhabited—and Amazonia was cast in national discourses as an empty and "unused" region—the eastern lowlands were considered open for colonization. (Note that the same notion of Indigenous lands as "unused" and awaiting colonization has been taken up by Brazil's current president, Jair Bolsonaro, who has advocated violence and genocide against Amazonians. He has said, "We're going to rip up Raposa Serra do Sol [Indigenous territory in Roraima, northern Brazil]. We're going to give all the ranchers guns," and that "it's a shame that the Brazilian cavalry hasn't been as efficient as the Americans, who exterminated the Indians"; both quotations and translations from Survival International [2019].) Many state-organized colonization projects in Peru during the 1960s failed (Schuurman 1979), but the spontaneous and unregulated colonization of the Urubamba Valley was successful and quickly transformed the region into a closely integrated tropical annex of Cusco's agricultural heartland.

The circumstances under which Andean migrants have come to reside in the Alto Urubamba have taken many forms. In some cases, these have been permanent migrations, but more often people have moved back and forth between lowland plots and the highlands, at least at the start. Indeed, throughout the twentieth century (and before, as I discuss in chapter 2), it was common for Andeans to engage in the kind of pendular migration that we would expect from the vertical archipelago pattern described earlier—working on small agricultural plots or taking other jobs in the lowlands at slow points in the highland agricultural calendar, then returning to their home communities. For example, this was the case among Quechua speakers in the highland community of

Kallarayan (Calca Province), who worked three-month contracts during the harvest season in the lowlands of the Alto Urubamba and Lares, but did not own land there themselves (Radcliffe 1986). Jane Collins (1984) reports a different case in the highland province of Huancané (Puno), where Aymara-speaking highland agropastoralists owned and worked coffee plots in the lowlands of Tambopata, while also earning money through wage labor in mines, agriculture and fish processing on the Peruvian coast, and work in the Bolivian city of La Paz (see also Collins 1985). Income from these activities supplemented the agropastoral activities back home in the highlands. An interesting variation on this theme comes from the highland-lowland transitional zone of central Bolivia, where the agricultural industry depends on seasonal laborers from the highlands, but where lowlanders also own agricultural and ranch lands in the highlands (Babel 2018, 28).

In other cases, kin groups have straddled highland and lowland centers and exchanged products among themselves. Antoinette Fioravanti-Molinié (1975) describes a case in which kinship networks controlled plots of land in La Convención (in what I have called the upper valley) and in the highland community of Yucay, in the Sacred Valley, in the 1960s and 1970s. Family members complemented their agricultural production and labor activities by traveling between those places. In some cases the home community was in La Convención; in others it was in Yucay. In this way, migrants in the Alto Urubamba remain closely linked to their kin back home, and the agrarian society of the lowlands has developed as an extension of the practices and networks of the highlands.

This kind of arrangement frequently develops into permanent residence in the lowlands. As noted by Carlos Aramburú (1984, 164–65; 1982, 22–23), some Andean migrants first establish a seasonal plot in the Alto Urubamba, then gradually take up permanent residence there as the plantations grow, while maintaining a connection to their home community. Finally, the migrants leave these agricultural plots to work in services and manufacturing in local towns and cities. This illustrates what often ends up being the next phase in the migratory process: moving from the lowlands to cities such as Cusco, Arequipa, or Lima. Note, for instance, that among the residents of the city of Cusco who reported in the 2007 census that they had lived somewhere else five years earlier, about one of every six reported coming from the lowlands (La Convención or Madre de Dios). Most of these people (or their parents) had surely originally made their way to the lowlands from the Andean highlands and used their earnings from lowland industries to establish themselves in the city. Like other Peruvian migrants, some of these people eventually continue their journeys onward to places like the United States (Berg 2017). When Andeans migrate from the rural highlands to the lowlands in search of economic opportunities, the money that they make there can be used to leapfrog back over the highlands into the urban centers of Peru (Skeldon 1977) and beyond (a fitting term for this process might be *slingshot migration*). Sarah Lund Skar (1994) provides a particularly illuminating case study about such connections between highland communities, settlements in the Amazonian lowlands, and urban life on the Peruvian coast. I now illustrate this process of rural-to-remote-to-urban migration with an ethnographic example from the Alto Urubamba.

From Rural to Remote to Urban: Three Generations of a Frontier Family

The rural-to-remote-to-urban migratory pattern I described above is illustrated by a man I came to know during my fieldwork, whom I shall call Alejandro. In 2009–12, Alejandro lived in a frontier settlement along the Urubamba River. Alejandro's parents were poor, monolingual Quechua-speaking campesinos, born in the 1930s in the rural highland province of Paruro. The scarcity of land in Paruro made their lives difficult, so after the Alto Urubamba malaria epidemic of the 1930s eased, and as roads were built into the frontier in the 1950s, they migrated there to find work on one of the large, old haciendas established in the seventeenth century. In this kind of arrangement—before the agrarian reform—laborers worked on land owned by an hacendado in usufruct, dividing their labor between their own plots and those of the hacendado.

Alejandro was born on the hacienda in the 1950s. Quechua was his first language, but, since he attended primary school in the 1960s, he also spoke a good deal of Spanish. He reported experiencing extreme discrimination, both because of his Quechua and his Quechua-inflected Spanish. The hacienda where he lived was expropriated during the agrarian reform in the 1960s, when he was still a child, which freed Alejandro's family of their commitments to the former hacendado. Now that they had years of experience with tropical agriculture, they decided to move down the valley in search of new land. By that time, most of the Alto Urubamba above the Cirialo River had already been colonized by Andean migrants (see map 1), so the family traveled beyond the frontier to a more remote, forested area that was still populated by Matsigenkas. Because

FIGURE 7 A hillside, inhabited until the 1970s by Matsigenkas, recently cleared by a family of Andean colonos, 2012. Photograph by the author.

Indigenous Amazonians had no legal basis through which to protect their land until the 1970s, Alejandro's family was able to claim a large forested area and undertake the difficult work of clearing it by hand for agriculture (a similar scene is shown in figure 7 above). They planted coffee on the upper slopes and cacao below. This was grueling and dangerous work, and it was common for such frontier pioneers to be injured or killed: hit by a falling tree; hurt in an accident involving a chainsaw (which few people from the highlands know how to use); bitten by a snake; simply lost in the unforgiving forest; or attacked by a fellow settler on the lawless frontier. These are the dangers of being a beginner in a new and unfamiliar landscape.

Alejandro and his family came into close contact with their new Matsigenka neighbors. These Matsigenkas opposed their presence but had no legal recourse through which to challenge their occupation of the land. However, they also welcomed the manufactured goods that Alejandro's family brought, as well as the opportunity for paid labor on their agricultural plots during the harvest season. Their children attended school together and came to know each other well. These Matsigenka families, whom I also know well, complained about the ecological devastation of their hunting and fishing areas caused by the agricultural activities of Alejandro and other local colonos. The depletion of fish and game forced them to turn to cash cropping to support themselves. They also became wary of the tendency of colonos—who are overwhelmingly young men—to pursue Matsigenka women. However, the nearby Matsigenkas also expressed satisfaction with the health post, restaurant, and Internet café that came along with Andean colonization, and they were grateful to Alejandro for marching alongside them in a recent protest against the incursions of the natural gas companies, which are a common adversary of Matsigenkas and colonos alike. Alejandro's brother-in-law also married a Matsigenka woman from a nearby community, linking their families as kin, and in 2009–12 their daughter went back and forth between her Matsigenka-speaking relatives in the community and her father's Quechua-speaking relatives in the frontier settlement. Today, Quechua, Spanish, and Matsigenka can all be heard in Alejandro's house, illustrating the complex social and linguistic dynamics of the coffee frontier.

Alejandro used his family's land wealth to consolidate his position as a major power broker in the region. He has achieved this status by being resourceful,

FIGURE 8 The frontier settlement of Ivochote, 2011. Photograph by the author.

tough, hardworking, astute, and ruthless in his pursuit of social advancement. Over the last few decades, he has invested his profits from agriculture into building a hotel, a restaurant, a discoteca, a fish farm, and a cement block manufacturing operation to supply the local construction boom. Local government officials now stay in his hotel, talk with him for hours in his restaurant, and seek his support in elections. He has gradually sold off parcels of his family's land—by now large, fully functioning coffee and cacao plantations—at a huge profit to newly arriving colonos. (Such is the financial reward that awaits the first colonos to arrive in a region.) In the 1990s, Alejandro successfully lobbied the municipal government to extend the road from Quillabamba into the area, which made his land much more valuable. The timing of these investments was felicitous: as the massive Camisea natural gas project began pouring millions of dollars into the region in the early 2000s, Alejandro was well positioned through his various commercial ventures to profit handsomely from the windfall. He now has the means to send his children to school in Cusco, where they live a comfortable life among the burgeoning Peruvian middle class—and where they can *ser algo* (be something), leaving agricultural life behind. In fact, Alejandro was already building a home in the city of Cusco during my fieldwork in 2009–12. He divided his time between Cusco and his business projects in the Alto Urubamba and invested in a few pieces of rebar and roofing material at a time. This phase of step migration—to the city of Cusco—was also gradual. His family hoped to continue on to Lima, and his son—who understands and speaks some Quechua but is more comfortable speaking Spanish—hoped to eventually live abroad in the United States or Europe.

This transition—from poverty in the rural Andean highlands, to years of arduous labor in the remote forests of the Alto Urubamba, to commercial success in a burgeoning frontier settlement, to middle-class comfort in an urban center (and possibly beyond)—has taken three generations. Alejandro's success comes from a combination of hard work, ruthless business sensibility, and luck. Like many colonos in the region, Alejandro's family see their time in the lowlands as a temporary step, albeit one that has taken decades, on the way to social mobility elsewhere. However, most colonos will not attain the kind of success that Alejandro's family has found. He and his family arrived early and worked hard, but they also repeatedly found themselves in the right place at the right time. The dream of social mobility for later-arriving colonos is often elusive.

Interethnic Marriage

Interethnic unions between Matsigenka women and colono men have become very common in the social milieu of the Alto Urubamba agricultural frontier, to the extent that they are now the norm rather than the exception in some comunidades nativas near the frontier. The gender disparity in such unions is due to the fact that colonos in the frontier zone are overwhelmingly young men. Many Matsigenka-colono couples and their children live in frontier settlements near comunidades nativas, in urban centers in the valley, or in communities or cities in the highlands; they are less common within the boundaries of comunidades nativas, where colono spouses are usually not permitted to live. Note that interethnic unions have been underreported in the scholarly literature about the Alto Urubamba, in part because most ethnographic studies of Matsigenkas have been conducted in comunidades nativas where colono spouses are not allowed to settle. In other words, what might look like an absence of interethnic marriage in some Alto Urubamba communities is actually because interethnic couples, by definition, are required to live elsewhere; a thorough accounting of kin networks in such communities usually turns up a great number of kin who married colonos and live somewhere else. However, some comunidades nativas have recently begun to admit colono spouses—usually with carefully restricted leadership and land use privileges—to stem the exodus of women from the communities. In a few of those places, colonos have nevertheless risen to become among the most influential people in the communities (Sánchez Vásquez 2009).

The frequency of interethnic marriage is due in large part to the sheer ubiquity of young Andean men on the coffee frontier (for a similar gender disparity among agricultural migrants on the Amazonian frontier of northern Ecuador, see A. Barbieri and Carr 2005). Working conditions in the most sparsely populated corners of the valley—where most Matsigenkas live—favor young, tough men who are unencumbered by family commitments back home. (High proportions of young, single men are characteristic of many frontier societies, a phenomenon that often corresponds to high rates of violence; see Courtwright 1998). According to the 2007 census, the district of Echarate—the most remote district in the province at that time, where most Matsigenka communities were located—was home to 119.8 men for every 100 women (INEI 2007). (The district of Megantoni was formed from the northern section of Echarate after my fieldwork.) In Quellouno, the district that includes the community of Yokiri described in chapter 3, there were 118.2 men for every 100 women. The 1972

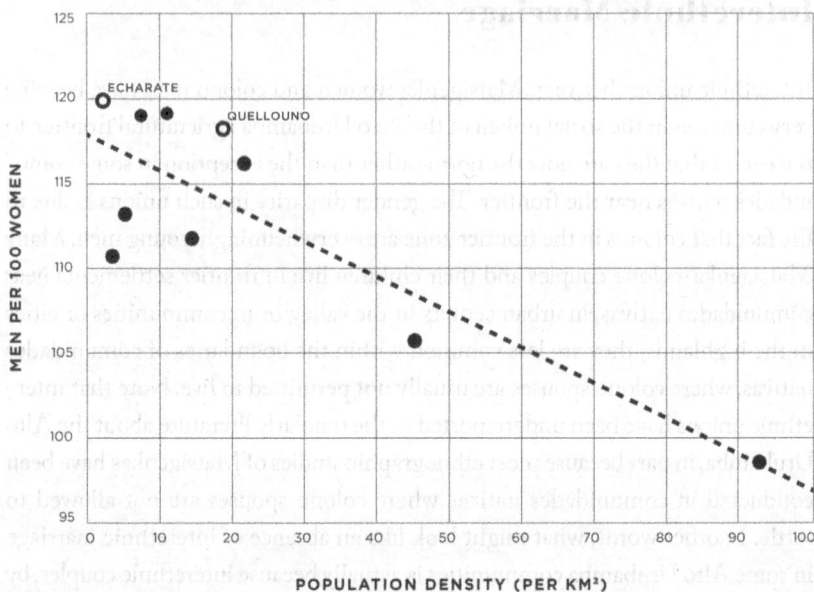

FIGURE 9 More remote districts—where most Matsigenkas live—tend to have higher proportions of men. Masculinity index (number of men per 100 women) versus population density (per km²) in the ten districts of the province of La Convención, 2007. Districts including Matsigenka comunidades nativas are indicated. Data source: INEI (2007). Graph designed by the author.

census reports an even more dramatic gender disparity: in the entire province of La Convención, there were 126.7 men for every 100 women (Encinas Martín, Perez Casado, and Alonso Ordieres 2008, 243). The correspondence between gender disparity and population density is illustrated in figure 9 above: the more remote, sparsely populated districts have higher ratios of men to women. Note that most Matsigenkas lived in Echarate and Quellouno during the 2007 census (indicated in figure 9), two of the districts with the highest proportions of men to women.

Many young colono men on the agricultural frontier seek out nearby Matsigenka women, in part because there simply aren't many other women on the frontier, and in part because of a certain sexual curiosity among many newly arrived colonos. Some Matsigenka women, for their part, find colono men to be more desirable partners than Matsigenka men because of their economic status and access to the world beyond the forest (Rojas Zolezzi 1998). It is common for

Matsigenka women to complain that Matsigenka men are *ociosos* (lazy), and that colono men, in contrast, work hard to provide for their families. Relationships between Matsigenka women and colono men have become very common—for instance, around a third of adult women in one comunidad nativa in the Alto Urubamba (and one man) had had a long-term, cohabiting relationship with a colono, either in a local frontier settlement or back in the colono's home community in the highlands. Most families in the same community also included at least one Matsigenka woman who still lived with a colono man nearby or in the highlands.

However, many Matsigenka families warned their daughters against becoming involved with colono men.[7] On the one hand, some of those men already had families back home in the highlands and did not intend to make an enduring commitment to a woman in the lowlands. Furthermore, when such relationships ended and the colono men returned to the highlands, the Matsigenka women were almost always left raising their children alone (usually these children were simply incorporated into the kinship networks of the comunidades nativas). Thus I more than once heard the Spanish refrain *No sueltes a tus hijas* (Don't let go of your daughters) among Matsigenka families. That is, if a Matsigenka woman is to live with a colono man, she should insist that he move to her land, so that she remains with the land if the relationship ends. Otherwise, she will be left with children to support but without land with which to feed them. This is, however, complicated in comunidades nativas where colono men are not permitted to live—and it is one of the reasons that some comunidades nativas have begun to admit colono husbands. This complex interplay between marriage, ethnicity, land, and children is a point of much concern on the Alto Urubamba frontier.

The ubiquity of young colono men in the valley has created a certain demographic instability: as Matsigenka women have left comunidades nativas to live with colono men in nearby communities, urban centers, and places back in the highlands, it has become more and more difficult for Matsigenka men to find wives. These men, in turn, have begun to seek out women in more remote Matsigenka communities where colonos have not yet arrived. Those Matsigenka men either move to the woman's community or bring the woman back to their own community closer to the frontier. This, in turn, makes it harder for the more remote Matsigenka men to find wives, pushing the same dynamic farther into the remote tributaries. The result of this process is the movement of men (both colonos and Matsigenkas) down the Urubamba River and up the remote tributaries, and the movement of women in the opposite direction—down the remote tributaries and up the Urubamba River to the region's towns and cities, and, in some cases, into the highlands and beyond. For instance, this is what happened with Ana María, the woman I mentioned earlier who in 2018 was integrated into highland life in Cusco and lived with a Quechua-speaking man. (Note that it is the gender asymmetry among Andean migrants that has created this migratory flow—if more Andean women lived on the coffee frontier, Andean men might not pursue Matsigenka women to the same degree.) The result of this process is that Quechua has moved downriver with men, while Matsigenka has moved upriver with women. As people move back and forth across the valley in this manner, they create an integrated, multiethnic, trilingual kinship network that spans the highlands and the lowlands (about which more below).

The Complexities of Ethnicity

Following this discussion of multiethnic families, an important question emerges: How is ethnicity attributed to, and experienced by, people who grow up with a foot in both worlds? As will be clear throughout this book, the ethnic categories at play on the agricultural frontier are contestable and contextual. First, who "counts" as ethnically Matsigenka or Andean depends on whom one asks. For instance, consider the case of an eleven-year-old boy named Óscar, the son of a Matsigenka mother and a colono father, who lived in a comunidad nativa that permitted both of his parents to live there. One day, Óscar visited me as I was recording a traditional song called "Saniri" (River Caiman) with an elderly, monolingual Matsigenka friend named Luis. Luis and I had the following exchange in Matsigenka:

NQE: Ikemi irirori pimatikanakerira?
(Does he understand what you're singing?)
LUIS: Tera! Inti ponyarona!
(No! He's a highlander!)

Óscar was trilingual, and he understood and spoke Matsigenka perfectly well. However, from Luis's perspective, the fact that his father was a Quechua-speaking agricultural migrant disqualified Óscar from Matsigenka ethnic membership, along with the linguistic and cultural competences that were thought to be necessary to understand a traditional song. However, when Óscar's father took him to visit other colonos in the neighboring frontier communities, he was universally considered Matsigenka—albeit one who spoke Quechua and was acquainted with rural Andean society. Thus Óscar was in the position of feeling like a perpetual ethnic outsider. However, people from multiethnic backgrounds like Óscar's often benefited from their close ties to colono society and the agricultural economy, and exerted influence among other Matsigenkas.[8] Diana Steele (personal communication) notes a similar phenomenon among university students in Cusco who had one Matsigenka parent: in Cusco they identified themselves as Matsigenka, while back in the Alto Urubamba they were called *ponyarona* (highlanders) by their Matsigenka families.

Along with perspective, social and institutional context is also relevant to such complexities of ethnicity. For instance, the conflicting conceptualizations of ethnicity described above between Óscar and Luis took place within a single community—however, such differences are flattened out in the eyes of state apparatuses like the census, which treats all members of comunidades nativas as Matsigenka, and the Bilingual and Intercultural Education program (EIB), which posits a homogeneous mapping between ethnicity, language, and legal territory. Another interesting contextual complication of ethnicity comes in relation to the coffee industry, in which Matsigenkas participate in the rural agrarian world that is associated with Andean society. For instance, one agricultural training workshop in Huillcapampa was attended by members of Matsigenka and colono communities, who sat side by side on long wooden benches and listened to lectures in Spanish about fertilizer and irrigation. The municipal agronomist opened the workshop by neutralizing the ethnic heterogeneity of the participants with the phrase "Todos somos campesinos" (We are all farmers)—employing a term that invokes both subsistence and Indigenous Andean ethnicity.[9] In this context in which Matsigenkas and colonos are linked in the common activity of coffee production, their ethnic differences recede into the background.

The Alto Urubamba as Just One World

It sometimes feels as though the Alto Urubamba is made up of two separate worlds: Matsigenkas at the bottom of the valley, Andeans at the top. It is possible to meet Quechua-speaking farmers above the current colonization zone who have never met a Matsigenka person, and who have only a dim awareness that their farmland was once forested and inhabited by Matsigenka people. This part of the Alto Urubamba is essentially a tropical annex of the rural Andean highlands (Gade 2016; Fioravanti 1974), and vestiges of historical Matsigenka presence persist only in scattered toponyms and in the stories of elderly colonos who arrived decades earlier. Meanwhile, not fifty kilometers to the north, one can spend time with monolingual Matsigenka speakers who live in remote corners of the forest, subsist exclusively on hunting, gathering, and horticulture, and interact only incidentally with Andean migrants.

But the Alto Urubamba is not two separate worlds; it is just one world. A view from the poles obscures what happens in between: a thriving trilingual frontier society mediates between the Amazon plain's remotest Matsigenka communities and the Andean highlands (and beyond).

The just-one-world character of the Alto Urubamba was made clear to me during a multiday soccer tournament held to celebrate the anniversary of a comunidad nativa on the coffee frontier in 2012. Hundreds of people traveled from nearby colono and Matsigenka communities to compete in the tournament, or just to eat great quantities of chicken, fish, and guinea pig and to drink and dance until the early hours of the morning. One morning during the event, I sat on a long wooden bench with three Matsigenka brothers in their twenties and thirties to watch a soccer match. The brothers had grown up on the estate of an Andean colono family that took over their family's land in the Yavero Valley in the 1950s; as a result, all three of the brothers were trilingual speakers of Matsigenka, Quechua, and Spanish. Two of the brothers lived in the comunidad nativa where the event was held, while the third lived in a nearby colono settlement; he had married a colona woman, and the bylaws of the comunidad nativa prohibited her from residing there. Regardless, the three brothers traveled to each other's land to reciprocate labor during each harvest season. The three spoke Matsigenka among themselves but switched to Quechua when the man's colona wife and her relatives came to talk with them. These relatives included a sister who also lived in the valley, as well as cousins who were visiting from a rural community in the Andes and were more or less monolingual Quechua speakers. The three brothers also greeted other Quechua-speaking acquaintances from nearby colono settlements, with whom they had attended school as children.

Clearly, these brothers were at home in the Quechua-speaking, agrarian social milieu that had taken hold in the Alto Urubamba—though they expressed to me that they never felt fully accepted among colonos, who regarded Matsigenkas as curiosities and outsiders in that milieu. But at the same time, two of the brothers had also recently returned from visiting cousins in a more remote Matsigenka community, a day's travel beyond the road network. Most people in that community lived from hunting, gathering, and horticulture, and many of the older people were monolingual Matsigenka speakers. When the two brothers traveled to that community, they only spoke Matsigenka to their cousins, and they were considered high-status visitors with special knowledge and experience. Following their recent visit, one of the children from the remote Matsigenka community came to stay with his cousins on the frontier, to help during the coffee harvest season and learn about life on the coffee frontier—a scout, responsible for reporting back about the changes making their way downriver. The brothers, thus, were comfortable in this kind of social milieu as well, and they functioned (at least in a limited sense) as intermediaries between rural Quechua speakers in the highlands and remote Matsigenka speakers in the lowlands. Indeed, this interregional social network also mediated the flow of goods: the three brothers sent their highland kin back to their home communities with bags full of fruit, coca, and yuca, and received manufactured goods from them, which in turn made their way to their more remote Matsigenka kin. It's not hard to imagine this kind of kin-mediated exchange network operating in the valley at earlier moments in history as well.

The soccer tournament, thus, struck me as a microcosm of the Andean-Amazonian interface in the Alto Urubamba. Here, interethnic marriage was ubiquitous and social networks connected Matsigenka and Quechua speakers in the valley within the context of the growing coffee economy. Social categories like race and ethnicity were also complicated and contextual. For instance, the two brothers who lived in the comunidad nativa were counted as Matsigenkas in the census, and their children attended a Matsigenka bilingual education program; the third brother, who lived in the colono community, was not counted as Matsigenka in the census, and his children attended a Quechua bilingual education program. Furthermore, these people on the coffee frontier maintained close social ties to remote Amazonian settlements as well as comunidades campesinas high in the Andes. The picture of the region that emerges from such patterns is of an unbroken network of kinship and interaction comprising people from remote Matsigenka communities all the way to agrarian communities in the highlands, mediated by the multiethnic and multilingual agricultural frontier.

Conclusion

In this chapter, I have offered a general introduction to the social world of the Alto Urubamba agricultural frontier during my fieldwork in 2009–12, focusing on the relationships between speakers of Matsigenka and Quechua. During that time, the road network was being cut through the valley's forests at a dizzying pace, bringing Matsigenkas and Andean migrants together around new multiethnic, trilingual frontier settlements like Huillcapampa. I introduced the Matsigenka, Quechua, and Andean Spanish languages, as well as Matsigenka society and culture as they have been discussed in the academic literature. I also presented census data to identify the process of rural-to-remote migration, whereby people from the rural Andean highlands have moved in great numbers to even more sparsely populated parts of the Alto Urubamba lowlands in search of land for the cultivation of coffee and other tropical crops. A Quechua-speaking man named Alejandro and his family typify this multigenerational process, which often ends with migrants finally leaving the lowlands to establish a life in urban areas. Rural-to-remote migration is an important process in southern Peru, though it has not received as much scholarly attention as migration directly from rural to urban areas (and to other countries).

Migrants in the remote regions of the Alto Urubamba frontier tend to be young men, and in areas around Matsigenka communities, nearly 120 men for every 100 women were counted in the 2007 census. Many of these young men formed relationships with Matsigenka women and either lived with them in the lowlands, brought them back to their home communities in the highlands, or left them to care for the children on their own. As a result of these unions between Matsigenka women and Andean men, Matsigenka men were forced to travel down the Urubamba Valley and into the more remote tributaries in search of spouses, whom they either joined or brought back upriver. Thus, at a regional scale, men and the Quechua language moved down the valley, while women and the Matsigenka language moved up the valley, in a pattern mediated by kinship. The frontier society that formed through this dynamic of migration and kinship was intensely multilingual, and ethnicity could depend greatly on perspective and context. I sought to show in this chapter that, as a result of this pattern of intermarriage and interaction, the Alto Urubamba constitutes *just one world*. That is, despite the scholarly and popular tendency to view the valley from the point of view of its poles, with distinct Andean and Matsigenka groups at either end, the valley is in fact home to a single, unified, trilingual network of people, brought together by the emerging agricultural economy.

I have also sought to illustrate the profound ecological and human stakes of the changes under way in the Alto Urubamba. This book is a micro-level look at the social relationships and interactions through which the Amazon rain forest is being transformed into farmland, and at the experience of living in this chaotic and unstable world. In this environment, people are fighting to establish a place for themselves amid great uncertainty. As we will see throughout the book, the agricultural frontier is a place of anxiety and environmental ruin, but also of hope, as people who have lived their whole lives as subsistence farmers or as hunter-horticulturalists glimpse the possibility of middle-class prosperity for the first time.

In the next chapter, I present a language-oriented history of the Alto Urubamba, to show how the patterns I described in this chapter have changed, and how they have remained consistent, throughout the centuries.

Chapter 2

Language and History at an Andean-Amazonian Crossroads

S ome Andean migrants who struck out into the forests beyond the Alto Urubamba frontier in the twentieth century had the uncanny experience of arriving in a landscape far from the reach of the agricultural economy yet finding themselves planting coffee among broad pre-Columbian agricultural terraces. Others—colonos and Matsigenkas alike—occasionally turn up ancient Andean stone axes as they clear and till their remote lowland fields. Road crews that have pushed the transportation network through tangled forests in the far corners of the valley find themselves crossing Inka roadbeds and ascending through traces of ancient settlements in the passes between far-flung valleys. (The fact that modern roads have only recently caught up with the network that was built and then abandoned by the Inkas hundreds of years ago is a remarkable statement about the ebb and flow of Andean projections into the valley.) These contradictory frontier experiences—the feeling of living at the vanguard of eastward Andean expansion while also being surrounded by the traces of a much earlier agricultural society—speak to the cyclical nature of Andean-Amazonian interaction in the Alto Urubamba. The region is, to use Paul Little's phrase, a "perennial frontier" (2001).[1]

The dynamics of interregional interaction that I described in chapter 1 have a long history in the Alto Urubamba. This chapter steps back from the ethnographic focus of the book and contextualizes the contemporary agricultural

frontier within a deeper, language-centered history of Andean-Amazonian interaction in the valley. I explore this history through written records, the accounts
of travelers in the region, archaeological findings, historical linguistics, and oral
histories that I recorded in the field. While much has changed over the centuries,
some of the patterns described in the previous chapter can be seen quite clearly in
previous historical moments. For one, the valley's particular combination of geographical inaccessibility and close proximity to the Andes has continually made
it both a haven for those seeking protection in its forests, and—paradoxically—a
tropical agricultural powerhouse and conduit of trade and mobility closely linked
with the adjacent highlands. Second, a close look at the records suggests that the
multiethnic and multilingual character of the contemporary frontier described in
chapter 1 also has a long history, as a varied assortment of people and languages
have come together in different kinds of relationships. One particular socioeconomic fact about the valley has often been at the center of this multiethnic and
multilingual character: from the Inka and colonial periods to the present, the
small local population has always been insufficient to supply labor for the tropical
agricultural industries, leading to the forced resettlement or voluntary migration
of people from other places, near and far.

I chose to include a historical chapter in this book because I hope to make
this case study relevant to broader concerns in South American history. As I
discussed in the introduction, recent historical and areal-typological linguistic
evidence has shown that various parts of the Andean highlands and the Amazonian lowlands have been closely integrated throughout the centuries and millennia. However, it is often difficult to use such evidence to arrive at a detailed
picture of the social worlds that lead to those kinds of patterns. By bringing
together the available evidence regarding Andean-Amazonian interaction in
the Alto Urubamba and contextualizing it within my own ethnographic study, I
hope to contribute to our understanding of how other such relationships might
have played out across South America.

I begin by orienting the historical linguistic panorama of the Alto Urubamba
within the broader context of South America. Then I turn to archaeological
and written evidence regarding the valley itself and follow its linguistic, social,
and economic history through the colonial period and into the nineteenth and
early twentieth centuries. The chapter ends with the malaria epidemic of the
1930s, which preceded the current burst of Andean migration that I discussed
in chapter 1.

Earliest Traces

To start at the beginning: humans have probably lived in the Alto Urubamba for millennia. No archaeological remains in the valley have been dated before the sixth century AD (Fonseca Santa Cruz and Bauer 2013), but humans have been in South America for at least 14,500 years (Dillehay et al. 2015). People were making foraging trips and perhaps settling in adjacent parts of the Andean highlands 12,000 years ago (Rademaker et al. 2014), and they were certainly living there permanently by at least 7,000 years ago (Haas et al. 2017). Meanwhile, foragers were producing shell mounds in the Bolivian lowlands 10,000 years ago (Lombardo et al. 2013). Given the Alto Urubamba's proximity to both of those places and its position as an interregional gateway between them, it is likely that humans first passed through the valley at a comparable time depth. No archaeological research has yet been conducted in the tropical parts of the valley that can tell us anything more specific about the area's early history of human habitation.

It is impossible to know what languages might have been spoken in the valley at that early time, but they probably did not include the ancestor languages of Matsigenka or Quechua, which are relative newcomers to the region. Matsigenka is a member of the Kampan sub-branch of the Arawak language family, alongside Nanti, Asháninka, Ashéninka, Kakinte, and Nomatsiguenga, which extend across a large expanse of the southern and central Peruvian Amazon. These languages are quite similar to each other—Lev Michael (personal communication) judges them to be more differentiated than Spanish and Portuguese, but less so than the whole Romance family, which is consistent with my own impression. This suggests that the whole Kampan sub-branch of the Arawak family likely split apart on the order of one thousand years ago. Only a small subset of that family moved up the Urubamba Valley toward the Andes, eventually becoming a dialect chain comprising Alto Urubamba Matsigenka, Bajo Urubamba Matsigenka, Manu Matsigenka, and Nanti, listed in order of similarity to each other (Michael 2008, 218).[2] These Matsigenka-Nanti varieties are similar enough today to permit mutual intelligibility even at the extremes. Thus, if we take one thousand years as an approximate time frame for the ramification of the whole Kampan Arawak sub-branch across the southern and central Peruvian Amazon, the small Matsigenka-Nanti subgroup probably made it to the Alto Urubamba, conservatively, no earlier than the fourteenth century (I owe this timeline to conversations with Lev Michael).[3] The earliest unequivocal written attestation of the Matsigenka language that I have found in the Alto Urubamba comes from 1801, and the toponyms (place names) appearing in earlier documents appear to come from a different language (or languages). Note that this relatively recent arrival of the Matsigenka language in the Alto Urubamba does not necessarily mean that the ancestors of today's Matsigenka people did not live there at that time—they may have adopted the Matsigenka language upon its arrival.

Southern Peruvian Quechua, for its part, probably expanded outward from its origin in central Peru between one and two thousand years ago (Emlen and Adelaar 2017; Heggarty and Beresford-Jones 2010; Cerrón-Palomino 2000). The Wari culture, which spread during the Middle Horizon (600–1000 AD), may have been associated with the Quechuan family's initial dispersal (Beresford-Jones and Heggarty 2011), or more narrowly with the dispersal of the Quechua II branch of the family (Adelaar 2012), which includes the varieties spoken in southern Peru.[4] In any case, Quechua was certainly widespread in the southern Peruvian highlands at the time of the European invasion in the sixteenth century, and it is possible that it was spoken there one thousand years ago or more (though probably not much more). It is not possible to know when Quechua first entered the Alto Urubamba after its arrival in southern Peru, but archaeological studies and Spanish colonial records show that some of the higher reaches of the valley (including Vilcabamba and Amaybamba; see map 3) were occupied from the highlands during the Inka period (1438–1532 AD). This probably means that Quechua was spoken there by that time at least, since Quechua was widespread in the adjacent highlands by then. Archaeological evidence points to sedentary highland populations in Vilcabamba as early as the sixth century AD, at the beginning of the Wari period (Meseth et al. 2015, 351; Fonseca Santa Cruz and Bauer 2013), and Late Intermediate settlements (1000–1400 AD) have been identified in Amaybamba (Wilkinson 2013). However, given the relatively recent chronology of Quechua expansion presented above, and given the complex multilingual mosaic of the nearby highlands during the Inka period (Mannheim 1991, 43–47), it is impossible to know for sure whether the people in those places would have spoken Quechua or some other language(s) at that time.

Thus, even though the Alto Urubamba has probably been inhabited by humans for millennia, we can only speculate about the last few hundred years of the valley's linguistic history. It is likely that prior languages in the valley overlapped with Quechua and Matsigenka, perhaps even relatively recently.

Such languages are probably the source of the great number of toponyms in the Alto Urubamba that are not attributable to any known language, and which are often quite inconsistent with the sound systems of both Matsigenka and Quechua. For instance, to name just a few inscrutable toponyms that are found only in historical sources (indicated by year) or are still used in the valley today, we find: Iguaraminuy (1552); Yuqua (1582); Usanbi (1586); Hondará (1610); Graz or Guaz (1790); Huinpuyu (1872); Chulituqui (1872); Erimuqui (1907); Echarati (later spelled Echarate); Maranura; and Yokiri.[5] These place names do not appear to be Matsigenka or Quechua. Notably, such unidentified toponyms are widespread in documents from the sixteenth to the early nineteenth centuries and become less common in more recent sources—it is only in sources from the late nineteenth century that Matsigenka toponyms take hold and come to predominate in the valley.[6] This suggests that these unidentified toponyms may have come from languages that preceded both Matsigenka and Quechua and overlapped with them both for some time before being replaced. For instance, Iguaraminuy—a distinctly un-Quechua and un-Matsigenka name for the Lucumayo Valley—was attested in 1552 just as it was being replaced with the Quechua toponym Amaybamba during the Inka period (Rostworowski 1963, 224; Gabai 1997, 251–52). This timeline of linguistic replacement is plausible, given that Matsigenka and Quechua probably had not arrived long before that toponym was recorded in 1552 (in the case of Matsigenka, perhaps only a century or two earlier, at the most).[7] The welter of groups of people that are named in written sources before the nineteenth century but then disappear in more recent sources—Pilcozones, Guanocaguas, Opataris, Manaríes, etc.—may have spoken some of these languages.

In addition to whatever unknown languages might have been spoken in the Alto Urubamba before Quechua and Matsigenka, languages from other places may also have had some presence in the valley in earlier times. For instance, a member of the Aymaran language family was spoken in some parts of the adjacent Cusco highlands during the colonial period (Adelaar and Muysken 2004, 174; Cerrón-Palomino 2000; Mannheim 1991), so people in the highland outposts of the Alto Urubamba may have brought that language with them in addition to Quechua. The Inka policy of long-distance resettlement may also have had some effect on the valley's linguistic fabric. For instance, around one thousand *mitmaqkuna* (resettled laborers) were brought to Amaybamba from Chachapoyas (Rostworowski 1963), a different Andean-Amazonian transitional area in northern Peru. They might have spoken the distinctive Chachapoyas variety of Quechua, or perhaps the so-called Chacha language that is thought to have preceded it (Adelaar and Muysken 2004, 167; Valqui and ZieMendorff 2016). In the early colonial period, resettled Cañari laborers, from present-day Ecuador, were also given land in Vilcabamba in exchange for military service against the Inkas in exile, and stayed there for centuries (Decoster and Najarro 2016). They may have spoken an early variety of Ecuadorian Kichwa—related to Cusco Quechua, but quite different—or perhaps an unrelated Indigenous Ecuadorian language that was subsequently replaced by Kichwa. In the seventeenth century, the Spanish sent over two thousand African slaves to work in the Alto Urubamba (Bowser 1974, 176). According to Baltasar de Ocampo, a group of these slaves staged an uprising alongside local people known as Pilcozones. He reports that the slaves spoke among themselves in "their language" (de Ocampo [1610] 1907, 240). We can only imagine what that language was, and what the sociolinguistic dynamics of the alliance between the African slaves and the Pilcozones might have been. Finally, the Yine language (also known as Piro), a more distantly related Arawak language located farther down the Urubamba Valley, has long been spoken by travelers through the Alto Urubamba (Gow 1991; Gade 1972; Camino 1977) and may have had an earlier presence there as well. However, no attempt has yet been made to document the linguistic traces of these countless passages through the Alto Urubamba.

All of this serves as a reminder that the Alto Urubamba has long been home to a great diversity of languages—some that took hold in the valley and others that were spoken by transient traders, conquerors, resettled colonists, slaves, and refugees—most of which are unknown to us today. A further complication is that the broader region was subject to catastrophic epidemics and demographic disruptions following the European invasion (Cook 1981; Wachtel 1977; Denevan 1992), and it is impossible to know which languages failed to survive that bottleneck. Indeed, recent research in other parts of the upper Amazon (e.g., in Ecuador; Loughlin et al. 2018) has shown that some pre-Columbian populations there were previously much larger, and had a more severe impact on the landscape, than after the epidemics and disruptions of the colonial period. Thus, whatever else the spotty evidence might tell us about the linguistic history of the valley, it certainly suggests that today's ethnolinguistic panorama is an unreliable guide to the past.

Evidence About Prehistoric Languages, People, and Interregional Connections

Following this introduction to the prehistory of languages and people in the Alto Urubamba, I now turn to the written and archaeological evidence that we can use to interpret the valley's history. The earliest reliable information comes from the archaeological record. There were sedentary agricultural populations in the Vilcabamba Valley during the Wari period (ca. 500–1000 AD; Meseth et al. 2015; Fonseca Santa Cruz and Bauer 2013), in places that were later inhabited by speakers of both Matsigenka and Quechua in the twentieth century (see map 3 below). During the Late Intermediate period (ca. 1000–1400 AD), Andean settlements extended over the Málaga Pass and into Amaybamba from the Sacred Valley (Wilkinson 2013). As mentioned earlier, it is likely that nonsedentary populations lived in the Alto Urubamba for millennia before this time, but traces of such populations are not often preserved in humid tropical forests.

Archaeological and ethnohistorical evidence suggests that the Inkas never gained direct control over the inhabitants of the Alto Urubamba lowlands, in part because their preferred state-building strategy of subjugating preexisting sociopolitical formations could not be easily applied to the region's sparse and relatively nonhierarchical societies (Covey 2006, 226–27; for more on the Inka projection into the lowlands, see Alconini 2004). Tropical diseases also discouraged Inka settlement (Le Moine and Raymond 1987), as did a more general aversion among highlanders to the topography and climate of the lowlands. The Inkas did, however, make some attempts to conquer parts of the Alto Urubamba, beginning with Pachacuti's campaign in Vilcabamba (Cobo [1653] 1890, 159; Renard-Casevitz 1981). The Inkas maintained a presence in Vilcabamba before escaping there to establish a capital-in-exile following the Spanish conquest. The Inkas also had coca plantations and royal estates in Amaybamba, just over the Málaga Pass from the Sacred Valley (Wilkinson 2013). However, given that the Inkas apparently did not pursue a policy of imposing Quechua on their subjects (Mannheim 1991), the people who lived there may have continued to speak other languages.

While Inka archaeological sites are found predominantly in the upper reaches of the Alto Urubamba, where the valley meets the highlands, there is evidence of occupation at lower parts of the valley as well. A road extended from the Sacred Valley and Ollantaytambo over the Málaga Pass (Wilkinson 2019), a primary point of access for the Inkas, and descended in one direction at least as far as the Yanatile River (Hassel 1907, 388; Bües 1942). Another road crossed the Urubamba River at Chuquichaca and led through Vilcabamba as far as Espíritu Pampa (Bauer, Cantarutti, and Halac-Higashimori 2016, 5). There were apparently traces of another road in the lower Yavero Valley (Hassel 1907, 377), near the communities of Huillcapampa and Yokiri (discussed in chapter 3). Some roads probably ended where river travel became possible (P. J. Lyon 1981, 8), and others likely led to earthen roads at lower elevations (A. W. Johnson 2003, 30–31). The Urubamba and Vilcabamba roads met (Renard-Casevitz, Saignes, and Taylor 1988, 87–88), creating a lowland road system from Vilcabamba and the Apurímac Valley all the way through the Alto Urubamba and Yavero Valleys to the Madre de Dios watershed.

One of the reasons for our limited knowledge of the Inka presence in the Alto Urubamba is that there simply has not been much archaeological research conducted in the lower parts of the valley—though many Matsigenka people are aware of ancient constructions in and around their communities. For instance, in March 2012 I accompanied a Matsigenka friend to an Inka or pre-Inka site called Mosocllacta, within the Matsigenka community of Chirumbia (see also Álvarez 1932; Ferrero 1966, 26–30), which has not been professionally excavated. Mosocllacta means "new town" in Quechua (spelled *musuq llaqta* in modern Quechuan orthography), but it is not clear when or why the site acquired this name. The site sits in a 1,950-meter pass connecting the Chirumbia, Yanatile, and Chapo watersheds, which is the most direct route between the lower Yanatile Valley and the Yavero Valley beyond (see map 3). A broad roadbed runs through the pass (figure 10) and disappears into the forests on either side. On the west side of the road (to the left in figure 10), there are stone terraces and the ruins of several buildings constructed with masonry walls. The site has been thoroughly looted.

Sites like Mosocllacta, some of which are near or within the boundaries of Matsigenka communities, suggest that there is a great deal more to be learned about the pre-Columbian highland presence in the Alto Urubamba. Indeed, the substantial scope of the ruins at Mosocllacta, at such a central point of access to the forests beyond, suggests that the site's builders must have had intimate knowledge of the lowlands and their people. Notably, it was not until the early 2000s that engineers finally built a modern road through the densely forested hills to Mosocllacta, finally catching up with the forgotten road network that had connected the Alto Urubamba to the highlands centuries before.

FIGURE 10 The pre-Columbian road at Mosocllacta Pass, facing north. Comunidad Nativa de Chirumbia, 2012. Photograph by the author.

The presence of overgrown pre-Columbian ruins in and around the Alto Urubamba, unfortunately, has fed an industry of overheated speculation about a legendary lost Inka city called Paititi. As the story goes, the Inkas fled the Spanish invasion with their gold and treasure to a remote corner of the adjacent Amazon, where it remains today. As the ever-expanding road network brings new parts of the eastern slopes into easy reach, and as deforestation and colonization uncover more and more traces of the region's long human occupation, legions of treasure hunters and amateur explorers have descended into parts of the forest in and around the Alto Urubamba (or, more benignly, have made their discoveries via Google Earth). By the time this book went to press, local and international news outlets were declaring the discovery of Paititi in this or that valley more than once a year. Some of these expeditions illegally target protected areas, endangering Indigenous Amazonians who are vulnerable to disease (Hill 2014). These adventures are based on a basic misunderstanding of the region's history: pre-Columbian Andean societies, in fact, had a substantial presence in the lowlands, and the many material remains there are simply a reflection of the prosaic concerns of accessing lowland resources rather than the hiding of secret treasure.

While the Inkas generally did not exert direct control over the inhabitants of the nearby lowlands, they did engage in sustained relations of trade. Some of the lowlanders who conducted this trade surely spoke Quechua in addition to their own languages, as attested by reports from the nineteenth century (see below). Lowland people supplied highlanders with coca, medicinal plants, fruit, wood, tobacco, live animals, animal pelts, and hallucinogens (Bélisle 2019) in exchange for tools, salt, and textiles from the highlands (Rosengren 2004, 19–20; Gade 1972, 209–10; Camino 1977, 128–29). Darryl Wilkinson (2018) argues that tropical bird feathers acquired from the lowlands were an important prestige good for Andean elites, and that their quantity in the highlands indicates an intense trade relationship. The Inkas also occasionally drew on the support of lowlanders as allies in military conflicts—for instance, several hundred lowland archers fought alongside the Inkas against the Spanish during the conquest (Hemming 1970, 330). The Inka vertical archipelagos included coca-producing areas in the tropical lowlands of the Madre de Dios watershed (Gade 1979; Renard-Casevitz 1981), and to a lesser extent in the Alto Urubamba (Wilkinson 2013). Andeans worked in these tropical coca plantations, though they apparently stayed for short periods of time out of fear of tropical diseases and attacks from Amazonians.

Sources about the Inka period tend to characterize the people of the lowlands as savages and cannibals, closer to nature than to humanity (Bertazoni Martins 2007). These stereotypes and misrepresentations persisted through the colonial period and still circulate in discourses about Indigenous Amazonians today. The most common term for lowlanders in sources about the Inka period was *Anti*, which refers in some cases to a specific group of people, while in others it is a more general designation for people from the eastern slopes. *Anti* also relates to Antisuyu, a wedge-shaped sector (*suyu*) of the Inka empire that projected northeast from the city of Cusco (Bauer 1998). There is some inconsistency in how this term is used as well: while in some sources it applies to a broad expanse of the eastern slopes, including the Urubamba lowlands, the Inka provincial divisions in fact placed the Alto Urubamba (along with the towns of Ollantaytambo and Lares through which it was accessed) within the Chinchaysuyu sector rather than in Antisuyu (Pärssinen 1992, 254–55; Zuidema and Poole 1982; Espinoza Soriano 1977; Julien 2000). Further complicating the matter, historical references to Anti people do not correspond consistently with the geographic designation of Antisuyu, and both terms apparently changed in meaning between the Inka and colonial periods. Meanwhile, the Quechua term *ch'unchu* (borrowed into Spanish as *chuncho*) also became common in the colonial period—and remains an offensive slur for Indigenous Amazonians today—though it began as a more narrow ethnonym for a group of people in the Madre de Dios watershed south of the Alto Urubamba (Renard-Casevitz, Saignes, and Taylor 1988).

In addition to these vague and inconsistent general terms, the colonial sources also present us with a dense tangle of more specific names for people in and around the Alto Urubamba before and after the European invasion: Manaríes, Pilcozones, Opataris, Guanucomarcas, Satis, Anaginis Antis, Moyo-Moyos, Ninaruas, Yanaximes, Paros, Sacapaqui, and others (cf. Bauer, Cantarutti, and Halac-Higashimori 2016, 39n14; Hemming 1970, 331; Renard-Casevitz, Saignes, and Taylor 1988). In-depth discussions of some of those names are presented by Renard-Casevitz, Saignes, and Taylor (1988), and Bauer, Cantarutti, and Halac-Higashimori (2016). Some names appear frequently in accounts of the Inka and colonial periods, while others are found once or only a handful of times, never to be seen again. For instance, we learn from a single source that the *chunchos guanocaguas* lived in the lower Yanatile Valley in the late eighteenth century (Oricaín [1790] 1906, 373), an area where Matsigenka speakers lived when the first reliable linguistic attestations appeared a short time later in the early nineteenth century. Whether these people were speakers of Matsigenka or another language (note that *guanocagua* does not appear to be a Matsigenka word), whether this is just the name of a single person representing an extended kin group (as often happened), or whether it is just an errant word jotted down thirdhand by a traveler with little understanding of the region, we can only speculate.

In any case, it is impossible to know what languages these people might have spoken. As I mentioned earlier, the ubiquity of non-Matsigenka and non-Quechua toponyms recorded in the valley before the nineteenth century—and the relatively recent arrival of Matsigenka and Quechua—suggest that we should be cautious about associating these named groups of people with contemporary languages and ethnic categories. This is especially true since many Matsigenka people today in fact migrated from other places beyond the Urubamba Valley during the twentieth century (see chapter 3 for a detailed case), such that a direct line cannot be drawn from the populations in the valley in earlier centuries to the category of people known as Matsigenkas today. Furthermore, the notion of a Matsigenka "ethnolinguistic group" is itself a twentieth-century construct without a reliable historical analogue, so it is not meaningful to equate such a contemporary category with named groups of people in the historical record. That is, while some Matsigenkas today may descend from people referenced in historical sources (e.g., the Manaríes), some of whom may have also spoken an earlier variety of the Matsigenka language, it is not the case that the Manaríes are "today's Matsigenkas."[8]

Neighbors in the Alto Urubamba

The people who produced the accounts of Inka and early Spanish involvement in the eastern slopes apparently found the lowlanders there to be incomprehensibly distant and foreign. However, this was just one perspective—an elite, imperial perspective, first on the part of the Inkas, then on the part of the Spanish—based on information gathered largely during expeditions in which the native inhabitants were encountered briefly, superficially, and often violently. There were other people, between the palaces of Cusco and the forests of the Alto Urubamba, who had a more prosaic and familiar experience of their neighbors at the Andean-Amazonian interface. Thus we should not conflate the elite Inka and colonial Spanish discourses recorded in early writing with a generalized highland attitude toward the lowlands. This difference in perspective remains true today: while people far from the Alto Urubamba tend to imagine Matsigenka people to be utterly foreign, the Andean colonos with whom they interact on a daily basis (and in many cases count as their own kin) have a much more informed and routine relationship with them.

The inevitability of familiar, if periodic, interactions between people in the highlands and the Urubamba lowlands comes from the organization of those societies themselves. The Andean social networks that extended vertically across a range of elevational zones brought highlanders into places adjacent to—or overlapping with—those frequented by lowland groups. Though the vertical archipelago pattern of discontinuous landholding (described in the introduction) did not play a major role in the Alto Urubamba during the Inka period itself (Gade 2016, 88), it is likely that some version of it functioned there beforehand, and subsequent links between the valley and the adjacent highlands certainly follow this pattern. For instance, we can see this in the ways that Andean campesinos from the Sacred Valley incorporated tropical land in the Alto Urubamba into their agropastoral activities in the mid-twentieth century (Fioravanti-Molinié 1975; Collins 1984). The Inka practice of sending *mitmaqkuna*—resettled populations from other areas—to work in the lowland coca fields persisted well into the colonial period, until Manco Inca's capture at Vilcabamba, when the valley had been largely depopulated (Gabai 1997, 252; Gade 2016, 98).

The seminomadic horticulturalists who lived in the lowlands, for their part, ventured to higher elevations as a matter of course on trade and hunting trips. There were also interethnic coca plantations in the Inka period, where highlanders and lowlanders worked side by side (Renard-Casevitz, Saignes, and Taylor 1988, 72), much as Matsigenkas and colonos worked together on the Alto Urubamba's plantations during the early twentieth century (see below), and as they do in the Camisea gas fields and municipal road crews today. Such Inka plantations would have mediated between highland and lowland societies, and they surely resulted in interethnic unions, demographic interchange, and multilingualism, as the coffee frontier described in this book does today. There were also interethnic settlements at the margins of Inka and Spanish control, in some cases inhabited by people fleeing the law or the burdens of *mit'a* (corvée labor). Indeed, the Amazonian lowlands have long been a place where Andeans have eluded the reach of the state, or where they have been banished as punishment for their crimes (a common sentence during the Inka period).[9] This, too, has continued to the present, as the secluded forests of the Alto Urubamba provide a haven for all manner of illegal behavior. Thus we find references to people of highland origin living among lowlanders in Vilcabamba and other places throughout the colonial period (Maúrtua 1906, 285; Oricaín [1790] 1906, 351, 372; Renard-Casevitz, Saignes, and Taylor 1988, 146). Such interregional contacts were probably even stronger before the Inka period, when smaller-scale political formations could maintain local relations across elevations without obligation to a centralized political structure in the highlands. (This was likely the kind of situation that led to the Yanesha'-Quechua contact described earlier.) For these reasons, we should be careful to recognize that the recorded discourses about Amazonian others reflect the elite Inka perspective rather than the experience of Andeans who actually lived at the highland-lowland interface.

The Multiethnic Borderlands After the European Invasion

The European invasion beginning in the 1530s, which occurred at the apex of the Inka period, witnessed points of both disruption and continuity in the relationships between highlanders and lowlanders in the Alto Urubamba. Most importantly, both Andean migrants and lowlanders were recruited to work in the colonial agricultural industries after the Inka period, where they came into close contact. The region also continued to serve as a place of refuge from the highlands, in this case from the Spanish colonial regime. This was true for people fleeing legal trouble and abusive labor obligations in the Andes as well.

The most high-profile moment of Andean involvement in the Alto Urubamba came during the Spanish conquest, when Manco Inca escaped from his Spanish captors in Cusco, laid siege to the city in 1536, and then retreated with his armies to Ollantaytambo and eventually the capital-in-exile of Espíritu Pampa in the forests of Vilcabamba. There the Inkas continued their attacks on the Spanish and their Native allies, and operated a neo-Inka state until it was finally defeated by the Spanish in 1572 (Hemming 1970). During this time, the Inkas were in contact with people variously called Antis and Manaríes, some of whom may have been forebears of some of today's Matsigenka people, and who might have spoken a prior variety of the Matsigenka language (note that Matsigenka speakers lived at the ruins of Espíritu Pampa in the early twentieth century, and continue to live nearby). These lowlanders helped facilitate the Inkas' escape and fought in their armies against the Spanish in the sixteenth century (Rodrí-guez Figueroa [ca. 1565] 1913, 189; Rosengren 2004, 22; Hemming 1970). On the other hand, the Manaríes also assisted the Spanish in their pursuit of the Inkas in Vilcabamba, suggesting that these alliances were opportunistic and localized (for more on this history from a lowland perspective, see Rosengren 2004, 21–24).

After the defeat of the Inkas of Vilcabamba in 1572, the newly established province of Vilcabamba saw amicable trade relations with Indigenous low-landers, particularly the Manaríes (Bauer, Cantarutti, and Halac-Higashimori 2016, 31–32). However, others, including the Pilcozones, were the targets of Spanish military campaigns. There were also fugitive Andeans and African slaves in the Alto Urubamba, some of whom lived among the lowland groups (see, e.g., de Quevedo 1900, 482; Regalado de Hurtado 1992, 97). As the Span-ish increased coca production in the lowlands (particularly in the Madre de Dios watershed), skirmishes with lowlanders increased (Daniel Gade [1979, 274] reports that armed guards called *matachunchos*, meaning "savage-killers," protected some frontier haciendas in the nineteenth century).

Even as the Inkas maintained their nearly forty-year resistance in Vilcabamba, the Spanish began a slow and halting colonization of the Alto Urubamba. There were short-lived mining ventures in Vilcabamba, and in 1539 Hernando Pizarro was given an encomienda—the right to the tribute of the Indians in a particular area, granted as a reward for military service—in Amaybamba (Julien 2000; Gabai 1997). This encomienda included the multiethnic group of laborers that remained from the Inka period, made up of people from the Andes and resettled mitmaqkuna from Chachapoyas and Cañar (most likely in addition to people from the lower valley as well). Pizarro had coca fields as low as the Yanatile Valley (see map 3), which were taken over from the Inka period (Covey and González 2008, 101; see also Gade 2016, 99). This is the very same place where Andean colono farmers were establishing coffee plantations in the early twentieth century. Gradually, haciendas were created farther and farther down the valley, and they were well established in the area around Quillabamba by the mid-seventeenth century. An hacienda was built in Echarati (as it was spelled at the time), near the confluence of the Yanatile and Urubamba Rivers (see map 3), in 1720 (Menéndez Rúa 1948, 30–34; Gade 2016, 311). Matsigenka speakers lived in this area in the nineteenth century, and probably did at this earlier time as well. Some of these haciendas prospered, supplying coca and sugarcane to the highland mining economy (Encinas Martín, Perez Casado, and Alonso Ordieres 2008, 38–39; Sala i Vila 1998, 402) until the valley's agricultural economy collapsed in the late sixteenth century. The development of farming in the region was limited by the short supply of labor, and the landowners recruited workers from wherever they could: the Indigenous population of the valley, African slaves, and highland migrants (Gade 1972, 215). Thus the agrarian society of the Alto Urubamba continued to be multiethnic, and surely multilingual, just as it had been during the Inka period. We can't be certain what languages were spoken there even at this late date, nor what the sociolinguistic situation might have been like—indeed, the Matsigenka language probably does not long predate this period in the Alto Urubamba. However, it is reasonable to assume that the presence of Andean and Amazonian laborers in the local plantations led to the same porous and interconnected sociolinguistic environment that it led to in the twentieth and twenty-first centuries.

The eighteenth century was a period of relative quiet in the Alto Urubamba. The rebellion of Juan Santos Atahualpa in central Peru (Brown and Fernández 1991; Castro Arenas 1973; Varese 1968) discouraged colonization, evangelization, and administration across much of the eastern slopes, though the Alto Urubamba did not experience a total rupture (Rosengren 2004). Skirmishes with lowlanders continued, and some haciendas were attacked, but the agricultural economy persisted without major interruptions. For this period between the colonial highland-lowland contacts of the sixteenth century and the concentrated geographical and economic interest of the nineteenth century, relatively little information is available.

By the mid-eighteenth century, relations of highland-lowland trade in the Alto Urubamba had picked up pace. The major point of interaction was the

Jesuit mission at Cocabambilla, on the Urubamba River above the confluence of the Yanatile River, near the modern town of Echarate (see map 3). At that time, highland-lowland trade in the Alto Urubamba was conducted by speakers of the Piro (or Yine) language, who traveled upriver from the Bajo Urubamba to meet highlanders at an annual trading fair. Piros raided Matsigenka settlements along the way, stealing women, children, and supplies for exchange with Andean traders. Some Matsigenka speakers fled into the interior to protect themselves from the Piro raids, creating the dispersed and remote settlement patterns still in evidence among Matsigenka communities today. In the nineteenth century, Matsigenka-speaking intermediaries along the Urubamba River appeased Piros with goods and slaves to prevent them from traveling up the tributaries to pillage the Matsigenka settlements themselves (Camino 1977). This system later became a mode of labor recruitment for the rubber industry (discussed below). The Matsigenka-speaking slaves worked alongside both Andean migrants and African slaves to fill the agricultural labor demands of the valley, and Matsigenka speakers were also brought to the highlands. Unfortunately, we know little about what happened to these Amazonians who were incorporated into Andean society.

The mid-nineteenth century saw a gradual revival of the valley's agricultural economy, facilitated by an expanding transportation network, new interest in agricultural products from La Convención (Encinas Martín, Perez Casado, and Alonso Ordieres 2008, 41), and military protection against the lowlanders' periodic attacks on colonos who were attempting to push the frontier beyond Cocabambilla (Nicolau 1907). The province of La Convención was created in 1857, as the Peruvian state sought a connection to the Amazon river network and the Atlantic Ocean beyond (Sala i Vila 1998, 424), which would grant the Cusco region a more prominent place in the national economy. The expanding road network would also open the possibility of agricultural colonization farther down the valley.

During the nineteenth century, the agricultural economy of La Convención began to intensify and shift from coca and sugarcane to crops such as coffee, cacao, fruits, and tea. The hacendados maintained a tight grip on the Alto Urubamba through most of the nineteenth century, until the first independent town—Quillabamba, the provincial capital today—was founded in 1881, allowing outside merchants to do business in the valley and breaking the monopoly of estate owners over the valley's agricultural industry (Fioravanti 1974, 56; Craig 1969, 281). Trade with lowlanders continued, and as the agricultural economy grew, landowners continued to draw on both Matsigenkas and Andean migrants for labor, particularly now that there were fewer African slaves in the valley (Gade 1972, 215–16; 2016, 316). Some Matsigenkas also sought refuge from the slave raids of the rubber period by working on local haciendas alongside Andean migrants; at the same time, Matsigenkas were also sold as slaves to the haciendas themselves, a trade that operated as recently as the 1940s (Gade 2016, 313–16). Given the constant recruitment of the labor of both Matsigenkas and migrants from the highlands, the agricultural labor force in the valley continued to be interethnic and multilingual, just as it had been for hundreds of years before that time. As I discuss below, Quechua was the lingua franca of the agrarian frontier society—particularly before Spanish became widely spoken in the mid-twentieth century—and Matsigenkas learned Quechua in those haciendas (see also the history of the community of Yokiri, described in chapter 3).

Beginning in the mid- to late nineteenth century, the trades in rubber and *cinchona* bark (used to make quinine, an antimalarial drug) transformed the economy of the Alto Urubamba. Between 1850 and 1890, the area around Chirumbia and Rosalina—still firmly within Matsigenka-speaking territory at the time—was a major point of trade for cinchona bark (see map 3). From 1880 until 1910, Matsigenka slaves, alongside some Andean migrants, collected rubber in the remote areas of the forest (Gade 1972, 217). Some of these slaves (particularly women and children) were recruited through the system discussed earlier, in which Matsigenka intermediaries supplied Piro traders with slaves and trade goods destined for the highlands (Encinas Martín, Perez Casado, and Alonso Ordieres 2008, 69–70; Camino 1977, 132; Valdez y Palacios 1971, 98). Matsigenkas were also recruited through debt servitude. The lawless rubber industry, and the diseases that accompanied it, devastated the Matsigenka-speaking population (Gade 1972, 217; Rosengren 2004, 30). Some Matsigenkas fled to the remote headwaters of the Urubamba tributaries, where many still live today, while others remained around the centers of the rubber industry along the Urubamba and Yavero Rivers (Rosengren 2004, 30). After the Peruvian rubber industry declined in the 1910s, raiders continued to enslave Matsigenkas to supply labor for the agricultural industry (Camino 1979, 138). In this way, the expanding agricultural economy continued to draw on a multiethnic labor force consisting of Indigenous lowlanders—whom at this point we can call "Matsigenkas"—as well as highland migrants.

In this period, Dominican missions became an important counterbalance to the violence of the rubber period and the abuse of Matsigenkas on haciendas.

The mission at Chirumbia was established in 1902, adjacent to the Rosalina hacienda, which was at that point the farthest extent of the agricultural frontier (Bowman 1912, 885). The Dominicans took in Matsigenkas from around the region and protected them from slave raids, which placed the missionaries in an uneasy relationship with the nearby landowners, who were constantly in need of labor (Rosengren 1987, 42). Ramón Zubieta, the founder of the mission at Chirumbia, described the religious purpose and placement of the mission in a 1905 letter:

> Since the savages in the whole region of the Urubamba and its tributaries are dispersed into families and small groups, it was necessary to visit them frequently, help them with their needs, and become familiar with them; with the goal of managing to baptize their children and obligate them morally to visit the Missionary in his residence; then, once this is all done, to form a settlement where the adults can receive frequent instruction, and the children can attend school and religious services, so that later they form a generation that is fundamentally different from that of their parents. (Zubieta 1905, 44; translation mine)

To a large extent, Zubieta's objectives were fulfilled over the course of the twentieth century: the missions established in the Urubamba Valley during that time are now nucleated, agrarian settlements, with greater similarity to neighboring colono communities than to the dispersed communities from which the Matsigenka residents came. Many Matsigenkas also encountered Spanish for the first time in these missions, and, after several generations of mission life, some speak more Spanish than Matsigenka today. Some also learned to speak Quechua from the workers in and around the mission, and as a result of the broader sociocultural integration of the mission into the surrounding colono society.[10] Recently, some Urubamba mission towns (now legally titled comunidades nativas) have begun to allow the colono spouses of Matsigenka people to take up residence there. As a result, one hears Quechua as much as Matsigenka in some of those communities today, particularly among the growing number of interethnic families. These missions remain major mediators between Matsigenkas and colono society. However, the Dominicans' goal of establishing an autonomous, enduring community of Catholic Matsigenkas has failed in an important respect: as Matsigenkas in mission towns have embraced commercial agriculture and joined the surrounding agrarian society, they have begun to abandon the missions and seek new opportunities in other places.

Andean frontier expansion, which had progressed gradually from the late eighteenth century onward, came to an abrupt end in the early twentieth century for two reasons: the collapse of the Peruvian rubber industry after World War I, and the great malaria epidemic that swept through the valley in 1933–35 (Craig 1969, 281–82; Hobsbawm 1969). A large proportion of the valley's non-Matsigenka population died or fled the valley during that time (Gade 1975, 28; Fioravanti 1974, 58), devastating the agricultural economy until the epidemic finally eased in the late 1940s. The Dominicans struggled to maintain their flocks as Matsigenkas abandoned the disease-stricken frontier and rejoined their kin in the forest, where disease did not spread as quickly because of the dispersed settlement pattern. At the same time, some Matsigenkas continued to work alongside the remaining Andean migrants on the haciendas, often forcibly, to offset the labor shortage caused by the epidemic. For many Matsigenka people, life in the valley was quieter for the moment; however, as we saw in chapter 1, the pace of frontier expansion bounced back in the 1950s and has continued with unprecedented intensity until today.

The Matsigenka Language in the Alto Urubamba, 1800–1930

What was the linguistic situation like during the period of frontier expansion described above, between the revival of the Alto Urubamba agricultural economy at the end of the eighteenth century and its sudden halt during the malaria epidemic of the early 1930s? It is during this period—finally—that we begin to have a clearer sense of the region's linguistic dynamics, including our first reliable information about the Matsigenka language in the valley. The first unequivocal attestation of the language in the Alto Urubamba that I have been able to find comes from an 1801 letter about the Franciscan missions in the valley (Maúrtua 1907, 48), which mentions the Matsigenka toponym Coribeni (from *kori*, "gold," and *-beni*, "watercourse").[11] A subsequent account of a Franciscan expedition through the Alto Urubamba in 1806 also mentions other Matsigenka toponyms still used today: Yriyapami (that is, *eriapa-ni*, "shotgun river," today Illapani), Chirumbia (from *tsirompi-ari*, "fern river"), and the aforementioned Coribeni (Izaguirre 1922, 320–41).[12] From that point forward, Matsigenka toponymy is ubiquitous in the written sources.

To understand where Matsigenka was spoken in the Alto Urubamba before Andean colonization pushed its speakers down the valley, we can look to the distribution of Matsigenka toponyms (see also Gade 2016, 298–300). In many places around the world, native toponyms have persisted long after the last speakers of those languages lived there, and thus attest to the languages' former geographical range—compare, for instance, the wide distribution of Celtic toponyms in Europe and Asia Minor, far beyond their current representation in the British Isles (Sims-Williams 2006), or Native American toponyms in parts of the United States where those languages are no longer widely used. Matsigenka toponyms are easily recognizable since they generally combine words for animals, plants, and other things with a set of suffixes denoting landscape features (Shepard et al. 2001).[13] In the Alto Urubamba, some of the most common suffixes are *-(h)ato* (small river), as in Toturoato ("snail river," cf. *toturo*, "snail"); *-(h)ari* (small river), as in Tsirompiari (meaning "fern river"; Hispanicized as Chirumbia, cf. *tsirompi*, "fern"); *-shi* (vegetation), as in Potogoshi (meaning "forest of genus *Ficus*"; Quechuanized as Putucusi, cf. *potogo*, a plant of the genus *Ficus*); *-ni* (watercourse; Mihas 2015, 110), as in Eriapani ("shotgun river," cf. *eriapa*, "shotgun"); and combinations thereof, as in Porenkishiari (meaning "river by the stand of *Renealmia* plants," cf. *porenki*, a plant of the genus *Renealmia*, suffixed with both *-shi*, "vegetation," and *-ari*, "small river").

To map the historical extent of Matsigenka in the Alto Urubamba, I compiled a corpus of toponyms containing identifiable Matsigenka nouns and suffixes, shown as dots on map 3. Data were collected from a variety of modern and historical sources.[14] (Quechua and Spanish toponyms, as well as the unidentified toponyms discussed earlier, are omitted.) Map 3 also shows today's comunidades nativas and other protected areas in the Alto Urubamba, shaded in gray. The places where Matsigenka toponyms lie outside of these protected areas were once inhabited by Matsigenka speakers before Andean colonos overtook the land (mostly before the comunidades nativas law of the mid-1970s); thus the map provides a visual summary of Matsigenka displacement. Other places mentioned in this chapter are also indicated. The main routes of twentieth-century Andean colonization are shown with arrows.

This map suggests that, since the nineteenth century, Matsigenka speakers have lived east of the Apurímac Valley, north and northwest of the Vilcabamba mountain range, north of the Yanatile River, and about as far east as Lacco in the Yavero Valley. One of the striking aspects of this geographical range is the diversity of environments that it encompasses: the language has extended from below three hundred meters in the humid Amazon plain past the Pongo de Mainique to the slopes of the snowcapped Vilcabamba Range, which includes high points of land up to four thousand meters within titled Matsigenka communities.

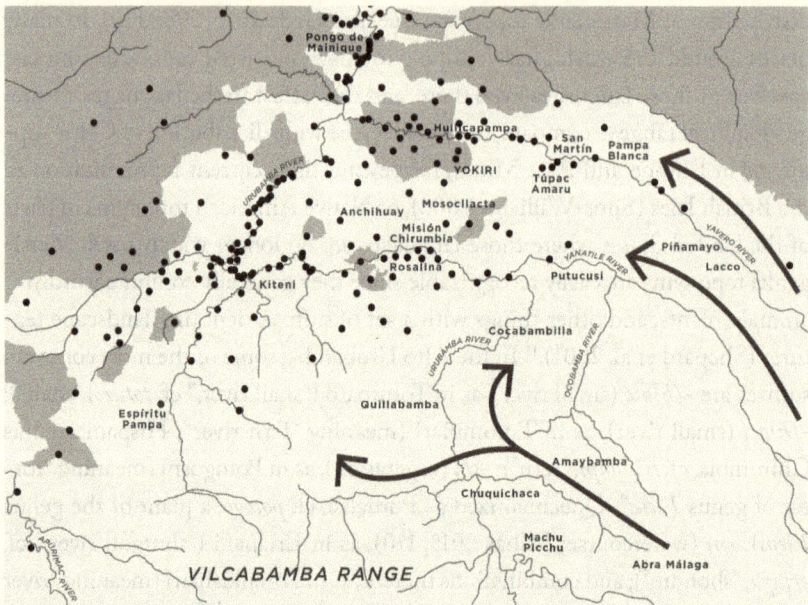

MAP 3 Matsigenka toponyms in the Alto Urubamba. Map designed by the author in QGIS. GIS data from Instituto del Bien Común. IBC-SICNA. Enero 2017, incluye información levantada en gabinete, AIDESEP-CIPTA, GEF PNUD, GOREL y PFS. Author's GPS data also used. Rivers and labels added by the author.

Matsigenka toponyms trail off in a rough line facing southeast; this is the direction from which speakers of Cusco Quechua have migrated down the major river valleys, as shown by the arrows indicating twentieth-century Andean colonization routes. A more detailed account of the displacement of Matsigenkas in the Yavero Valley is given in chapter 3.

Historical accounts also provide helpful anecdotal information about where Matsigenka was spoken in the Alto Urubamba in earlier times. For instance, Hiram Bingham (1914a) describes encountering "campas," almost certainly speakers of Matsigenka, during an expedition to Vilcabamba in 1911. These people worked on a sugarcane plantation in Conservidayoc and inhabited the ruins of Espíritu Pampa (map 3), not far from the contemporary Matsigenka communities of Inkaare and Tivoriari, where many residents today speak both Matsigenka and Quechua and routinely travel near Espíritu Pampa (see the concluding chapter of this book for more). Indeed, a toponym that Bingham recorded within the ruins, Eromboni, is a plausible Matsigenka toponym (with the ubiquitous suffix -*ni*, "watercourse"), though its meaning is not clear. He also mentions the name Tendi Pampa (Bauer, Fonseca Santa Cruz, and Aráoz Silva 2015, 129; Bingham 1914b), which likely comes from Matsigenka *tindi* (meaning "papaya"; *pampa* is a ubiquitous Quechua term for "flat place").

Matsigenka may also have been spoken farther up the Urubamba Valley in earlier periods—the data in map 3 only go back to the nineteenth century, after centuries of Inka and colonial agricultural involvement that might have displaced the language if it had been spoken in the upper valley in earlier times. Notably, the upper limit of Matsigenka toponyms is at the nineteenth-century frontier—it was at around that time that modern cartography and the administrative practice of recording standardized toponyms began in earnest (Orlove 1993). Thus Matsigenka toponyms may have existed farther up the valley before that time without being recorded. Furthermore, it is also possible that there are, in fact, toponyms of Matsigenka origin farther up the Urubamba Valley, from before the nineteenth century, but that these words have been so transformed in the mouths of generations of Quechua speakers that they are no longer recognizable as Matsigenka. For instance, near the confluence of the Yanatile and Urubamba Rivers, where Matsigenka speakers have not lived since the nineteenth century, Quechua speakers have accommodated the Matsigenka toponym Potogoshi (forest of genus *Ficus*) into Quechua phonology as Putucusi (map 3). I would not have recognized the origin of this toponym if my Matsigenka friends had not alerted me to it. Such a process might explain some of the many inscrutable toponyms mentioned earlier. However, I have not seen evidence to support the assertion that Matsigenka was spoken nearly as high as Machu Picchu, or even Quillabamba (Casevitz 1972, 215–16)—though it would not be surprising if Matsigenka speakers did venture up the valley, particularly during times of waning highland influence.

Multilingualism on the
Agricultural Frontier, 1800–1930

One of the recurrent themes of this chapter has been the perennially multiethnic nature of the Alto Urubamba's agrarian society. The valley has long been home to encounters between lowlanders and Andeans in search of land and work. Furthermore, because the valley's population has often been insufficient to supply labor for the local agricultural industry, people have come from a wide variety of other places—some by choice, others by force—to work and live there. These include thousands of mitmaqkuna (resettled laborers) who were brought from other parts of the Andes during the Inka period; African slaves during the colonial period; settlers, temporary laborers, and fugitives from the Andes, who have arrived in periodic waves from prehistory to the present; and the Native people of the valley themselves, who have circulated through local agricultural centers to various extents. As I discuss in the rest of this book, the agrarian society of the Alto Urubamba retains this multiethnic character today, though the people, the languages, and the socioeconomic circumstances that bring them together have changed over the centuries.

The valley's multilingual and multiethnic character can be seen in the early-twentieth-century frontier below the confluence of the Yanatile and Urubamba Rivers (see map 3). In 1926, the mission at Chirumbia was home to 60 Matsigenkas and 14 Quechua-speaking Andean colonos, while more than 140 Matsigenkas lived and worked alongside Andean colonos in the nearby haciendas of Santusari, Illapani, Rosalina, and Cochayoc (Martínez 1926, 702). Many of the Andeans were seasonal laborers who came to the Alto Urubamba to work for a few months at slow points in the highland agricultural calendar; the Matsigenka people, for their part, tended to circulate between the mission, the haciendas, and their more remote forest settlements. The result was an unbroken network of interaction that extended from the rural Andean highlands to Matsigenka settlements far beyond the Alto Urubamba frontier. Though it is not often remarked in the written record, this surely involved some degree of interethnic marriage, or at least the birth of children to colono fathers and Matsigenka mothers (as today, many of these children were probably incorporated into Matsigenka communities when the colonos returned to the highlands). In this view, lowlanders and highlanders in the Alto Urubamba were part of an interregional and multilingual social network, and the space between the Andes and Amazonia had the character of a continuum rather than a boundary.

The agrarian society of the Alto Urubamba has long been associated with Quechua, since Spanish only became widely spoken among rural Andeans following the institutionalization of public education in the countryside over the last few decades. Thus the Matsigenkas who have participated in the agrarian society have tended to learn Quechua. Indeed, as I describe in chapter 4, being a successful coffee farmer in the valley today requires acquitting oneself in a range of interactions in Quechua. Many Matsigenkas on the coffee frontier today also form families with Andean colonos, and many of these families are trilingual in Matsigenka, Quechua, and Spanish; before the mid-twentieth century, such interethnic families were bilingual in Matsigenka and Quechua, and Quechua was the primary language through which Matsigenka people participated in the broader society. Quechua was also spoken by Matsigenka intermediaries who dealt with traders beyond the frontier in the nineteenth century (Marcoy 1875, 382, 398, 419, etc.)—particularly the men (Hassel 1907, 372)—while some highlanders also spoke Matsigenka (Marcoy 1875, 403).

The linguistic influences between Cusco Quechua and the attested varieties of Matsigenka have been relatively minor. It is possible that there were other varieties closer to the Andean frontier that were more heavily affected by Quechua (as in the case of Yanesha' in central Peru) but that these did not survive the demographic and socioeconomic circumstances of that contact. In general, the Matsigenka varieties closest to the frontier exhibit stronger influence from Quechua, and more recently from Spanish, though these varieties are also the ones undergoing the most rapid intergenerational language shift. All Matsigenka varieties have borrowed some Quechua terms for products, trade goods, tools, deities, and other things, while I have been able to identify only one unequivocal Kampan Arawak loanword in Quechua: *sayri* (tobacco), from *seri* (also meaning "tobacco," though it is not clear whether this came from Matsigenka or another Kampan language). Table 1 shows some terms shared by Quechua (as listed in the dictionary of the Academia Mayor de la Lengua Quechua [2005]) and Matsigenka as it is spoken beyond the frontier (listed in Snell 2011). Most of the terms can be reconstructed in Proto-Quechua (as presented in Emlen 2017b); thus we can be sure that they originate there and were borrowed into Matsigenka. *Seri* (tobacco) comes from Proto-Arawak *yuerɨ (tobacco) (see Payne 1991), and thus was likely borrowed into Quechua. This is unsurprising, given that tobacco is a tropical crop. This term was likely borrowed during or before the colonial period, since it is present in the 1608 Quechua dictionary of González Holguín (Renard-Casevitz 1981, 116–17; González Holguín 1608); thus it is not certain which Kampan language it came from. Other cases of Kampan loans in Cusco Quechua may include *anpi* ("cotton"; cf. Matsigenka *ampei*, Asháninka *ampehi*, "cotton") (Kindberg 1980, 12) and *unkucha* (a type of tropical root vegetable; cf. Matsigenka *onko*, the same type of vegetable, and *ongo*, of the same meaning in the closely related Nomatsiguenga language) (Shaver 1996). These terms also refer to lowland cultivars that have made their way to the highlands. However, since none of these terms can be

TABLE 1 Lexical items shared by Matsigenka and Cusco Quechua

MATSIGENKA	CUSCO QUECHUA	PROTO-QUECHUA	PROTO-ARAWAK
ampato (toad sp.)	bamp'atu (toad sp.)[a]		
ampei (cotton)	anpi (cotton)		
bampi ~ ampi (medicine)	bamp'i– (medicine, to cure)	*hampi– (medicine, to cure)	
aryo (really, indeed)	ari (yes)	*ari (yes)	
chopi, chopisere (soup, food)	chupi (soup)		
inti (sun)	inti (sun)	*inti (sun)	
ktipi– (to carry in a bundle)	q'ipi– (to carry in a bundle)	*qipi– (to carry in a bundle)	
kori (gold)	quri (gold)	*quri (gold)	
koriki (silver, money)	qulqi (silver, money)		
kororo (larva)	kuru (worm)	*kuru (worm)	
michanti (stingy person)	micha (to be stingy)	*mitʂa (stingy)	
onko (tropical root vegetable)	unkucha (tropical root vegetable)		
pachakamu, pachakami (deity)	pachakamaq (creator deity)	*pacha (world), *kama– (create)	
pampa– (flat place, to be flat)	pampa (flat place)	*pampa (flat place)	
ponyarona (Andean)	puna runa (resident of the high grasslands)	*puna (high grasslands), *runa (person)	
seri (tobacco)	sayri (tobacco)		*yueri (tobacco)
sopai (devil, demon)	supay (devil, demon)		
tanta (bread)	t'anta (bread)	*tanta (bread)	
varaka (slingshot)	warak'a (slingshot)	*waraka (slingshot)	
viracocha (white person, Andean)	wiraqucha (deity, Inka ruler, white person)		

Matsigenka data from Snell (2011) and the author's fieldwork. Cusco Quechua data from Academia Mayor de la Lengua Quechua (2005) and the author's fieldwork. Proto-Quechua reconstructions from Emlen (2017b), Emlen and Adelaar (2017), and Emlen and Dellert (forthcoming). Proto-Arawak reconstructions from Payne (1991).

[a]Though bamp'atu (toad) is not reconstructible in Proto-Quechua by the criteria of Emlen (2017b), the term is widespread in the Quechuan and Aymaran languages and probably originates in the Andes.

reconstructed in either Proto-Quechua or Proto-Arawak, the directionality of borrowing remains uncertain, as do the time depth and the specific Quechuan and Kampan varieties involved.

Clearly, the influence between Matsigenka and Cusco Quechua has been modest—it is nothing like the case of Yanesha', which took on a great deal of Quechua loanwords and also underwent some Quechua grammatical and phonological influence (to such an extent that its phonology patterns, typologically, with the Andean languages; see Michael, Chang, and Stark 2014). However, an important caveat is that most Matsigenka and Quechua sources have been compiled relatively far from the contact zone and thus represent the varieties of each language that are least likely to exhibit contact effects. On the Alto Urubamba frontier, where I conducted my fieldwork, there has been quite a bit more contact influence among Matsigenka, Quechua, and Spanish. For instance, Matsigenka in Yokiri (see chapter 3) includes the verb *pirik-* (to make a wall), from Quechua *pirqa* (wall), which I have not encountered outside of the frontier. Matsigenka words for flora and fauna are used in the local Quechua and Spanish, as well as some culturally specific terms—for instance, Matsigenka-Spanish bilinguals use the verb *chagompitar* (to tie a baby in a sling), from the Matsigenka verb *tsagompu-* of the same meaning.[15] I heard Matsigenka speakers express time with Spanish roots, as in *osinkotanake* (it's five o'clock—ing)—here the Spanish numeral *cinco* (five) is used as a verb in Matsigenka. Perhaps most significantly, the Matsigenka-Nanti inventory of nine vowels (Michael 2008, 225) appears to be reduced in some parts of the Alto Urubamba, which is what we would expect as a result of contact with Quechua, which only has three vowel phonemes. This question requires more detailed acoustic phonetic analysis.

Conclusion

This chapter has offered a linguistic history of Andean-Amazonian interaction in the Alto Urubamba. I began with the earliest periods of human presence in and around the valley and argued that the Matsigenka and Quechua languages were probably relatively recent arrivals. Those languages likely coexisted until relatively recently with an earlier language (or languages), which is reflected in a large number of unidentified toponyms in the valley. I then traced the history of interregional contacts in the valley through the Inka period, the Spanish colonial period, and the postcolonial period including the Dominican presence, up through the eve of the current period of Andean expansion beginning in the 1950s (which is described in chapter 1).

Throughout this chapter, I have drawn attention to a couple of recurring themes. First, a major fact of Alto Urubamba demographics throughout history has been that the region's population has normally been insufficient to supply labor for its agricultural industries. This has led to the forced resettlement or voluntary migration of people from other regions, especially Andeans from the neighboring highlands, but also African slaves and laborers from other parts of Peru and Ecuador. The result has been a perennially multiethnic and multilingual frontier, in which people from other places have intermingled (and likely intermarried) with the valley's local inhabitants. Second, while trade networks have played an important part in the connections between the Andean highlands and the Amazonian lowlands, so too have relationships between neighbors in the Alto Urubamba. I have sought to show that both forms of Andean-Amazonian contact have been important in the history of the valley.

I include this chapter in the book because I wish to contribute the case study of the Alto Urubamba to a broader understanding of interregional connections in South America. Interdisciplinary research suggests that other places in the Andes and Amazonia have been closely connected throughout the centuries and millennia, but it can be difficult to know with any precision how those relationships might have functioned at those early times. Focusing on the interplay between multilingualism, labor, kinship, gender, resources, and migration that we find in the Alto Urubamba (both today and in the past) may help us interpret the nature of those other relationships as well.

In the next chapter, I move on to explore how the social system that I introduced at the regional level in chapter 1, and historically in chapter 2, played out among the ninety-four residents of a single community called Yokiri in the lower Yavero Valley.

Chapter 3

A Community Forms

On a single densely forested hillside tucked into a remote corner of the lower Yavero Valley sits a small community called Yokiri. Yokiri was established by people from a wide range of places and circumstances in the nearby Amazonian lowlands and Andean highlands, including remote forests far beyond the agricultural frontier, the nearby Dominican mission at Chirumbia, a handful of haciendas in the Yavero Valley that used enslaved Matsigenkas as laborers, and a part of the rural highland province of Paucartambo. These people came together between the 1970s and the early 2000s amid the upheavals and dislocations of the coffee frontier, and intermarried to form the community. In 2009–12, the community's heterogeneous formation meant that each household was a site of substantial cultural and linguistic variation—indeed, in a sense, each family had its own history—and most people born in the community since its establishment were trilingual. Consistent with the gendered nature of the Matsigenka/Quechua relationship described in chapter 1, men from interethnic families tended to use Quechua more frequently, while women tended to use Matsigenka more frequently, though most people could speak and understand all three of the community's languages. The community members also maintained close ties to colono and Matsigenka kin across the region, both inside and outside of comunidades nativas. During my fieldwork in 2009–12, the Yokiriños (as they call themselves) were managing the community's transformation from the remote, sparsely populated patch of forest it had been in the 1970s into a thriving agricultural landscape, integrated into the rural agrarian society that had come to surround them.

Yokiri's formation and its place in the broader Andean agrarian society provide an illuminating ethnographic case study in the social and linguistic dynamics of the coffee frontier, described at a regional scale in chapter 1 and historically in chapter 2. This chapter begins with an introduction to Yokiri and then presents the community's history as it resulted from Andean migration into Matsigenka territory. The chapter concludes with a discussion of the sociolinguistic patterns that have emerged in Yokiri, introducing the more in-depth discussion that will follow of language use in Yokiri and other multiethnic frontier communities (chapters 4, 5, and 6).

Yokiri

During my fieldwork in Yokiri, the community's population comprised ninety-four people living on 3,390 hectares of land (around 34 square kilometers, or 13 square miles)—roughly the size of the island of Manhattan below Harlem—making it one of the smallest comunidades nativas in the region by both area and population. The community, pictured in figure 11, stretches from the Yokiri River at the valley bottom to the ridgeline above that marks the eastern and southern extent of its watershed. The hillside is traversed by a network of footpaths connecting the widely dispersed homes. A road, which links the community to nearby colono settlements and the broader coffee frontier beyond, was built by the people of Yokiri themselves and opened in 2008, though in 2011–12 it had not yet settled into the landscape and was impassable in the rainy season. Most of the Yokiri Valley is still covered in dense rain forest, now dotted by small cleared plots of coffee, achiote, and fruit.

Yokiri's topography is precipitous indeed. The highest point of land (2,280 meters, or 7,480 feet) and the lowest point of land (780 meters, or 2,560 feet)—a difference of 1,500 meters, almost 5,000 feet—are separated by a mere 5.8 kilometers (3.6 miles) of distance on the map. The community's homes are scattered across this vertiginous slope. This vertical arrangement and the fact that the hillside is blanketed in dense forest make traveling through the landscape a difficult task: trips between even neighboring houses can involve an elevation change of several hundred meters or more, and it is often necessary to clear one's way with a machete along even the most well-established paths. During

FIGURE 11 The Yokiri Valley. North-facing view from the community's southern border. The clouds in the distance sit above the Amazon plain. Photograph by the author.

the few hours it takes to climb the 5,000 feet from the Yokiri River to the towering ridgeline above, one passes through a diverse range of ecological and climatic zones. Yokiriños live vertical lives, just as Andeans do—they cultivate and gather a wide variety of products between the hot valley floor and the cool, mist-shrouded hilltops. More than a dozen streams, most of which are small enough to jump across even in the rainy season, cut through the thick vegetation and converge into the Yokiri River, a dangerous torrent that is impassible except by means of a couple of wobbly footbridges. The Yokiri River runs its brief ten-kilometer course into the Yavero River, which in turn joins the Urubamba River, then the Ucayali River, and finally the Amazon River beyond before discharging into the Atlantic Ocean some 6,500 kilometers (~4000 miles) away.

Yokiri's single hillside is hemmed in by the larger Matsigenka community of Matoriato to the west (the right-facing slopes to the left side of the photograph in figure 11) and the colono communities of Huillcapampa to the north (in the background), Nueva Luz to the east (across the pointed hills on the far right), and Otingamía to the south (behind the camera's view). These places are also shown on map 3. Farther north lies the Santuario Nacional Megantoni, a massive protected area of steep, forested hills that marks the end of the Andean foothills (in the far background of the photograph in figure 11). Beyond this, below the distant clouds in the photograph, is the vast and mostly undeveloped Amazon plain, inhabited by Matsigenkas, Nantis, and other Indigenous Amazonians. To the south and east of Yokiri lies Cusco's tropical agricultural heartland, occupied mostly by Quechua-speaking campesinos who have swept down the valleys over the last half century, clearing forest, displacing many of the original Matsigenka inhabitants, and incorporating the remote lowland hills into the rural agrarian expanse of the Andes. Yokiri lies, thus, right where the remote Amazon plain and the rural Andes met in 2011–12—though this point of articulation is constantly moving and has already expanded farther into the forests pictured in the middle distance of the photograph in figure 11 since then.

Settlement Layout and Organization

In 2011–12, the ninety-four people of Yokiri lived in twenty households widely dispersed across the landscape—around one household per 1.7 square kilometers. Most households consisted of a couple, their children, and occasionally an elderly parent or adopted child, but the houses were generally not physically close enough to be considered part of a larger "residence group" (Michael 2008, 5), "hamlet" (A. W. Johnson 2003), "kin cluster" (Baksh 1984), or "local cluster" (O. Johnson 1978), which are characteristic of other Matsigenka and Nanti settlements.

Most people in Yokiri belonged to one of two extended kin groups, the members of which each tended to live in the same general—though overlapping—areas of the Yokiri Valley in 2011–12. There was also a primary school, with around thirty students and two or three resident teachers, depending on the year. In some years the teachers were Quechua-Spanish bilingual colonos, and in other years they were Matsigenka-Spanish bilinguals, some of whom also spoke some Quechua, from the state bilingual education program. Children who pursued secondary education had to attend a school in one of the nearby colono communities, a situation that is common in some places in the Alto Urubamba. There was also a *comuna* (communal agricultural plantation) a thirty-minute walk from the school, where the men (and, during a busy harvest, the women) cultivated coffee, achiote, and other crops to support community investments and projects.

The primary school area, which served as the community's central public space during my fieldwork in 2011–12, is pictured in figure 12. At the center is a large open space for playing soccer and volleyball, drying coffee, and holding community celebrations. Along the periphery of the open space are the primary school (the large metal-roofed building), a small storage building to the left, a community kitchen (the barely visible thatch-roofed building), the *salón comunal* (the community meeting hall, the building with the largest flat metal roof), and a warehouse (the narrower metal-roofed building next to the salón comunal). In 2012 I worked on a construction crew with the community members to build a new school and community building, which were finished after I departed. Electricity has since been brought to Yokiri for the first time. This area of Yokiri has changed since 2012, but in this chapter I limit my description to the time of my residence in the community.

When I first arrived in Yokiri, the men of the community and I spent two days building the warehouse with the narrow metal roof on the left of figure 12. This structure was partitioned into three rooms, two of which were for community storage and one of which was my residence. As I mentioned in the introduction, the labor those men performed on my behalf indebted me to them, and I reciprocated by working with them on their coffee plantations, often staying over in their homes for two or more days at a time. The room that we built for me measured about two by three meters (six by nine feet). I took water for bathing and washing from a small pipe nearby that carried water from a frigid spring about half a mile away. Inside the structure, I had a wooden sleeping platform raised about a meter (three feet) above the ground, a propane tank, a small wooden table for cooking, an antenna for my shortwave radio, and a folding solar panel that I put on the roof to charge my recording equipment. The walls of the structure did not touch the ground, since the torrential flooding that periodically washed across the landscape would simply carry the structure away if the water could not pass through it; nor did the walls reach the metal roof, which would have trapped the oppressive heat in the middle of the

FIGURE 12 The school area in Yokiri, 2011. The author's living space was in the structure with the narrow metal roof to the left of the soccer field. Photograph by the author.

day. For this reason, the full, wonderful cacophony of forest creatures filled my ears in the evenings, and all manner of insects and animals were free to visit. I cooked, ate, and wrote field notes by candlelight in the evenings, but the light attracted such a barrage of insects through the gaps in the walls that I would end up blowing out the candle and going to sleep at seven or eight o'clock every evening. (At close to two thousand meters in the cold, wet cloud forest, the most notable insects near my house were not the swarms of small mosquitos that create a nuisance in the Amazon plain, but rather the solitary, menacing creatures, sometimes larger than my hand, that made their home in the cracks and crevices of my room.) My living arrangement was complicated by the fact that I am a chronic sleepwalker, which led to situations that were at turns terrifying and humorous, but which always provoked perplexed amusement in my hosts. It also gave them something to gently mock me about, which was the stuff of friendship on the coffee frontier.

The central location of my quarters allowed me to visit all of the homes of Yokiri relatively easily, and since Yokiriños frequently passed through the school area, I received visitors almost every day. Some of these visitors lingered in the evenings, and we played volleyball and chess as the sun set over the hills (two of the men had learned to play chess while working in the gold mines of Puerto Maldonado; though I am a decent chess player, I could rarely keep up with them). The other two rooms of my building served as a warehouse and community store, and since I was the only one except the schoolteachers who lived in that central location, I was deputized as the store manager. As I discuss in chapter 4, this gave me a close perspective on the community's participation in the regional agricultural economy. I received much of my food from my Yokiriño friends, either as gifts or by trading manufactured goods such as soap, candles, batteries, pens, and bullets. I bought the rest of my supplies by hiking two hours down to the nearby colono settlement of Huillcapampa (and three hours back up), a trip that I made every two to three weeks. During these trips, I used the solar-powered public telephone in Huillcapampa—the only telephone in the whole lower Yavero Valley in 2011–12—to call my loved ones back in the United States.

Yokiri's highly dispersed settlement layout and much of the community's social life were consistent with the so-called "family-level" pattern of social organization described in chapter 1. That is, people tended to limit their relationships, interactions, and social commitments to members of their own families and to spend much of their time in their own far-flung homes and fields. Indeed, the preference for family-level interaction was reflected by the layout of the footpaths in Yokiri: only the homes of people within the same kin groups were connected, since non-kin rarely visited each other's homes. The exclusive patterns of visiting among the two major kin groups made Yokiri more like two distinct hamlets superimposed onto the same territory.

But while these patterns continued to play an important role in Yokiri, two profound—and, in a sense, contradictory—sociopolitical transformations had begun to alter the residents' tendency toward dispersed settlement and family-level social organization. First, as the road network steadily expanded toward Yokiri, eventually passing through the community itself in 2008, Yokiriños began to participate in the coffee economy—and with it, the local agrarian social world—alongside their new Andean neighbors. This meant adopting a range of new discursive practices, which I discuss in depth in chapter 4.

The second sociopolitical transformation that has broadened Yokiri's inter-actions and commitments beyond the family level has been its embrace of the notion of the "community" as a unit of social organization spanning kin groups. As I discuss in chapter 5, this was carried out in large part through Spanish public speech in the monthly asambleas (community meetings), as well as work in faenas (communal work parties). Since the community mode of social orga-nization served in large part to differentiate Yokiri and protect its autonomy from the rural agrarian society that has come to surround it, this mode of orga-nization stood in a contradictory and occasionally problematic relationship to the trend toward regional incorporation discussed in chapter 4. People in Yokiri created, managed, and kept separate these domains of social life through differ-ent kinds of speech—in all three languages—as they engaged with each other as family members in some moments and as members of a centralized agrarian community with a formal political structure in other moments.

A Brief History of Yokiri

I now present the history of Yokiri by following the paths of four families who came together in the community over the last several generations. Throughout this section, I offer transcriptions from my recordings (in Matsigenka, Quechua, and Spanish) in which Yokiriños tell this history in their own words.

The formation of Yokiri played out through a particular convergence of geog-raphy, law, and timing. In the 1970s, the wave of migration from the nearby highlands had worked its way through the area from two directions. One group of colonos, represented by the arrow beginning to the right in map 4, made their way down the Yavero Valley from the east, through Lacco, Piñamayo, Calangato, San Martín, and Estrella, eventually arriving in Huillcapampa in the late 1970s (some of these places are marked on map 4). Meanwhile, another group of colonos, represented by the arrow on the left side of map 4, pushed their way overland from the Urubamba River in the early 1900s, up the Chapo and Boyero Valleys by the 1950s, and eventually to Otingamía—adjacent to Yokiri—around the 1960s. Yokiri is the point at which these two waves of colonization converged in the mid-1970s.[1]

In the mid-1970s, at the same time that the waves of colonization through the Yavero Valley and Otingamía had converged on two sides of the Yokiri Valley, the Peruvian comunidades nativas law was passed. This law grants communal territorial rights to Indigenous Amazonians in Peru, and the Matsigenkas in the Yokiri Valley used it to title most of their land and protect it from colonization. This happened not a moment too soon: a colono family in Huillcapampa had already beaten them to titling the northeastern tip of the Yokiri

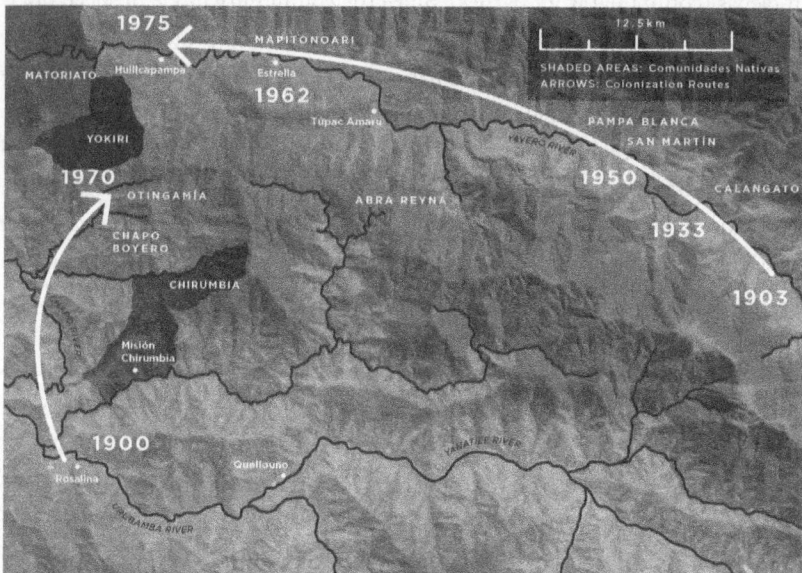

MAP 4 The colonization of the Yavero Valley. Map data: Google, Landsat, DigitalGlobe, Instituto del Bien Común. IBC-SICNA. Enero 2017, incluye información levantada en gabinete, AIDESEP-CIPTA, GEF PNUD, GOREL y PFS. Author's GPS data also used. Rivers and labels added by the author.

Valley, which is why the community does not extend all the way to the Yavero River today (see the top left of map 4). More migrants were arriving from the Andes every day, and the Indigenous land titling would have become impossible just a few years later.

Because the quantity of land the community could claim was proportional to its population, and because a large population of children would be needed to petition the government for a school, the one Matsigenka family that lived in Yokiri in the mid-1970s set about recruiting new community members to join them (for a similar case among the Ashéninka of central Peru, see Killick 2008a). As I discussed in chapter 1, there were many Matsigenkas around the region who now lived interspersed with Andean colonos because their land had been taken over, or who were unsatisfied with their current lot for one reason or another; these people were invited to claim land in Yokiri. Some Yokiriños refer to this scramble to populate Yokiri with Matsigenkas as their own *colonización* (colonization) of the valley. This had the effect of drawing people with a claim to Matsigenka ethnicity out of the surrounding colono milieu, thereby tightening the association between ethnicity and territory both within and outside of the comunidades nativas.[2] Crucially, it also led to the community's current heterogeneous makeup and close integration with the frontier society, since most of the Matsigenka people who came to Yokiri had already lived among colonos—in many cases within interethnic kin networks—for decades by that point.

As these families arrived in Yokiri from around the region, they married together in a manner that laid the blueprint for the community's subsequent social and political organization: with only a few exceptions, all of the siblings from one arriving family married all of the siblings from another. The result of this process was two tightly knit kin groups that dominated the community in 2009–12. By the logic of Matsigenka kinship practices mentioned in chapter 1, the cross-cousins of these marriages would, in theory, become ideal marriage partners (A. W. Johnson 2003; Rosengren 2017), and indeed this pattern has been borne out among some of the children of those newly formed kin groups. The advantage of this system is that it allows young people to marry someone already residing in the community (O. Johnson 1978, 92–93) rather than leaving the community (thereby depleting its population and threatening its land base) or allowing a spouse to occupy land inside the community (another risky proposition). However, it is too early to tell whether cross-cousin marriage will be practiced widely among these families in the future, since many Yokiriños are more interested in colono spouses than in their own community members, and since cousin marriage is stigmatized in colono society.

While many Matsigenka people heeded the call to move to Yokiri between the 1970s and the early 2000s, others declined the invitation.[3] Some—mostly women, per the gendered dynamics of migration described earlier—had already established families with colonos and therefore would not have been permitted to join the community even if they had wanted to. Others simply preferred the electricity, roads, and commercial goods of colono society to the remote, undeveloped forests of Yokiri, even if they would be entitled to free land.[4] In many cases, those who moved to Yokiri and those who stayed behind belonged to the same kin groups and still visited each other frequently.

Juan

The story of Yokiri begins with a trilingual Matsigenka man whom I shall call Juan (1915?–1980), whose life I also mentioned in chapter 1. Juan grew up in the porous early-twentieth-century frontier milieu, when the Rosalina hacienda marked the frontier zone between the colonized upper valley and the lower valley inhabited mostly by Matsigenkas (map 3). This frontier zone was characterized by close contact between colonos and Matsigenka people, particularly as they worked together on local haciendas.

As a child, Juan lived with his father, a bilingual Matsigenka and Quechua speaker born in the late nineteenth century by the headwaters of the Anchihuay River (map 3). Juan's father was a *koraka*, a kind of Matsigenka leader who traditionally had multiple wives and recruited laborers to work on the plantations of large landowners. He also collected resin from the katarompanaki tree (used to make incense) for trade at Rosalina and Chirumbia. Juan and his father, therefore, were deeply embedded in the multiethnic and multilingual society of the early twentieth century, where they mediated between Matsigenka people, colonos, and Dominican missionaries. This position required Juan to speak both Matsigenka and Quechua; he learned both of those languages as a child, as well as Spanish at the Chirumbia mission school.

According to some reports, most of Juan's family, including all of his several siblings, were killed in a slave raid when he was a child, perhaps in the late 1920s or early 1930s. At this point, his father sent him to the safety of the Dominican school at Chirumbia, where he was instructed in Spanish and

FIGURE 13 Two Yokiriños at the Artillería Pass, 2012. Otingamía and Chapo-Boyero are pictured in the background, and Urusayhua, the mountain on the left of the horizon, marks the point of the eighteenth- and nineteenth-century frontier. On a clearer day, the snowcapped peaks of the Vilcabamba Range are visible on the horizon. Photograph by the author.

learned about Christianity and commercial agriculture. He also spoke Quechua, which he had learned while staying with his father on local haciendas and among the many Andean colonos who worked in and around the mission. However, like many Matsigenkas, Juan did not take to mission life, and he returned to the Chapo Valley to collect katarompanaki resin and work seasonally on colono coffee plantations. As he grew older, he took on his father's role of brokering between Matsigenkas and colonos seeking labor for their coffee plantations, which was always in short supply (particularly after the malaria epidemic described in chapter 2). Over the coming decades he moved back and forth across the Andean frontier, between Anchihuay, Avantiari, and Otingamía, eventually entering the Yokiri Valley as far north as the Yavero River (map 4). While he mostly spoke Matsigenka with his kin, he continued to conduct close relationships with colonos in Quechua, as well as with the Dominicans in Spanish.

After leaving Chirumbia in the 1930s, Juan married a monolingual Matsigenka-speaking woman named Eugenia, who lived in the Chapo drainage (beyond the frontier), and he moved there to work on her parents' land. This marriage was consistent with the pattern of men on the frontier seeking women farther in the forest and bringing Quechua with them. Eugenia's parents had come to the Chapo Valley after fleeing slave raids in the Kumpiroshiato Valley, near what is now the comunidad nativa of Shimaa, probably around 1920 (note that Eugenia's extended family was probably among the people in Allen Johnson's classic ethnography of Matsigenkas in Shimaa; see A. W. Johnson 2003). The flight of Eugenia's family from the Kumpiroshiato Valley illustrates the violent displacements that took place during this terrifying period in the Alto Urubamba, when Matsigenkas were being rounded up in *correrías* (slave raids). According to one of Juan and Eugenia's grandsons, Eugenia's family was attacked by a slave recruiter, who killed some of the men and children and put the women to work as cooks. That night, some of the surviving Matsigenka men managed to free the captive women, and the group fled up the Urubamba River to seek refuge at the Rosalina hacienda and in the nearby Dominican mission at Chirumbia, where they would be safe from the slave raids. Juan and Eugenia's grandson—an old man living in Yokiri at the time of my fieldwork—tells the harrowing story in Matsigenka in transcript 2. Spanish elements are underlined.

Transcript 2

Yagapitsaiganakeri itsinanetsite yomperaiganakaro itsinanetsite.$_1$ Hehe acaso yapakuaigairo iaigaira anta ivankoegiku.$_2$ Yovashi maika inintake irogaigakerira intonkaigakerira yogashi maika okanti maika pashini, "Ampa shigaiganaera," ipokai ishigaigi tsitenigite.$_3$ Ipokaigi tsitenigeti okutagitenake anta maika iaigaera.$_4$ Okantagani maika iromperaigaemparora onkotaera okantagani anta itsamaitaigira ikogaigake, "Arimera nontonkakerime chapi.".$_5$ Ishigakagaiganakaro maganiro pine tsinane okyaenka pine jóvenes okya antaroigankitsi hehe.$_6$ Ogashi maika ipokaigakera pe..$_7$

[The slave recruiter] went around stealing [the Matsigenka men's] wives away from them, he forced their wives to work.$_1$ Yes, they wouldn't let [the women] go once they went to their houses.$_2$ They wanted to kill [the Matsigenkas], to shoot them, so one [of the women] said, "We'd better escape," and [the Matsigenka men] came running in the night.$_3$ [The men] came at night, at dawn, so that they could leave.₄ When [the slave raiders] looked for [the women] so that they would cook where [the slave raiders] were working [and realized that they had escaped, they said,] "We should have shot them yesterday.",₅ [The Matsigenka men] had helped all the women escape, all the young women, that's right.₆ So that's why they came here [to this region of the Alto Urubamba].₇

Once Eugenia's family was established in Chapo, in the vicinity of the mission at Chirumbia and the Rosalina hacienda, Juan moved there to marry Eugenia and work on her father's land. They continued to circulate between local haciendas, where they worked and spoke Quechua alongside Andean migrants, and their families' more remote plots of land, where they spoke Matsigenka with their kin.

Juan lived in this region for decades until his death in 1980, and he had more than a dozen children with four consecutive wives (Yokiriños do not know what became of Eugenia, who may have died or moved to a different valley). Several of these children would eventually join their father in the Yokiri Valley and marry members of families across the region to establish the community; others went on to join other comunidades nativas in the area. Some of the women married colonos and lived with them nearby or in the highlands. Others migrated to the highlands or left to work in mining ventures in Madre de Dios and were never heard from again. Many of those who have remained in contact visit each other frequently even decades later. Thus Juan's sprawling kin network includes people in both colono settlements and Matsigenka communities; speakers of Matsigenka, Quechua, and Spanish (in all combinations); and people who live in the remote lowlands, rural highlands, and cities across Peru. Some of Juan's descendants continue to mediate between Matsigenka speakers and Andean colonos today.

In the 1950s and 1960s, the pressure from Andean colonization began to increase as newly arriving colonos moved their way through Chapo-Boyero in search of land. Chapo-Boyero can be seen in the foreground of figure 14; when the family's scattered plots in this area were taken over, they were gradually displaced up the valley to Otingamía, the hillside in the background of the photo.

Around 1973, once Quechua-speaking Andean migrants had colonized Chapo-Boyero and begun to encroach upon Otingamía, Juan finally moved his family over the Artillería Pass into the Yokiri Valley permanently. The Artillería Pass is the carved notch in the hillside at the top left of figure 14, where the new road—flanked by landslides visible in the photograph—crossed over into the

FIGURE 14 Chapo-Boyero (foreground), Otingamía (background), and Artillería Pass to Yokiri (top left). Viewed from the south. Photograph by the author.

Yokiri Valley on the far side in 2008 (the photograph in figure 13 was taken from the Artillería Pass, looking back across Chapo-Boyero and Otingamía, in 2012). The family's claim to land back in Otingamía continued until the 1990s, and some of the family members remained there, until one of Juan's sons traded the family's ninety-hectare tract of land there for several head of cattle.

While moving to the Yokiri Valley allowed Juan's family to stay ahead of the wave of Andean colonos who were quickly climbing through Chapo-Boyero and Otingamía from the south, in the 1970s a different group of Quechua-speaking Andean colonos were on their way down the Yavero Valley toward Yokiri, past Estrella and Huillcapampa, from the east (see map 4 above). Many of these colonos came in the late 1970s when a devastating flood in the highland district of Lares (province of Calca) destroyed their land. They were led by a Salesian priest who sponsored a series of expeditions into the valley.[5] One of Juan's children describes their arrival down the Yavero Valley, in Matsigenka, in the following transcript:

Transcript 3

Hehe pairani nanti aka pitaigatsi naro hehe.₁ Pairani acaso ainyo ponyarona, mameri.₂ Hehe ipokakera pareri ikantagani yoga pareri ikantagani yoga [name].₃ Ogashi ogashi itentaigakarira okantagani ogashi maikari itsamaitaiganakera kara.₄ Hehe game inti irirori game game itimavageigi katonko anta okantagani kan-

tinka kentiarenaku kara.$_5$ . . . Pairani nopokaigakera <u>acaso</u> ainyo ponyarona, hehe.$_6$
<u>Recién</u> maika itimanakera maika itsamaitanakera hehe.$_7$

Yes, we were the ones who used to live here, yes.$_1$ <u>It's not like</u> there were any
highlanders earlier, there weren't any.$_2$ Yes, when the <u>priest</u> came, what's his name,
the <u>priest</u> is called [name].$_3$ So he brought [the colonos] along, so that they could
work there.$_4$ Yes, if it hadn't been for him, they would [still] be living up the river
there, [the colonization would have stopped] right in Kentiarena.$_5$ . . . When we
came, <u>it's not like</u> there were highlanders, that's right.$_6$ <u>Just now</u> there are beginning to be [people] who [are coming] to work.$_7$

Most of these colonos, who had grown up in the highlands of Lares and
Calca and were unaccustomed to tropical life, had trouble adapting to the
remote lowland frontier and returned home within a year or two. But a few of
the toughest and most motivated families stayed, and they taught successive
colonizing families to survive in this new and unfamiliar environment. Because
of the great quantity of fertile land they were able to claim in the sparsely
populated lower Yavero Valley of the 1970s, these first-arriving colono families
are now some of the wealthiest and most powerful people in the region. This
sudden influx of colonos put pressure on the northern and eastern sides of
Yokiri, and by the time Juan died in 1980, his family found themselves hemmed
in between the colonos of Otingamía to the south, Nueva Luz to the east, and
Huillcapampa to the north, with the Matsigenkas of the recently titled comunidad nativa of Matoriato to the west. The time-tested Matsigenka strategy of
migrating farther into the forest to avoid the oncoming wave of colonos was no
longer possible, and Juan's family became sedentary for the first time.

Luckily for Juan's family, it was at this pivotal moment that the Peruvian
comunidades nativas law was passed, and they quickly titled their land to halt
the spread of colonization from the Yavero Valley into the Yokiri Valley. Upon
his death in 1980, Juan left his land to his children as well as his new son-in-
law José (described below) for that purpose. But before the titling process was
completed, a colono from Calca established himself in the northeast corner of
the Yokiri Valley. This colono argued that he arrived in the valley before Juan
moved permanently from Otingamía, and he told me repeatedly that Juan's
family were the ones who had invaded his land ("Me están invadiendo"—a
strategic inversion of colonist-Indigenous discourse). This conflict illustrates
the tensions that arise from different conceptions of land occupation: For Juan's

family, scattered plantations and seasonal visits in the traditional Matsigenka pattern constituted use of the Yokiri Valley. For the colono from Calca, only permanent residence and clearing for agriculture counted as occupation.

In the 1980s, the nonprofit organization CEDIA helped Juan's family finally acquire the title to their land in the Yokiri Valley as a comunidad nativa. However, since the amount of land that a comunidad nativa could claim depended on its population, as did the establishment of a school, it was in the family's interest to gather as many Matsigenkas together as possible in the Yokiri Valley (as we will see below).

José

Another side of Yokiri is represented by a man whom I shall call José, a Quechua-Spanish bilingual who grew up in the nearby Andean highlands. In the late 1970s, he migrated to the Yavero Valley and took up residence in Yokiri with a Matsigenka woman named María.

In the 1950s, José's father worked as the administrator of an hacienda in what is now Manu National Park, to the south of the Urubamba Valley. His mother, a member of the Huachipaeri ethnic group, worked there as a laborer. José's parents both died when he was a young child, and he grew up in the care of his father's family in the city of Paucartambo, where he spoke Quechua almost exclusively. In the 1970s he learned that a group of campesinos from Calca were planning an expedition to colonize the Yavero Valley, and he joined them—in part to find land, and in part to reconnect with his Amazonian heritage. In transcript 4, he tells me in Spanish about how he left Paucartambo and gradually migrated down the Yavero Valley to Yokiri:

Transcript 4

JOSÉ: Recién he entrado a los catorce años a la escuela, yo mismo como era huérfano.[1] Así esta temporada recién estaban allí creando escuelas en zonas rurales.[2] No había escuela.[3] Paucartambo, ajá, mas abajo de Paucartambo, Challabamba, Acobamba he entrado ya catorce años ya.[4] Así, pues.[5] Yo he crecido.[6] Familia de mis padres son hartos.[7] Hay Huamanes, también hay Mendozas, porque mi papá había sido Gregorio Huamán Mendoza.[8] Entonces yo bajé acá abajo más arriba de Lacco, más arriba, allí estuve una temporada ya jovencito así, después me iba hacia [donde] mis familias.[9] Ya estuve era diecinueve, veintidos años.[10]

Escucho están colono–entrando ya a colonizar a Yavero.$_{11}$ Ya habrán regresado pues, "¡Hay nativos, pucha, ay!"$_{12}$ Yo pensaba que estaba mi raza pues.$_{13}$ Bajé junto con esos colonos pe en el setenta y nueve.$_{14}$

NQE: Porque, este mismo río Yavero llega hasta Paucartambo, ¿no?$_{15}$

JOSÉ: Claro, claro, pero yo he llegado vueltas así pues por Yanatile.$_{16}$

NQE: Ah, por Yanatile has ido.$_{17}$

JOSÉ: Entonces, bajé entonces, no había sido mi tribu sino había sido matsigenka, ajá.$_{18}$ Yo estaba allí con los [solteros].$_{19}$ Acá estaba mi señora anterior que es María.$_{20}$ Había estado ya madre soltera, con ella hemos conversado ya hemos convivido con ella.$_{21}$ Así pues.$_{22}$

JOSÉ: Only then did I enter school, at fourteen years old, all by myself since I was an orphan.$_{1}$ At that time they were just setting up schools in rural areas.$_{2}$ There was no school.$_{3}$ In Paucartambo, yes, below Paucartambo, Challabamba, Acobamba, I entered when I was fourteen years old.$_{4}$ That's right.$_{5}$ I grew up.$_{6}$ I have lots of relatives on my father's side.$_{7}$ There are Huamanes, and there are Mendozas, since my father was Gregorio Huamán Mendoza.$_{8}$ Then I came down here a little bit above Lacco, farther up, and I was there for a while as a young man, and then I went [farther down the valley] to where my relatives were.$_{9}$ I was nineteen, twenty-two years old.$_{10}$ I heard that some people were colonizing–that they were entering [the valley] to colonize the Yavero.$_{11}$ Some must have come back, "There are Amazonians, wow, oh no!"$_{12}$ I thought they were my race.$_{13}$ So I went down together with those colonos, in 1979.$_{14}$

NQE: Because, that same Yavero River goes all the way up to Paucartambo, right?$_{15}$

JOSÉ: Yes, yes, but I went the long way around, through Yanatile.$_{16}$

NQE: Oh, you went through Yanatile.$_{17}$

JOSÉ: So I went down, it ended up not being my tribe, but rather the Matsigenkas, that's right.$_{18}$ I was there with [the single men].$_{19}$ My previous wife was here, María.$_{20}$ She was a single mother, and we discussed things, and then we lived together.$_{21}$ That's right.$_{22}$

María and José had two children before María's death in the early 1980s; at that point, José remarried another woman in Yokiri, with whom he had several more children. José's children are all trilingual and understand themselves to have both Andean and Matsigenka heritage. Indeed, their ethnic identity is fluid and contextual: when they interacted with neighboring colonos in local events and meetings during my fieldwork, they participated as equals, and their

FIGURE 15 A Yokiriño family, 2012. Artillería Pass, overlooking Otingamía. Photograph by the author.

interlocutors had only passing awareness of their exceptional status as members of a comunidad nativa. Likewise, in community meetings in Yokiri and in public expressions of Matsigenka ethnic identity organized by the Matsigenka Council (COMARU), they were generally regarded as unproblematically Matsigenka—though on occasion their legitimacy was challenged in such contexts (for instance, I discuss in chapter 5 the perils of using Quechua in Yokiri's community meetings).

José's experience in the rural agrarian society between Paucartambo and the lower Yavero Valley made him a skilled and determined tropical agriculturalist, and he was the most outspoken advocate for Yokiri's integration into the coffee industry. After all, José migrated to Yokiri in the 1970s as a colono hoping to make a living as a farmer, a desire that distinguishes him from some of the other families who migrated to Yokiri precisely to avoid the expanding agricultural frontier. The degree of Yokiri's involvement in the coffee industry thus remains a tense—and racialized—subject among people of various backgrounds in Yokiri (as I discuss in chapter 4).

Ana

Another important facet of Yokiri's history is illustrated by the story of a woman I shall call Ana, who came in the 1980s from the recently abandoned Dominican mission at Chirumbia.[6] Ana was born in the Madre de Dios watershed around 1940 and was brought to Chirumbia by the Dominicans as a teenager. When she arrived in Chirumbia, she was introduced to Carlos, the Matsigenka boy whom the missionaries had arranged to be her husband, and in the late 1950s the couple settled down near the mission and began a life working in the priests' fields and pastures. They had twelve children, nine of whom survived beyond childhood, and lived a life that was carefully managed by the priests. They were not allowed to drink alcohol or use shamanic plants such as tobacco or ayahuasca, and they were expected to spend their days working in the mission's coffee, cacao, and fruit fields.[7]

The priests intended to transform Matsigenkas like Ana and Carlos from dispersed horticulturalists and hunter-gatherers with animist beliefs into Catholic, Spanish-speaking cash croppers living in nucleated settlements. But the Dominicans' purpose was not simply to transform them into colonos, but rather to create an independent community of Matsigenka Christians—that is to say, they were meant to remain ethnically distinct from the surrounding colono society but socially, religiously, and economically indistinguishable.[8] The Matsigenkas of Chirumbia were in close contact with neighboring colonos (many of whom leased land in the Chirumbia Valley from the Dominicans and took it over when they left), and many learned Quechua. Over the years most of them learned to live more or less like colonos, and today most of them use the land in Chirumbia much the way the neighboring colonos do.

Since the Dominicans withdrew from Chirumbia in the early 1980s, colono spouses have been permitted to live in the community, and now many of the residents are either colonos or the children and grandchildren of Matsigenka-colono unions, despite Chirumbia's legal status as a comunidad nativa. Quechua is now at least as prevalent in Chirumbia as Matsigenka, and Spanish is widely spoken. The colonos' entrance into Chirumbia has been distressing for some of the Matsigenka residents, and after Ana and Carlos's family learned of the community forming in Yokiri, they abandoned their land in Chirumbia and migrated there in the early 1990s. They headed north across the Chapo and Boyero Valleys, first to Otingamía, where some of Juan's family was still working. Ana explains this in Spanish in the following transcript:

Transcript 5

Mi esposo ha dicho, "Mejor como están entrando, pues tenemos que irnos." Por eso hemos venido a este lado donde este cómo se llama Juan, a conquistar a Otinganía.[9]

My husband said, "Since [the colonos] are beginning to enter [Chirumbia], we have to leave." That's why we came over here where, what's his name, Juan [lived], to conquer Otinganía.

Ana's use of the verb *conquistar* (conquer) here is significant: since she saw herself in competition with Andean colonos for untitled tracts of land in the interior, she did not consider her migration to be entirely different from that of the colonos who had come from the highlands. Indeed, when Ana and her family moved to the Yokiri Valley in the early 1990s, some members of Juan's family saw them as more colono-like than Matsigenka-like: they were Catholics and adept cash croppers, they accumulated manufactured goods, they were not accustomed to life in the forest, and their Matsigenka, to the extent that they spoke it, was heavily influenced by both Spanish and Quechua. Even today some of the oldest members of Juan's family refer to Ana and Carlos's family as *ponyarona* (highlanders), despite the fact that the neighboring highland migrants consider them all to be simply Matsigenkas. Thus some of Yokiri's families who come from Chirumbia face a degree of ethnic uncertainty, and in Yokiri their familiarity with colono society has put them in the position of mediators between Matsigenkas and the colonos around them.

During their gradual migration through Chirumbia, Otingamía, and Yokiri, the teenagers of Ana's family began to start families of their own. Two of these teenagers, who had experienced the social and material possibilities of agrarian life while living in Chirumbia, protested the move deeper into the forests of Yokiri and departed for the Andean highlands in search of a new life. However,

FIGURE 16 A Yokiriño man and his grandson, 2012. Photograph by the author.

they found the highlands to be more difficult and unwelcoming than they had imagined, and they both returned within a few years and married members of Juan's family instead. Two of Ana's other teenaged daughters married Andean colono men who had recently colonized Otingamía, and they and their children still live there and occasionally visit their kin in Yokiri. These children are also trilingual, but since they do not reside in a comunidad nativa, there are not many contexts in which their Matsigenka ethnic status is publicly invoked. The next generation of their children will likely have only the vaguest connection to Matsigenka ethnicity—despite occasional contact with their Matsigenka cousins on the adjacent hillside—and will likely be Quechua-Spanish bilinguals. The rest of the siblings of this family married several siblings of a single family in Yokiri, forming one of the two major kin groups of Yokiri. The children of those unions, unlike their cousins in Otingamía, are mostly Matsigenka-Spanish bilinguals but also speak some Quechua.

For Ana's family, the move to the dense forests of Yokiri and Otingamía was a major change from their carefully controlled lives at the Dominican mission. The children had all been born in Chirumbia (with the exception of the youngest son, who was born in Otingamía after their departure), where they had never learned to hunt, practice traditional horticulture, or survive in the forest. Neither had they acquired the aspects of Matsigenka culture practiced by other families in Yokiri, and they had little experience with the cosmology, folklore, and ecological knowledge of their peers. Some of the younger family members were also Spanish-dominant and mixed Spanish with their Matsigenka, to the extent that they spoke Matsigenka at all. This all changed, however, when they arrived in Yokiri—after the migration, their lives were filled with new kinds of knowledge and skills, and they began to speak Matsigenka much more frequently and acquired a fuller lexicon relating to the forest and its inhabitants than they had learned in Chirumbia. Thus, contrary to the patterns of language shift and cultural assimilation that are so often associated with Indigenous experiences of expanding frontiers, Ana and her family have become more regular speakers of Matsigenka and practitioners of Matsigenka culture over the last few decades. Indeed, Ana's children and grandchildren speak Matsigenka more regularly and confidently than she does. This presents a remarkable contrast to their cousins in Otingamía, who have become incorporated into the rural, Quechua-speaking agrarian society and have little awareness of the Matsigenka language.

Cristina and Ángel

The fourth and final Yokiriño family discussed in this chapter comprises Cristina and Ángel, whom I mentioned at the beginning of chapter 1, and their several children. They heeded the call to move to Yokiri in the early 2000s, coming from San Martín, an area farther up the Yavero River (see map 4).

In the 1920s, Ángel's parents were born in Calangato (alt. Talangato), and Cristina's parents were born in Piñamayo (both are areas still farther up the Yavero from San Martín, toward Lacco). These places were inhabited by Matsigenkas when Andean colonos swept down the Yavero Valley over the course of the twentieth century, before the passage of the comunidades nativas law in the 1970s that gave Matsigenkas a legal means to protect their land. Thus, when the Dominican missionary priest Wenceslao Fernández Moro visited the same area in the 1930s, he noted, referring to a group that probably included Cristina's and Ángel's parents, that "here the Matsigenkas mix together with the *civilizados* [i.e., Andean colonos] as they work for the landowners. . . . We might call them 'civilized,' since they fit right in with the laborers on the [Calangato and Hacienda Pampa] haciendas" (1934, 72–73; translation mine).

After working alongside colonos on those haciendas until the 1940s, Cristina's and Ángel's parents fled their abusive labor arrangements and traveled farther downriver, past the colonization frontier, to San Martín, Pampa Blanca, and Amancaes, which were inhabited only by Matsigenka people at that time (see map 4). They started families around Pampa Blanca, and Cristina and Ángel were both born in the vicinity in the early 1950s. However, the wave of Andean colonization quickly caught up with them again in the mid-1950s. Large landowners claimed the land around San Martín, and they enslaved the Matsigenkas they found there. This was not a form of chattel slavery, in which people are bought and sold as property, but rather a kind of estate slavery in which the landowners are entitled to the residents' labor. The Matsigenkas there were not free to leave or to refuse to work, under threat of beating or carrying an onerous labor debt. Cristina and Ángel reported that their families owed three days of work in the landowner's coffee plantations and had the rest of the week to work in their own small subsistence plots. Landowners also kept Matsigenka people from fleeing by engaging them in relations of bonded labor in exchange for manufactured goods: the landowners offered goods like clothes, machetes, and cooking pots up front, which the Matsigenkas were then required to pay off with exploitative and open-ended labor obligations.

For instance, in transcript 6 below, Ángel and Cristina report that their families were forced to dig a mule trail for colonos under conditions that they likened to those in Werner Herzog's 1982 film *Fitzcarraldo*, in which Indigenous Amazonians are made to do the dangerous work of dragging a steamship over a pass between two rivers (see Brown 1982). This film was screened by the local Dominican missionary priest the evening before our conversation, and it resonated with the older people of Yokiri who had experienced forced labor firsthand.[10] As in chapter 1, Ángel speaks Spanish here, and Cristina speaks Quechua. Spanish elements are underlined.

Transcript 6

CRISTINA: Primerota monteraq ñanta kichanku.₁ Masta tiyanku kay ukhupi ñanta ruwaqtinkuña.₂ Hinapi ñanpi tiyanku chaymanta anchuña–₃

ÁNGEL: "Ojalá que hace ellos pues nativos–"₄

CRISTINA: Nativoraqchu kichanku ñanta.₅

ÁNGEL: Hace obligar también, "Abras camino," así era antes pues.₆ He visto pues
video cuando era noche igualito esto antes.₇

CRISTINA: First it was still just forest, [and then] they opened a path.₁ More of
them came to live here in the forest once they made the path.₂ In that way
they lived by the path, and then it [became] wide–₃
ÁNGEL: [They said,] "Let's make the nativos make it–"₄
CRISTINA: The nativos opened the path.₅
ÁNGEL: They ordered [us], "Open the path," that's how it was.₆ I saw it on the
[Fitzcarraldo] video that night, it used to be just like that.₇

Ángel's and Cristina's parents all passed away when they were young children, and both were raised in the homes of extended family members, and by
the colonos themselves, in San Martín. They were married as teenagers in the
mid- or late 1960s. They continued to work on the colonos' land as servants
and laborers and learned Quechua from a very young age, but they continued
speaking Matsigenka at home. They briefly attended school, but Ángel learned
more Spanish than Cristina, who does not feel comfortable speaking it.

Ángel and Cristina had six thoroughly trilingual children, four of whom
survived past adolescence. In the mid-1990s, Yokiri's school was in danger of
closing for lack of students, so the Yokiriños sent word up the valley that they
needed Matsigenka children to help keep it open. Ángel and Cristina's eldest
son was attending Yokiri's elementary school at that time, and he reported back
to his parents and siblings that there was land available in Yokiri. Because they
had married each other instead of marrying colonos—unlike many of their
kin—they were accepted there in 2000. The eldest son told me that the community admitted them because they were able to speak Matsigenka, which is an
important marker of Matsigenka identity. All of the members of Cristina and
Ángel's family told me that they are now much happier in Yokiri, where they
have plenty of land for themselves and their children, and where they are free
of the traumatic circumstances of their childhoods.

Ángel and Cristina left behind a large network of kin in San Martín, who
married colonos and were therefore not welcome to move to Yokiri (for instance,
all of Cristina's three sisters married colono men and still lived around San
Martín; their children became incorporated into Quechua-speaking colono
society). Interestingly, these San Martín relatives were given Spanish surnames,

while their extended kin in the Dominican mission at Chirumbia were given Matsigenka surnames (referencing local plants and animals), assigned by the priests to emphasize their ethnic difference. This difference in surnames obscures the close kin ties between the Yavero and Chirumbia Matsigenkas and makes the Yavero Matsigenkas even more invisible amid colono society. Cristina's sisters occasionally visited Yokiri during my time there in 2011–12, often with their children and colono spouses, to participate in public events as well as to assist during the harvest season. Ángel and Cristina's family, therefore, is part of a close-knit kinship network across the Yavero Valley that crosscuts the division between the comunidad nativa and the colono society—indeed, the only reason that such a division exists now is because the creation of Yokiri allowed the Matsigenkas who hadn't married colonos to remove themselves from that society. These kin networks extend far into the rural communities and cities of the Andean highlands, and Ángel's and Cristina's siblings travel to those places to visit their kin.

Ángel and Cristina's migration to Yokiri represented a move out of the rural, Quechua-speaking agrarian society and back into something more like the traditional Matsigenka lifestyles of their early childhoods and their parents' and grandparents' generations. Though they grew up speaking Matsigenka in their homes from the 1950s to the 1980s, by the 1980s and 1990s they had both begun to shift to Quechua and, to a lesser extent, Spanish—Ángel in particular had all but abandoned Matsigenka for Quechua. Moving to Yokiri meant recuperating their Matsigenka, which was difficult for Ángel. They describe this change in Spanish in the following transcript:

Transcript 7

ÁNGEL: Sí, acá cuando yo he venido he recordado yo, si estaría arriba, ¿qué voy a saber?$_1$ Hubiera olvidado ya.$_2$ Más he venido estoy recordando–$_3$

CRISTINA: Escuchando escuchando ya está recién está recordando había estado olvidando pe.$_4$

ÁNGEL: Yes, when I came here I [began to] remember [how to speak Matsigenka], if I had [still] been upriver, how would I know it?$_1$ I would have forgotten it already.$_2$ When I came [to Yokiri] I began remembering–$_3$

CRISTINA: Listening, listening, just now he's remembering [it], he had been forgetting it.$_4$

Language Histories in Yokiri

My intention in presenting this fine-grained history of Yokiri has been to show how people from a wide variety of places and circumstances have come, in the context of the last century of Andean colonization, to make their lives together on a single hillside in a remote corner of the Alto Urubamba. I have also sought to show how, as a result, the region's three languages came to be spoken by the Yokiriños in various combinations. The picture that emerges from this historical account is one of remarkable sociolinguistic heterogeneity. Among the ninety-four people who lived in the community in 2011–12, some were near-monolingual Matsigenka speakers who experienced Andean colonization from the community's periphery; some were Quechua-Spanish bilingual farmers who migrated from the rural Andean highlands in search of land; others were Spanish-Matsigenka bilinguals raised as Catholic cash croppers in the nearby Dominican mission; and others still were Matsigenka-Quechua-Spanish trilinguals who grew up enslaved on land that was taken from their families.

Remarkably, the marriage patterns through which the diverse families of Yokiri came together—whereby all of one set of siblings married all of another set of siblings—meant that this sociolinguistic heterogeneity was present even at the level of each household. In a sense, each household in Yokiri had its own sociolinguistic history. This family-level heteroglossia has also meant that each of the three languages was spoken under almost every roof, and thus that most children born since the community's founding were exposed to all three. The gendered distinction between Quechua as a language of men's agricultural work and Matsigenka as a language of women's domestic work was also mapped onto language acquisition among the youngest generations: men in trilingual families tended to favor Quechua, while women favored Matsigenka. Roughly speaking, Quechua was transmitted patrilineally in such families, while Matsigenka was transmitted matrilineally.

In addition to the house-to-house linguistic variation in Yokiri in 2011–12, it is also important to note the intergenerational quality of linguistic variation. Indeed, it was rare for a generation in any of these families to have the same linguistic repertoire as the preceding one; however, the intergenerational change in linguistic repertoires varied considerably from one family to the next. Consider the summary of such changes among Juan's descendants, shown in table 2 below. (This summary is a rough heuristic intended to give a synopsis of broad historical patterns, without putting much linguistic analytical weight on

TABLE 2 Language use by generation in Juan's family

GENERATION	YEARS	MATSIGENKA	QUECHUA	SPANISH
1: Juan	1915?–1980	X	X	X
2	1945?–	X		
3	1971–	X		X
4	1996–			X

the evaluations.) Juan spoke Matsigenka, Quechua, and some Spanish because of his work as an intermediary between Matsigenkas and colono landowners, but when he moved his family past the frontier to Otingamía and Yokiri, his son (generation 2) did not learn to speak Quechua and Spanish as well as he did. This son's daughter (generation 3), in turn, learned Matsigenka as well as Spanish as a result of the community's increased integration into Peruvian society, particularly through the presence of schools. Finally, a daughter from generation 4 (a teenager at the time of my fieldwork) only spoke Spanish comfortably.

The changing linguistic repertoires of José's family are shown in table 3. José's father was a monolingual Quechua speaker, and José learned Quechua, and later Spanish, in the highlands of Paucartambo. He went to Yokiri and married a Matsigenka-speaking woman, and his son (generation 3) grew up trilingual. The young daughter of generation 4, however, mostly spoke Spanish.

Ana's parents were born in the Madre de Dios watershed around 1920 and spoke only Matsigenka (table 4). When Ana was taken to the mission at Chirumbia, she learned to speak Spanish, and her own daughter (generation 3) acquired Matsigenka and Spanish. Later this daughter moved away from Chirumbia to live for several years with a man in the highland district of Ocongate, where she learned to speak Quechua. Her teenage daughter (generation 4), however, only spoke Spanish.

Cristina's and Ángel's parents were born far beyond the advancing Yavero Valley agricultural frontier around 1910 and grew up speaking only Matsigenka. Cristina's mother is represented in generation 1 of table 5 (Cristina's and Ángel's family histories are very similar, but only Cristina's is outlined in table 5 for simplicity). Cristina and Ángel were raised by colonos and acquired Matsigenka, Quechua, and, to a lesser extent, Spanish. Their son (generation 3) was raised the same way; however, this son's own children (generation 4) spoke

TABLE 3 Language use by generation in José's family

GENERATION	YEARS	MATSIGENKA	QUECHUA	SPANISH
1	1925?–		X	
2: José	1952?–		X	X
3	1978–	X	X	X
4	2008–			X

TABLE 4 Language use by generation in Ana's family

GENERATION	YEARS	MATSIGENKA	QUECHUA	SPANISH
1	1920?–?	X		
2: Ana	1940–	X		X
3	1968–	X	X	X
4	1990–			X

TABLE 5 Language use by generation in Cristina's family

GENERATION	YEARS	MATSIGENKA	QUECHUA	SPANISH
1	1910?–?	X		
2: Cristina	1952?–	X	X	X
3	1980–	X	X	X
4	2002–		X	X

Quechua and Spanish comfortably but did not (as far as I could tell) speak much Matsigenka.

These family histories demonstrate that intergenerational changes in linguistic repertoires have been neither uniform nor unilinear; rather, they have been embedded in specific and contradictory experiences of the region's long history of social upheaval. However, a notable point of consistency across the six families is that by 2009–12, the youngest generations were embracing Spanish while moving away from both Matsigenka and Quechua. Note, though, that this is a view from within the comunidad nativa of Yokiri—some young women in Yokiri found colono spouses outside of the community and acquired Quechua after they left (since colono spouses were not permitted to live there). Thus trilingualism was more common outside the legal boundaries of the comunidad nativa than inside them. Another important observation about the linguistic histories of these families is that each generation in each family also included other siblings and cousins, many of whom followed different life paths over the last century. Some married colonos and joined the agrarian frontier society decades earlier; some moved to more remote comunidades nativas; others migrated to Cusco and other cities around Peru. Thus, if we were to sketch Juan's, José's, Ana's, Cristina's, and Ángel's full family trees, we would find a stunningly diverse range of sociolinguistic histories, experiences, and locations, even within the same kin networks. This is the point I wish to make with my preceding discussion of the Alto Urubamba as *just one world* in chapter 1.

Conclusion

In this chapter, I have described the formation and sociolinguistic life of a small community called Yokiri. Yokiri was established by a group of families who came together between the 1970s and the early 2000s to take advantage of the comunidades nativas law, which grants territorial rights to Indigenous Amazonians. These families came to the Yokiri Valley from a remarkably diverse set of places and circumstances: remote hamlets in the forests far beyond the agricultural frontier, the Dominican mission at Chirumbia, the mid-twentieth-century frontier milieu of the Yavero and Urubamba Valleys, and a rural area of the nearby Andean highlands. Most of the chapter has been dedicated to showing how four of those families navigated the upheavals of frontier expansion as they eventually made their way, along very different paths, to the Yokiri Valley. When they arrived, all of the siblings from two of the families married together to form a single kin group, while all of the siblings from two other families did the same, forming a second kin group. This process consolidated the community's hold on the territory, kept the families' allegiances contained to the community itself, and created the two tightly knit networks that represent the core of the community's political life. I also showed how this process of community formation led to a situation of dense and intimate multilingualism. Since each of Yokiri's major founding families came from a very different sociolinguistic background, Quechua, Spanish, and Matsigenka were each found in most of the households they created. Most children who were born after Yokiri's founding were trilingual.

This chapter concludes the first part of the book, which has presented the social life of the Alto Urubamba frontier at regional, historical, and family-level scales. In chapter 1, I gave a broad view of the encounter between Andean migrants and Matsigenka people as the agricultural frontier moved through the valley during the late twentieth and early twenty-first centuries. Chapter 2 examined these issues from a deeper historical perspective and showed that the valley has long been home to a multiethnic, multilingual society that connects the Andean highlands and Amazonian lowlands. Chapter 3 explored how frontier expansion was experienced by several of the multilingual families who traveled across the region and eventually married together in the Yokiri Valley.

The second part of this book builds on this sociolinguistic description of the Alto Urubamba by examining the everyday linguistic practices that are involved in frontier expansion through the Alto Urubamba. As people in communities like Yokiri negotiated a place for themselves in the new socioeconomic and ecological order, they began to embrace the agrarian society that came to surround them (chapter 4), while also pushing back and carving out a space for autonomy and resistance against it (chapter 5). These efforts were mediated through the use of language. People also began to speak about the landscape in new ways, each of which was associated with particular communicative contexts, ideologies of land use, and even ideas about what kinds of beings exist in the world (chapter 6).

PART II

Speaking on the Frontier

Chapter 4

Speaking as a Farmer

Imagine, for a moment, what it is like to establish oneself as a coffee farmer in a remote corner of the Alto Urubamba frontier. This process—of transforming a forested landscape into an economically viable coffee plantation—is not only difficult, dangerous, and lonely, it is also extraordinarily complicated. More often than not, one must first identify a forested parcel of land that lies far beyond the road network, spend months clearing it with axes, machetes, and chainsaws, and burn the cleared vegetation. Since coffee is a technically demanding crop, one must acquire sophisticated knowledge of varieties, soil types, processing techniques, and the like. A false step at any point may ruin the product. Then, once the coffee is grown, harvested, and processed, one must find a means of transporting it to the nearest road to meet a merchant, sometimes a journey of a day or more. The merchant may arrive, or he may be delayed indefinitely by the region's interminable landslides. He will not be able to communicate easily with the farmer if there is no cell phone coverage, as was the case in most of the region in 2009–12. If the merchant and farmer finally manage to meet, the relationship turns quickly from cooperative to adversarial—one must hold one's ground with the shrewd and savvy coffee merchant, who tries to extract as much coffee as possible, of the highest quality possible, for as low a price as possible. What's more, most people in the Alto Urubamba must learn these varied skills of cultivation, processing, and distribution on the job: highland colonos often have little experience with tropical agriculture, and few Matsigenkas have practiced much commercial agriculture at all. (I was surprised to learn just how few people, in this region of catastrophic deforestation, know how to use a chainsaw.) It is in this sense that the Alto Urubamba agricultural frontier is a society of beginners, struggling to forge a path for themselves in an economy that is at once grueling, labyrinthine, and unfamiliar.

When I first came to the Alto Urubamba to study multilingualism, I had no idea that I would also, necessarily, be studying the day-to-day functioning and expansion of the coffee industry. But as it happens, most people in the valley spend most of their daylight hours managing their relationship to this economy—and thus most of their day-to-day linguistic interactions also involve coffee production in some way. Conversely, after spending a great deal of time with farmers and merchants, I came to understand that many of the challenges on the way to success in the coffee economy are themselves linguistic and communicative in nature: acquiring complex technical information in Spanish during training workshops; negotiating in Quechua for a good price; or dispatching a teenaged motorcycle messenger to a far-flung crossroads to intercept a merchant and warn him, in Spanish or Quechua, about a road that has been washed away by the previous night's rain. Seen this way, there is little difference between studying the day-to-day life of multilingual speech and the micro-level social dynamics of coffee production on the Alto Urubamba frontier. They are one and the same.

However, going about the countless daily linguistic tasks demanded of coffee producers is not merely a matter of knowing how to speak Quechua or Spanish. Rather, each interactional genre related to the coffee economy is indexically associated with particular linguistic registers and modes of participation. Municipal training workshops are hours-long, relatively monologic discourse contexts in which an assembled group of farmers listens attentively to an agronomist giving instructions in a technical variety of Spanish. Leverage among farmers and merchants is established in rowdy, highly dialogic Quechua joking sessions that take place among small groups of people on the dusty roadsides of the frontier. These kinds of interactions and registers are structured by language ideologies that, in turn, are embedded in broader ideas about institutions and sociality. To participate in a training workshop, for instance, is to acknowledge the role of the state in agricultural development, while roadside joking in Quechua draws on the sociality, morality, and humor of the rural Andean social world. Therefore, to become a farmer is not just a matter of adopting particular lexicogrammatical codes, or of gaining "language skills," narrowly defined. It is also a matter of knowing how to express displeasure through silence, dominance through joking, and reconciliation through small talk. It is a matter of adopting wider-ranging connections between language and social life, and of imagining oneself as belonging to different kinds of publics—a Peruvian public, or an agrarian public, each of which is associated with different spaces, ways of speaking, and types of moral obligation. In this sense, coffee production, language use, and the local social universe are inseparable.

This is the language-ideological terrain on which Matsigenkas and colonos encounter each other on the Alto Urubamba coffee frontier; it is also the social and linguistic matrix in which coffee is grown and distributed. (As I wrote this book, I often looked down into my mug of coffee and tried to imagine, like Marx [(1867) 1978], the inconceivably vast network of relationships—and words—that brought those beans to my door.) Crucially, since colonos tend to have more experience with all of these discursive practices than Matsigenkas do, they enter the coffee economy on surer footing. Thus, in this complex and competitive market, language has real implications for socioeconomic inequality, as we will see below (such connections between language, capitalism, and inequality have been explored recently by Heller and McElhinny [2017]).

For Matsigenkas, coffee production is an arena of socioeconomic integration in which they participate in, and become part of, the rural agrarian society around them, as incipient farmers. Agriculture is their common ground with their colono neighbors. Interestingly, this process of regional, national, and global integration is mediated in part through the Quechua language. In the highlands, by contrast, Quechua is ideologized as a language of the home and village, in opposition to Spanish, the language of broader national and global integration. This disjuncture shows just how local and contingent these social indexicalities can be.

In this chapter, I explore the linguistic life of coffee production in the Alto Urubamba, taking examples from the community of Yokiri and other places around the valley. My goal is to show how a farmer must speak to survive in the coffee economy, and how speaking in these ways also involves adopting far broader cultural conceptualizations of language use. All of this is embedded in the rural social milieu that has extended into the valley from the Andes. The chapter begins with an introduction to the basics of coffee production in the Alto Urubamba, and then it discusses the use of Spanish during municipal training workshops. These are important contexts for interaction with the state apparatus and engagement with scientific agricultural discourses, and they involve a technical register of Spanish through which Matsigenkas and colonos inhabit the social persona of the modern coffee farmer. Then I turn to the transportation and sale of coffee, as seen through three moments of interaction: the negotiation of terms by farmers and merchants at the beginning of the harvest season; the circulation of (sometimes coded) information via the provincial radio station; and the actual moment of sale, in which the coffee and money change hands. These interactional contexts involve registers, participant frameworks, and discursive skills of various kinds. The chapter thus offers a language-centric description of a few important moments in the process of coffee production. In the next chapter ("Speaking as a Comunero"), I contrast these integrative aspects of the coffee economy with public speech in asambleas (community meetings), through which communities differentiate themselves from the encroaching frontier society. Comparing these two domains of speech and social action demonstrates that the opposed tendencies of integration and autonomy manifest in particular types of interactions, which are each associated with particular languages, registers, and spaces.

Producing Coffee in the Alto Urubamba

Why would farmers in the Alto Urubamba subject themselves to the frustrations and anxieties of such a demanding endeavor as coffee production? The answer, of course, is that coffee is where the money is—or at least where it might be, given the volatility of local prices. The Peruvian coffee trade was thriving at the beginning of the twenty-first century: arabica exports grew by an average of 11 percent annually between 1990 and 2017 (International Coffee Organization 2018), with the most recent peak coming during my fieldwork in 2009–12. The total area under cultivation has grown rapidly as farmers have colonized the Amazonian foothills east of the Andes, from 162,661 hectares in 1990 to 399,523 hectares in 2014, an increase of 146 percent (FAO 2015, 139). The industry has grown to meet the tastes of the burgeoning global middle class, which consumes more and more coffee every year. For instance, China's coffee consumption grew—amazingly—by an average of 16 percent annually between 1994 and 2004 (International Coffee Organization 2015), and, at the time of writing, Starbucks was opening an average of more than one store *every day* in China (Starbucks Corporation 2016).[1] The world's soaring demand for coffee has outpaced supply, in part because the crop is best grown in only a few places on Earth: high elevations in rainy areas close to the equator.[2] Importantly, the areas of Peru that are suitable for coffee cultivation are some of the poorest in the country, because they tend to be remote, underdeveloped areas far from the country's economic centers. The maturing coffee industry has come to employ nearly a million people in those places, raising a great many people out of poverty (Bean and Nolte 2017). The majority of these farmers work on small- and medium-sized farms (Tulet 2010, 134), with 95 percent of Peru's coffee producers cultivating less than five hectares (MINAGRI 2019; for more on the distinction between these producers and "big coffee," see Reichman 2018). Many sell their coffee through small, locally organized *cooperativas* (cooperatives). Coffee also represents an alternative to the illegal production of coca leaf, which grows in much the same ecological niche. However, this strategy depends on high coffee prices to make the crop more attractive. In 2019, a decline in coffee prices drove some producers into the illegal coca trade, where they could earn between 70 and 120 soles (21–36 dollars) per day (Taj 2019), instead of the 40 soles (12 dollars) per day that they could earn by producing coffee (Carranza 2019).

Coffee is a delicate and temperamental crop, and successful production, even for the lower-quality domestic market, requires exacting conditions and techniques. First, farmers cut down a patch of forest and burn the cleared vegetation, often in a remote area beyond the road network, where land is cheapest. Then they choose a variety of coffee, taking into account the plot's elevation, orientation with respect to the sun, and soil conditions, all of which vary greatly across the region (people in the Alto Urubamba grow arabica coffee, with a preference in Yokiri for the Caturra variety). For instance, the small Yokiri Valley ranges from 780 meters in elevation (2,560 feet) at the river bottom to 2,280 meters (7,480 feet) at the ridgeline—with the two extremes just 5.8 kilometers (3.6 miles) of distance apart—encompassing most of the 500-to-1,500-meter elevation range suitable for the diverse varieties of arabica coffee. The diversity of ecological niches within this small hillside presents a major challenge to a novice coffee cultivator: a variety that thrives in one farmer's plot might fail in another's due to subtle differences in elevation, sun exposure, and soil chemistry. The only way to choose the right variety is through consultation with *extensionistas* (agricultural extension agents) who make recommendations regarding varieties, the necessary fertilizer cocktail (based on laboratory results), and appropriate shade crops for the specific conditions in each plot. This process brings farmers into a relationship of close dependence on the state apparatus and frequent interaction with its representatives—which, as we will see below, requires the use of a technical register of Spanish. Often the first state representatives to arrive in the farthest reaches of the frontier are extensionistas.

Growing coffee is complicated indeed, particularly for beginners. During a workshop in 2011, the novice farmers of Yokiri were instructed that seeds for new coffee plants must be chosen from the third to ninth branches from the bottom of a healthy, four-to-eight-year-old plant, peeled, fermented for twelve to sixteen hours, washed and dried in the shade until they reach 25 percent humidity, and then planted in sifted alluvial soil. Once the seeds are transplanted from the seedbeds, they must be planted at carefully measured distances from each other and meticulously interplanted with other crops that provide ample shade (such as banana and avocado). Once the plants begin to grow, weeds must be constantly cleared from beneath them and they must be regularly pruned.

Once the plant has matured, the farmer must harvest only the reddest and ripest coffee fruits, being careful not to mix them with unripe fruits, which can ruin a whole sack. In the Alto Urubamba, farmers practice "wet processing": they wash the fruits and sort them by immersion in a bucket, letting the bad and unripe fruits float to the water's surface to be skimmed off. The fruits are then run through a carefully adjusted hand-cranked pulper to remove the cherries from the seeds. A poorly calibrated pulper can crush the seeds or leave them with too much of the cherry intact. From here, the seeds are carefully pushed by hand over a sieve, through which they fall into a tiled fermentation pool (these materials and specifications are provided by state extensionistas). When the water is drained from the pool, the seeds are left to ferment for a prescribed period of time (usually more than a day). Then the seeds are washed and left out to dry in the sun (see figure 17) until they reach exactly 12 percent humidity, at which point they are bagged in one-quintal sacks (around one hundred pounds) and brought to the road for sale. Farmers who live in remote areas must synchronize the multistage harvesting process to conclude upon the arrival of the merchant: the coffee cannot sit long in the sacks, nor will a merchant wait for a farmer who has not finished the work. The lack of communication infrastructure and the poor condition of the roads often confound such coordination, and I have seen more than one sack of coffee rot on a roadside.

Any errors throughout this long and complicated process can ruin the product, and even the successful management of these variables often only yields coffee suitable for the domestic market. Producing export-quality coffee, which

FIGURE 17 Drying communal coffee on the soccer/volleyball field in Yokiri, 2011.
Photograph by the author.

commands a higher price, is still beyond the capabilities of many people in
the Alto Urubamba, and considerations about systems like Fair Trade Certi-
fication (S. Lyon 2010) were distant abstractions in 2009–12 (particularly for
Matsigenka farmers). Since the current growth sector of the Peruvian coffee
economy is specialty coffee (Tulet 2010), an army of extensionistas has been
dispatched across the frontier to help farmers improve their product. These
difficulties of coffee production are only redeemed by the high price that the
crop can command: when I arrived in Yokiri in 2011, merchants were buying
coffee at close to 500 Peruvian soles (around $179 at the time) per quintal. This
was more than twice the prices for cacao and achiote, the two other important
commercial crops grown in the valley. However, early in the 2012 harvest, the
price offered by some merchants plunged to as low as 300 soles (around $111)
per quintal, which demonstrates how vulnerable farmers in the region can be to
fluctuations in the market. At the time of writing in 2019, global coffee prices
were in the midst of a deep dive, driving farmers to other crops. (The high
price of coffee during my fieldwork is one of the reasons it figures more prominently than other crops in this book.) Complicating these uncertainties further
are diseases like coffee rust (*roya* in Spanish), a menace to coffee plantations
worldwide since at least the nineteenth century (Waller, Bigger, and Hillocks
2007).[3] Coffee rust devastated the crop in some areas of Peru—reaching a peak
in 2011–12—leading to confrontations between farmers and police over government relief (Taj 2013). However, coffee rust has been brought under control

since then, and the Peruvian coffee industry (though still fragile) has recovered its frenetic pace. Prices, though, remain volatile.

Workshops: "Todos Somos Campesinos"

Since the foreseeable future of the Peruvian coffee industry is in specialty and high-quality exports—a cruel twist of fate for the region's new farmers—coffee-producing districts in Peru have implemented state training programs to help farmers navigate the complex process of improving their product. In the Alto Urubamba, these were funded in part through revenues from the Camisea natural gas project, and they served both colono and Matsigenka communities. Municipal extensionistas held monthly workshops in enrolled communities and visited the farmers' plantations to monitor their progress and consult on all manner of technical details. They also provided fertilizer, herbicide, and tiles and cement for the fermentation pools. Some participants were also brought on *pasantías* (site visits) to successful coffee farms across the region to observe their techniques. Interactions with extensionistas were the only interactions that some farmers had with agents of the state for months at a time.

I often joined the extension agents on such visits, and I was struck by how difficult it was to improve and standardize the production practices of the region's dispersed farmers. On one occasion, when we arrived in a colono coffee plantation after a hike of several hours, we found two dogs asleep on top of the drying *seleccionado* (select) coffee, which provoked in the extension agent a look of pure anguish. Another time, I accompanied the same extension agent to a Matsigenka friend's far-flung plantation, where I had spent the whole previous day helping him harvest his high-quality seleccionado coffee as part of a municipal improvement program. After crossing waist-deep streams and crawling up and down steep jungle paths for hours, the extension agent arrived, drenched in sweat and gasping for air, and noted before he even put down his bag that the Matsigenka man's coffee pulper was poorly adjusted and had crushed most of the beans that we had picked the day before. He could only shrug his shoulders, offer some advice, and mark the man's coffee as a loss on his plastic-covered clipboard. These poor souls face the unenviable task of enforcing the byzantine demands of high-quality coffee production among farmers who may be poorly equipped or unmotivated to accept them. However, the experience this extension agent had with the Matsigenka farmer was more encouraging than in other places. He told me that in a different community nearby, only a small fraction of the hundreds of high-quality coffee seedlings he had delivered were picked up, while the rest were left to die on the roadside. Whole communities had abandoned the program.

When I attended coffee workshops in colono communities and comunidades nativas, I was struck by what an important interactional setting they were— both for the functioning of the local agricultural economy and as a centerpiece of the region's sociolinguistic ecology. On the one hand, as a technical matter, they were central to the emergence and improvement of the valley's coffee production. At the same time, they were also an important site for the establishment of a rural agrarian public in which both colonos and Matsigenkas participated together, side by side, as farmers. For instance, in 2012 I attended a coffee training workshop in the Yavero Valley with a large mixed group of Matsigenka and colono farmers, on the land of a particularly successful local producer. Some farmers had walked for hours from their remote patches of forest in the hills above the Yavero River, while others arrived in overflowing truck beds from up and down the valley. In the morning, we sat in a shady coffee grove and listened to lectures about herbicides; at lunch, we lined up dutifully for bean and beef soup, provided by a team of municipal chefs. In the afternoon, we toured a greenhouse, a pulping machine and fermentation tank, and a huge drying platform. The atmosphere was jovial and celebratory—the life of a frontier farmer can be lonely, and such events are often their only chance to socialize. Over the course of more than nine hours, the extensionistas spoke constantly, explaining in great technical detail the proper application of this or that fertilizer and the best method for pruning this or that variety of plants.

Transcript 8 gives an example of this kind of talk. Here an agronomist stood before a group of about fifteen Matsigenka and colono farmers and showed them how to set up a coffee pulper and fermentation pool. He stood next to the machine and pointed out the proper positioning of the various parts and their role in the production of high-quality coffee. He was a Quechua-Spanish bilingual, but as a representative of the state, he spoke Spanish in this meeting (with occasional humorous, informal asides in Quechua).

Transcript 8

De esta parte de la despulpadora, debe haber un espacio por lo menos de ochenta centímetros a este cajón [*thumps box with fist*].₁ ¿Para qué?₂ Para que la pulpa pueda amontonarse y puedan palear a un costado, ¿no?₃ . . . Luego, si nosotros tenemos un cajón con este tipo de piso bajado, y el tubo, no vamos a necesitar mucha agua.$_4$ Por su propio peso van a entrar todos los cerezos.$_5$ Solamente vamos a necesitar una manguerita acá [*points behind the box*] para que no se pegue la pulpa.$_6$ Bajo esas condiciones, acá adelante [*points to front of pulper*] va a pasar con bastante melaza.$_7$ Y la melaza nos garantiza una buena fermentación.$_8$ . . . ¿Por qué queremos aprovechar la melaza?$_9$ Porque tiene contenido de . . . ? [*waits for farmers to mumble along*] . . . potasio.$_{10}$ Que es un abono que necesita para rellenar los granos.$_{11}$ Esa es la función: el desarrollo y crecimiento de los granos.$_{12}$ El potasio.$_{13}$

From this part of the pulper, there should be a space of at least eighty centimeters to this box [*thumps box with fist*].$_1$ Why?$_2$ So that the pulp can pile up and you can shovel [it] to one side, no?$_3$ . . . Later, if we have a box of this type with a lowered bottom, and the tube, we won't need much water.$_4$ The cherries will enter under their own weight.$_5$ We'll just need a little hose here [*points behind the box*] so that the pulp doesn't stick.$_6$ Under those conditions, it will come out here [*points to front of pulper*] with plenty of mucilage.$_7$ And the mucilage guarantees us a good fermentation.$_8$ . . . Why do we want to take advantage of the mucilage?$_9$ Because it contains . . . ? [*waits for farmers to mumble along*] . . . potassium.$_{10}$ Which is a fertilizer that it needs to fill out the seeds.$_{11}$ That is the function: the development and growth of the seeds.$_{12}$ Potassium.$_{13}$

For lack of a better term, we might call this discourse genre *agricultural workshop talk*, and the associated register *agricultural workshop Spanish*. This was similar, of course, to the form of Spanish used in workshops dedicated to other purposes, but it featured its own technical lexicon. Indeed, the position of the agronomist as an agent of the state brought this kind of interaction in line with other official state interactions—public meetings, for instance, which partook of some of the same enregistered features (see chapter 5).

This discourse genre was usually performed by an agronomist standing before a group of farmers, who were either seated or congregated around a piece of equipment, as in transcript 8. It was quite monologic, with the exception of occasional backchannel. The agronomist often elicited a response from his audience by pausing before a significant word, indicating that he expected them to demonstrate their knowledge by completing his sentence. For instance, in sentence 10 above, he began the clause "porque tiene contenido de . . ." (because it contains . . .) and waited for the farmers to join him in stating the answer, ". . . potasio" (. . . potassium). This usually elicited a quiet, half-hearted, and sometimes conflicting mumble among a subset of the participants (and a few embarrassed glances among those who had answered incorrectly). This mode of participation invoked a sort of schoolhouse interaction between teachers and students and positioned the agronomist as an educator among novices. Another way in which the agronomists kept the attention of the farmers was to introduce a degree of dialogism through frequent tag questions, like "¿no?" (sentence 3), and questions that they would pose and then immediately answer themselves, as in, "¿Para qué? Para que la pulpa pueda amontonarse" (Why? So that the pulp can pile up) (sentences 2–3). This was also a frequent feature of other kinds of public, monologic speech, as I discuss in my presentation of asamblea (community meeting) oratory in chapter 5.

For our purposes, what is most significant about the agricultural workshop talk discourse genre and its associated Spanish register is the kind of presupposed knowledge that makes it intelligible. For instance, consider a statement like "debe haber un espacio por lo menos de ochenta centímetros" (there should be a space of at least eighty centimeters) (sentence 1) from the perspective of a Matsigenka farmer who grew up far beyond the agricultural frontier without a formal education, who might have only the vaguest sense of what both "eighty" and "centimeter" might mean—and who might not speak much Spanish to begin with. The same is true for *potasio* (potassium), a technical notion that can only be interpreted through a particular conceptualization of the physical properties of the earth that is usually acquired in school. Many older people with little formal education, Matsigenkas and colonos alike, find such discourses perplexing. I was surprised at how attentive the farmers remained during this nine-hour onslaught of technical speech; note that the interaction in transcript 8 lasted less than a minute and presupposed several different types of complex information. It is no wonder that the farmers had trouble implementing such techniques when they returned to their remote patches of forest, and why they might have drifted away from this confounding and frustrating economic routine. It is also clear why people who do not possess the linguistic skills to keep up in this kind of interaction might not attain the financial rewards of high-quality coffee production.

Finally, I wish to point out that these workshops were a particularly important site for the interactional mediation of the valley's interethnic encounter. These were some of the only times when Matsigenkas and colonos sat side by side—and they did so as farmers. By nodding along to the same speeches, chuckling at the same jokes, eating the same lunch, and mumbling the same answers to agronomists' elicitations (". . . potassium"), they participated in a common agrarian public that backgrounded their ethnic differences. This was a context in which Matsigenkas experienced belonging in the Andean agrarian society that had come to surround them. As an agronomist proclaimed at the beginning of one workshop, after taking stock of just how multiethnic his audience was: "Todos somos campesinos" (We are all farmers). This inclusive impulse can be seen throughout the excerpt in transcript 8 above: "the mucilage guarantees *us* a good fermentation" (sentence 8); "if *we* have a box of this type with a lowered bottom" (sentence 4). In addition to everything else that it requires, becoming a farmer on the Alto Urubamba frontier means recognizing oneself in this "we"—as an agrarian subject, among agrarian coequals.

Moving Coffee in Yokiri

As one travels down the Urubamba Valley and into its remote tributaries, beyond the mature mechanisms and routines that move coffee so efficiently through the old agricultural juggernaut of the upper valley, the infrastructure's hold on the land gradually loosens. The broad, smooth roads give way to bumpy dirt tracks; sturdy bridges become fewer, and drivers find themselves plunging through creekbeds with water flowing over the top of their tires; cell phone coverage grows patchier and eventually blinks out entirely. Finally, past the end of the road, the newest farmers are on their own in the forest, clearing land, planting coffee, and struggling to secure a reliable, remunerative means to sell their product.

In 2009–12, finding someone to buy one's coffee in the remote corners of the Alto Urubamba frontier was difficult, particularly for farmers who were not part of a cooperativa. In these places, farmers generally met merchants by the nearest roadside rather than transport their coffee to a distant town. The closest road could be far away, and in some places coffee merchants only traveled through the region once a week—when the roads were passable—even during the busy harvest season. This could be a problem, since there is a short time window in which coffee must be sold after it is processed and dried. Farmers had to improvise solutions by gathering information from friends and neighbors and from battery-powered radios that broadcasted programming from the provincial radio station; by promising merchants favorable terms in exchange for a firm commitment to arrive at an appointed time; and by hatching backup plans in case those arrangements fell through (and, often, concealing those backup plans, which sometimes violated the terms of their other agreements). Resourcefulness, persuasion, deception, and effective information management were essential to surviving in this economy. As I argue in this section, these are linguistic skills as much as they are economic skills.

Before the farmers of Yokiri built their road in the late 2000s, pictured in figure 18, they hauled their coffee via mule to the road terminus in the Yavero Valley. In the mid-1990s this terminus was at Túpac Amaru, a small, ramshackle settlement at the foot of the formidable Abra Reyna pass (map 4), a day or two's walk from Yokiri. Only a couple of sacks of coffee could be transported on these arduous trips, which took Yokiriños away from their homes for most of a week. The road moved closer and closer over the years, gradually making it possible to produce more coffee and to sell it with less effort. In the late 1990s the road arrived in Huillcapampa, at the valley bottom below Yokiri, and then it reached Yokiri itself a couple of years before I first visited the community in 2011 (see figure 18). During my time there, the road had still not settled into the landscape, and it was washed out by mudslides in several places for much of the year. During that time, the community was only reachable by a three-hour hike from Huillcapampa; I made this hike back and forth every few weeks to buy supplies, call my loved ones on the solar-powered telephone, and talk with friends in town.

Figure 19 shows a small landslide that blocked the road to Yokiri in 2012. The Yokiriños and I cleared the road before the arrival of Edison, the community's primary coffee merchant at the time. The Yokiriños are adept at this kind of work, and they use all kinds of ingenious solutions to manage the landscape. Here they redirected a small channel of water away from the stream running across the road and used it to carve away the debris heaped on the road. This careful, small-scale feat of hydraulic engineering dissolved the mudslide much faster than we could have done with our shovels and picks. Becoming a coffee farmer on the Alto Urubamba frontier requires learning to do day-to-day battle against the landscape in this manner.

Landslides that cut the valley off entirely during the harvest season were a major problem for farmers and merchants alike during my fieldwork. The farmers needed to harvest and sell their coffee as it ripened and could not wait for days or weeks for the municipality to send a front-end loader to clear the debris. Merchants, meanwhile, made financial projections based on how much coffee they expected to collect from week to week, and they could find themselves coming up short if they couldn't get around a landslide. Municipal road crews were under a great deal of pressure to resolve these problems quickly. When

FIGURE 18 The muddy road through the cloud forest of Yokiri, 2012. Built by the community members in the late 2000s. Photograph by the author.

no road crew was available, people on the frontier often made what they called an *escala*, in which farmers brought their harvest via truck or mule to one side of a landslide and then carried their products through the mud and debris to the merchants waiting on the other side. This allowed the flow of products and money to cross the landslide even if the trucks couldn't make it. However, it could also be dangerous to walk across a muddy and partially collapsed road platform.

Edison and Yokiri

During the time I lived in Yokiri in 2011–12, Edison, a Quechua-Spanish bilingual merchant, was the primary buyer of the Yokiriños' coffee. Edison was born

FIGURE 19 Yokiriños clear a landslide to open the road for Edison, 2012. Photograph by the author.

in the late 1960s in the growing provincial capital of Quillabamba and was raised in a family of agriculturalists and traders who had migrated from the adjacent highlands. As a child he helped his family in their coffee and cacao plantations, and he accompanied his father on trips up and down the Urubamba Valley selling bottled soft drinks and learning how to fix cars, trucks, and agricultural machinery in the region's tiny frontier settlements (many of which are large towns today). As a boy in the late 1970s, he witnessed the triumphant arrival of the first train in Quillabamba from Cusco.[4] Edison's experience in the remote frontier comes in part from his time as a soldier during the internal war of the 1980s and 1990s, when he fought against the Sendero Luminoso in the lowland forests between the district of Vilcabamba and the Apurímac Valley. During my fieldwork, he kept a pistol in his truck as he drove through the same valleys, some of which came to be controlled by heavily armed cocaine smugglers who used the Sendero Luminoso name. Edison is kind and generous, but he is also tough and unflinching in the dangerous frontier environment. He became the provincial government's first choice when they had to transport large amounts of cash through unstable parts of the frontier.

Edison first came to Yokiri in July 2011, after the community's previous merchant, Gregorio, was ambushed and robbed late at night on the road from Otingamía. The assailants allegedly set off dynamite on the road as Gregorio

FIGURE 20 A coffee merchant's truck in Artillería Pass above Yokiri, 2011. Photograph by the author.

approached, pulled him from his truck, and relieved him of a large sum of cash. Gregorio was terrified by the attack and never returned. Edison, who was armed and adept at defending himself in the lawless frontier, saw an opportunity to operate where other merchants were afraid to go.

He and the Yokiriños came to an arrangement after a tense and serious negotiation. Edison promised (1) to arrive on prearranged days, with greater frequency during the peak of the harvest season; (2) to attend and help sponsor some community celebrations, particularly those that required the transportation of sound systems, generators, and Catholic ritual items from Quillabamba; and (3) to bring market goods from Quillabamba for sale when he arrived in Yokiri. This way, Yokiriños would not have to spend a full day traveling to the *plaza* (market) of Huillcapampa to buy staples. Edison's wife Gladys, who often accompanied him on these trips, would load their truck with great quantities of fish, rice, eggs, machetes, *chuño* (dehydrated potatoes), *ch'arki* (dried meat), live chicks and ducklings in a cardboard box, bullets, soap, batteries, flashlights, and anything else that she might be able to sell in Yokiri and on the way. Gladys's goal was to travel into the frontier loaded with market goods, and Edison's goal was to return loaded with coffee; thus they made money on both ends (and they tried never to have an empty truck). Yokiri, in turn, committed to (1) reserve at least 50 percent of their harvest for sale to Edison, and (2) make a storehouse available so that Gladys would not have to haul her durable wares back and forth across the frontier for each visit. The storehouse was adjacent to my house, and I was eventually deputized as Gladys and Edison's storekeeper. I was authorized to sell wares to the community on Gladys's behalf and to look after sacks of coffee that farmers brought to the road early for Edison. This put me at the center of the community's commercial life, which was an invaluable fieldwork experience.

For Yokiri, the arrangement with Edison and Gladys ensured a reliable and punctual buyer for their coffee, crucial in a remote place like Yokiri, as well as easy access to market goods. In turn, the arrangement decreased Edison and Gladys's risk by guaranteeing that they would have business upon their arrival—indeed, if they arrived in Yokiri and the farmers did not show up, or had sold all their coffee to another merchant, Edison and Gladys would stand to lose quite a lot of their investment in the trip (hundreds of dollars of gasoline and perishables, as well as the time away from Edison's other work as a personal driver and mechanic). As a result, each party had quite a lot of leverage against the other, since a failure by either party to honor the agreement would mean a substantial financial loss for the other. However, Edison remained the dominant participant in the commercial relationship (for a similar case among Ashéninkas and mestizo traders in central Peru, see Killick 2008b, 320).

There were many moments in which speaking was important in the process of selling coffee in Yokiri and other similar places. I now focus on three such moments: negotiations between farmers and merchants, often in Quechua, in which the parties competed for leverage; the use of radio broadcasts to pass information among various people on the frontier; and the somewhat anticlimactic moment itself at which coffee and money changed hands, which was as significant for what it avoided—indexical invocations of the bargaining discourse genre—as for what it included.

Gaining the Upper Hand

Edison and Gladys and the Yokiriños arrived at the agreement outlined above through a long and contentious negotiation. The terms of this agreement would establish the economic parameters of the whole harvest season and thus had major implications for each party. There were a couple of main issues up for debate: First, Edison wanted to space out his trips, thus reducing his travel costs, while the Yokiriños wanted him to visit more frequently. Second, there was disagreement over the proportion of each farmer's coffee that would be reserved for Edison: Edison wanted a larger commitment, while the Yokiriños wanted the flexibility to sell more of their coffee to other merchants if Edison didn't arrive on schedule or if another merchant turned up offering a better price. There was also quite a bit of disagreement within the community itself over this arrangement, with one prominent Yokiriño arguing that they should not restrict themselves to any such limitations—as he declared in Spanish during one meeting, "¡El negocio es libre!" (Trade is free!). However, the most important variable, the price that Edison would offer for the coffee, was not up for debate at that moment, since regional prices fluctuate throughout the harvest season and cannot be predicted.

Quite a bit of interactional maneuvering and posturing went into this kind of negotiation. Each party sought to frame their own commitment as overly generous and to devalue the other's. Both feigned willingness to walk away from the negotiation altogether. These positions played out interactionally—usually with words, but often with gestures: offers were met with stony silence or conspicuous glances at wristwatches, suggesting that one or the other party might break off the negotiation at any moment.

Edison was an adept practitioner of this sort of subtle interactional combat. The Quechua exchange in transcript 9 below took place as Edison was considering forming a commercial relationship with Yokiri. Here, a newly established Matsigenka-speaking farmer (F) discussed his modest coffee and cacao production with Edison (E). Edison was skeptical (or at least performed skepticism) that Yokiri's small harvest was worth the investment of time and capital that would be required to drive all the way to the remote Yokiri Valley. The farmer, anxious to secure a buyer, attempted to ease these concerns by representing his coffee as high in quality and thus worth more. He also exaggerated his yields, which were in fact much lower than the thirty-five annual quintales that he reports in line F1. As a seasoned merchant, Edison had the leverage in this relationship, and he repeatedly interrupted the farmer (lines E1 and E5) to press him further about quantity. That is, each time the farmer attempted to steer the conversation toward quality, which he saw as his point of leverage, Edison redirected it to quantity, where the farmer was most vulnerable. Edison is a native speaker of Quechua, so his superior grasp of that language also gave him the upper hand against the Matsigenka farmer, who was not able to keep up in this adversarial and fast-paced Quechua interaction.

The interaction took place in Quechua, with numerous Spanish borrowings and code-switches. Spanish elements are underlined, brackets indicate overlapping speech, and dashes indicate self-interruptions.

Transcript 9

F1: A veces wisch'unman hasta treinta y cinco quintales hinallaman,
   pero cali[dad

E1:   [Kay watata hayk'ata [pallaranki

F2:   [kay wataqa yaqa chunka tawallayuqman
   chayani, pero—pero urquni—calidad es.

E2: ¿Calidad?

F3: Calidad es pues.

E3: Ya, cacaotarí?

F4: Cacao[ta

E4:   [Pallankichu mana[chu?

F5:   [Pallaniyá—[ah

E5:   [Hayk'a quintalta kay watapi?

F1: Sometimes it might produce up to around thirty-five quintales,
   but high quali[ty

E1:   [This year how much [did you harvest

F2:   [this year I'm getting up to around forty,
   but—but I harvest—it's high quality.

E2: High quality?

F3: Yeah, it's high quality.

E3: Okay, and cacao?

F4: Cacao[

E4:   [Do you harvest it or [not?

F5:   [I definitely harvest—[um

E5:   [How many quintales
   this year?

At stake in such adversarial interactions were the terms that the farmers and merchants would eventually reach, if they reached them at all. Managing the subtleties of competition and positioning in such discourse was thus a skill with serious economic implications, and the inability to use Quechua effectively in these contexts was a liability.

Radio Quillabamba

Crucial to the functioning of the Alto Urubamba coffee economy in 2009–12 was a radio station called Radio Quillabamba (91.1 FM / 1210 AM). Radio Quillabamba was established and operated by the Dominican missionaries in the provincial capital, and it was the only broadcaster powerful enough to reach the entire valley. It spilled out of homes, roadside bars, and mechanic shops between the bustling urban centers and the remotest frontier outposts; on some busy mornings, one could walk from one side of any given town to the other and overhear the broadcast almost without interruption. Farmers placed radios on pieces of cloth on the ground or hung them from branches to listen to the music and commentary while they worked. Most programming was in Quechua and Spanish, and it offered music, interviews with local politicians, Catholic religious content, long advertisements for nutritional supplements and medical treatments, and information about the coffee economy. Most significantly for the social dynamics of coffee production, there was also a daily program in which valley residents could pay one Peruvian sol (about $0.30 at the time) to have a message addressed, twice a day, to a specific person or group of people within the broadcast area. This program served an important function in the circulation of information in the Alto Urubamba frontier, including among farmers and merchants, and it was central to the day-to-day functioning of the coffee economy.

Before exploring the role of Radio Quillabamba in the dynamics of coffee production, it is important to first consider the radio station's importance in the frontier society of the Alto Urubamba more generally. In particular, Radio Quillabamba mediated the experience of belonging to an agrarian public—among both colonos and Matsigenkas—in the Alto Urubamba. To tune in was to imagine oneself alongside an aggregate of co-listening farmers, brought together by the common endeavor of coffee production and consuming the same information, jokes, debates, and moral discourses in real time. (It also had a Catholic bent, which alienated some of the Evangelical colonos in the valley, particularly during the frequent religious programming.) Farmers on the Alto Urubamba frontier discussed the information and opinions they had heard on Radio Quillabamba among themselves. Radio programs often serve a comparable function of mediating imagined social groupings among listening publics (Spitulnik 1996). This was one important day-to-day context in which Matsigenkas experienced their own integration into colono society, and they experienced it through Quechua and Spanish.

However, the Matsigenka Council (COMARU) also ran an hour-long weekly radio program called *Iriniane Mavaintini* (The Voice of the People), which was conducted entirely in Matsigenka and featured information about issues specific to comunidades nativas.[5] This included schedules for upcoming meetings and protests, legal notices, and death announcements, as well as Matsigenka songs and poems, which were part of an effort of cultural revival (a common use of Indigenous radio programming in Amazonia; see Ennis 2019). Through *Iriniane Mavaintini*, Matsigenkas participated in a very different public, defined in opposition to the agrarian public invoked through the rest of Radio Quillabamba's programming.

In addition to providing important information specifically intended for Matsigenkas (also with a Catholic orientation), the program served a pointed political function: for one hour a week, thousands of colono listeners who did not understand the Matsigenka language were reminded of the Indigenous Amazonians living among them as *Iriniane Mavaintini* came on in their homes. On a couple of occasions I was staying with colono friends when the program came on, and it was fascinating to see them pause and listen intently to the unfamiliar language. This weekly event, in which the presence of Matsigenka people in the valley was momentarily invoked in the consciousness of thousands of colonos, was as effective an ethnopolitical statement as any organized protest. There also was a further layer of interpretation to this phenomenon: Matsigenkas, as they listened, were acutely aware of how their colono neighbors were experiencing the program. Matsigenka people in multiethnic homes and spaces, in particular, suddenly felt more Matsigenka than ever when the program came on. Thus, while Radio Quillabamba's normal Quechua and Spanish programming provided a context in which Matsigenka people participated in a regional agrarian public, *Iriniane Mavaintini* provided a brief, weekly moment in which Matsigenka speakers stood apart—sometimes defiantly—from that public.

It is not an exaggeration to say that moving coffee in the lower valley depended vitally on Radio Quillabamba in 2009–12. People in far-flung corners of the frontier needed to communicate with each other to coordinate their agricultural activities, and since there was little cell phone coverage there during my fieldwork, the Radio Quillabamba message program was often the only way to reach someone. Every morning and evening, the colono radio hosts in Quillabamba read aloud messages intended for specific recipients across the valley; people who heard a message addressed to a neighbor or friend often checked in to make sure they had received it. The program also included messages such as birthday wishes to friends or pleas from concerned relatives who could not find their loved ones in the vast frontier and wanted them to come home. Many notified people working in remote corners of the valley that a parent or a sibling was sick or had died, and the radio announcers had the difficult task of delivering such sad news to their listeners nearly every day. Messages for colonos were usually read in Spanish and then repeated in Quechua, since many did not understand Spanish. Matsigenka speakers sometimes requested that their messages only be broadcast in Spanish. The radio hosts were considered hilarious and virtuosic Quechua speakers, and they often embellished the messages with their own commentary, speculation, and special voices. This included an interesting *mock Quechua* voice, which was used to create a loving caricature of an elderly Quechua-speaking man, and featured phonological and grammatical characteristics stereotypically associated with Quechua. Many people in the Alto Urubamba tuned in just to savor this sort of verbal artistry.

An example of people using this program to organize their coffee production activities is given in transcript 10, parts a and b. Here, a farmer named Walter Mamani has traveled to the highlands to recruit workers to help harvest, process, and transport his family's coffee (as everywhere in this book, these names have been changed). He paid to have a message broadcast back in the valley to his wife, Sonia Mendoza, to update her on his progress. In 10a, the radio announcer first uses Spanish to identify Mrs. Mendoza in the remote frontier settlement of Nueva California and then reads Walter's handwritten message aloud from a notebook. Then the announcer restates the message in Quechua (10b). Spanish is underlined, and Quechua is in plain type.

Transcript 10

a: Nueva California, Sonia Mendoza en Nueva California, de parte de tu esposo Walter Mamani: "Esta tarde estaré bajando con cinco personas más el carro. No debes preocuparte de nada. Saludos en casa," nintaq.

b: Nueva California anchaypiraq Sonia Mendoza qusachayki Walter Mamani nimushasunki: kunan tarde payqa haykumushan. Phisqa personata café palla-

nankupaq riki pusayamushan. Carrupi haykumushanku chayqa amas preocupa-
kunkiñachu. "Saludos," nintaq, "wasipi kaqkuna, llapaykichispaq napaykuy."

a: Nueva California, Sonia Mendoza in Nueva California, from your husband
Walter Mamani: "This evening I will be coming down with five people, as well as
the truck. Don't worry about anything. Greetings in the house," he says.

b: There in Nueva California, Sonia Mendoza, your husband Walter Mamani is
telling you: this evening he's coming in here, [and] he's bringing five people to
pick the coffee. They're coming in in the truck, so don't worry about anything
anymore. "Greetings," he says, "to the ones who are in the house, to all of you,
say hello."

The participant framework in this message tells us much about Radio Quillabamba and its place in the rural agrarian society. Here we can see that the
announcer aligns himself with his Quechua-speaking listeners by using Quechua as a metalanguage to discuss Spanish messages. In this way, he creates
a sort of folksy, intimate familiarity with his audience, in opposition to the
more formal language of the messages themselves, which are usually in Spanish. In 10a, he begins by reading the Spanish text directly from the page, so
it is addressed to Sonia Mendoza in her husband's first-person voice ("I will
be coming down . . ."). To use the terms of Erving Goffman (1979), Walter
Mamani is the *author* (the composer of the message) and *principal* (the person
responsible for the message); the radio announcer is the *animator*, the person
who speaks the message aloud. Quechua is the metalanguage of the message in
10a: at the end, the announcer closes the directly quoted Spanish text with the
Quechua *nintaq* (he says).

Then, in 10b, there is a shift in footing, corresponding to a switch in language.
The radio announcer now translates the message and offers his own interpretation in Quechua, as animator (speaker), author (composer of the specific words),
and principal (person to whom responsibility for this particular utterance falls).
This change from Spanish to Quechua indicates that the announcer is now
adopting a social role aligned with his Quechua-speaking listeners. It is also a
shift in deixis. For instance, Mr. Mamani's Spanish construction *estaré bajando*
(I will be coming down) takes Mr. Mamani's place in the highlands as its deic-
tic point of reference. However, the radio announcer's Quechua translation

haykumushan (he's coming in here) takes the audience's position in the Alto Urubamba lowlands as its point of reference.

In these ways, Quechua is the metalanguage through which the announcer aligns himself with his listeners and reconsiders the Spanish message from their perspective. He moves back and forth between these footings by switching between the two languages, which are indexically associated with different social identities. Thus the experience of using and listening to this program, in Quechua, was also central to the self-conception of farmers as fellow agrarian subjects on the coffee frontier. As such, listening to Radio Quillabamba was one discursively mediated context in which Matsigenkas participated in, and imagined themselves as part of, the rural, Quechua-speaking Andean society.

In the case of Edison and Gladys and the Yokiriños, Radio Quillabamba was also an important medium for managing the economic and diplomatic relations between them. On more than one occasion, Edison and Gladys were blocked by landslides, which prevented them from arriving in Yokiri as they had agreed with the community. In October 2011, Edison, Gladys, and I spent hours clearing a small landslide with picks, machetes, and shovels (pictured in figure 21). We recruited the colonos who lived near the road to help and then slept in the back of Edison's truck to continue work at dawn—only to be forced to turn back when we encountered a much larger slide a few kilometers farther on. In situations like this, the Yokiriños (who may have been unaware of the landslides) might accuse Edison and Gladys of failing to honor the terms of their agreement. This would force Edison and Gladys to make some sort of concession to repair the relationship. In these cases, a message via Radio Quillabamba explaining their ordeal after the fact might help Edison and Gladys maintain their good standing with the community.

One of the interesting aspects of these messages is how they were produced with respect to the particular limitations and affordances presented by the medium (Barker 2008). Radio Quillabamba was a unidirectional medium, broadcasting messages to thousands of homes across a vast swath of the Alto Urubamba lowlands. In this way, it functioned somewhat like an airport or hospital paging system. However, the public nature of this system presented a problem, since many messages were sensitive or private. Protecting the flow of information was important for day-to-day coffee production—for instance, some farmers wished to obscure the fact that they were doing business with two different coffee merchants despite an exclusivity agreement. One solution to this kind of problem was to include a request that the intended recipients travel to

FIGURE 21 Edison, Gladys, and the author (not pictured) on the road to Yokiri, 2011. Preparing to spend several hours clearing a small landslide. Video still by the author.

the nearest solar-powered public telephone, found in some frontier settlements, to call a particular number. However, this added another potentially costly step in the communicative process, since it might take a day or two for the farmer to reach a phone.

Another solution to the privacy problem was to send encoded messages. This was particularly helpful if the matter was time-sensitive and the sender could not simply broadcast a telephone number and wait for the recipient to call back. Transcript 11 gives an example of such an encoded message, in which a woman named Alejandra refers obliquely in Spanish to *lo conversado*, "the thing [we] talked about" (translated into Quechua, with a switch in subject, as *parlasqaykichista*, "the thing that you [pl.] talked about"), in a transmission addressed to her sister.

Transcript 11

a: <u>Raquel Santa Cruz en Zonaquishiato de parte de tu hermana Alejandra: "Lo conversado te estoy enviando al Señor Braulio López esta noche, y debes esperar al paradero. Los que escuchen, favor avisar."</u>

b: Zonaquishiato anchaypiri Raquel Santa Cruz <u>a ver</u>, Raquel Santa Cruz ñañachayki Alejandra nimushasunki parlasqaykichista apayamushansi—riki apayachimushansi. <u>"Te estoy enviando,"</u> nintaq. Wiraqucha Braulio López paywansi apayachimushan chayqa kunan ch'isi chayqa suyanaykichis kanqa <u>paraderupi</u>. Uyariqkuna willaripuychis.

a: <u>Raquel Santa Cruz in Zonaquishiato, from your sister Alejandra: "I'm sending the thing we talked about to Mr. Braulio López tonight, and you have to wait at the bus stop. Whoever is listening, please tell [her]."</u>

b: Raquel Santa Cruz there in Zonaquishiato, <u>let's see</u>, Raquel Santa Cruz, your sister Alejandra is telling you that she's bringing—she's sending the thing that you talked about. <u>"I am sending [it] to you,"</u> she says. She's sending it with Mr. Braulio López, so tonight you have to wait at the <u>bus stop</u>. Listeners, please tell her.

However, while it was often desirable to obscure information in a message, having the ear of thousands of overhearers could also present an opportunity. Almost every day during my fieldwork, a message was broadcast that publicly shamed delinquent debtors. The rural economy of the frontier depended on informal loans in which farmers borrowed money from merchants and relatively well-heeled colonos in the local towns to make investments in their coffee operations. These loans were supposed to be paid off once the farmers sold their product during the harvest season. However, when coffee prices dropped—as they did during my fieldwork in 2011—farmers might find themselves unable to pay their debts. Creditors often put pressure on their debtors by broadcasting threats over Radio Quillabamba, which were intended to be overheard by thousands of people. This discourse strategy, which took advantage of the particular affordances of the medium itself, was meant to tarnish a person's reputation. To the extent that this strategy changed people's behavior—and, anecdotally, it seems that this pressure was often effective—it played a role in the circulation of capital and maintenance of funding liquidity in the valley.

In the example of public shaming in transcript 12 (parts a–c), a well-known local creditor whom I will call Roberto Quispe Vargas called out Ruth García Huamán and his other debtors, and urged them to come and pay off what they owed. The radio announcer read the message in Spanish (12a) and then restated it in Quechua (12b). The announcer also used Quechua as a metalanguage, as above—and a moral one at that—to insert his own commentary and reactions: for example, "Oooh chay tawa wataña?" (Oooh, four years already?) and "Qunqarapurankichu imachá pasakunpas imanaqtin?" (Did you forget, or what happened?). Then he added his own extemporaneous elaboration by playing out a dramatic dialogue between Mr. Quispe and his debtors (12c), demonstrating that they should not be afraid to contact him. The debtor in this dialogue spoke Quechua, and Mr. Quispe spoke Spanish, creating a distinction between the two voices and indexing the socioeconomic disparity between them. Radio Quillabamba listeners relished these improvised, semifictional verbal dramas. Again, here Spanish is underlined and Quechua is in plain text.

Transcript 12

a: Ruth García Huamán en Ozonampiato, Echarati, de la parte del Señor Roberto Quispe Vargas.[1] Debe aproximarse a cancelar su cuenta pendiente que debe hace cuatro años–oooh chay tawa wataña?[2] Si no cancelas, se le procederá judicialmente.[3] Aproximarse a [address].[4] También se le hace llamado a todos los deudores a acercarse a cancelar las deudas.[5] O sea, los días jueves, sábados y domingos suchuriyamuychisyá.[6]

b: Chaymi chay willakuycha kasqa Ruth García Huamán haqay Ozonampiato Echarati anchay uraypi.[7] Wiraqucha Roberto Quispe Vargas nimushasunki suchuriyamunayki cuentachaykitaqsi kashan pendiente yaqa tawa wata hunt'aña uuuuy cuatro años, ¿ah?[8] Qunqarapurankichu imachá pasakunpas imanaqtin?[9] Si no cancelas, "Bueno pues tendré que proceder en otra forma, judicialmente," nimushasunkitaqmi.[10] Chayraykuyá suchuriyaramuy ñawpaqchanta kay [address].[11] . . . Así mismo se está haciendo llamado a todos que le deben también, por adelantos, ¿no?[12] Al Señor Roberto Quispe Vargas.[13] Vengan a ver vuestra situación, a cancelar vuestras deudas.[14] Especialmente les está esperando los jueves, sábados y domingos.[15] Hamuychisyá chay cuentachaykichista arreglarapuychis.[16]

c: "Wiraqucha Roberto, wakichallantaraq apakamushayki."[17] "Muy bien pues, muy bien, ¿el resto cuándo vas a traer?" nispa.[18] "Qhipayakunayá" acaso–como wiraqucha Roberto muy buena gente, acaso pay mana–mana llapanta apamunayki.[19] Q'ipiykitachu mochilaykita qichurisunki manamá mana chaynachu sino que hamunayá, hay que venir a conversar.[20]

a: Ruth García Huamán in Ozonampiato, Echarati, from Mr. Roberto Quispe Vargas.[1] You have to come by to pay off your outstanding account, which you owe from four years ago–oooh, four years already?[2] If you don't pay it off, he will take legal action against you.[3] Come by [address].[4] Also, he's making a call to all the debtors to come by and pay off their debts.[5] That is, on Thursdays, Saturdays, and Sundays, come by.[6]

b: So, that little message was for Ruth García Huamán, down in Ozonampiato, Echarati.₇ Mr. Roberto Quispe Vargas is telling you that you have to come by, your <u>account</u> has been <u>outstanding</u> for almost four whole years, <u>uuuuy four years, ah?</u>₈ Did you forget, or what happened?₉ <u>If you don't pay,</u> "Okay, well, I'll have to proceed in a different manner, legally," he's telling you.₁₀ So before that, come by [address].₁₁ . . . <u>Likewise, he's making a call to everyone who owes him, for advances, no?</u>₁₂ <u>To Mr. Roberto Quispe Vargas.</u>₁₃ <u>Come check your situation, to cancel your debts.</u>₁₄ <u>He's especially waiting for you on Thursdays, Saturdays, and Sundays.</u>₁₅ <u>Come and settle your accounts.</u>₁₆

c: "Mr. Roberto, I'm bringing you just a part."₁₇ <u>"Okay, okay, when will you bring the rest?"</u> he says.₁₈ "Some time later"—<u>it's not like—since</u> Mr. Roberto [is] a good person, it's not like he—you don't have to bring it all.₁₉ He's definitely not going to take away your bundle or your <u>backpack</u>, it's not like that, <u>rather</u>, you have to come, <u>you have to come talk</u> [to him].₂₀

In my description of the Radio Quillabamba message program, I called Quechua a metalanguage, in the sense that it was the language with which the Spanish discourse was framed and commented upon. For instance, Spanish reported speech was marked with Quechua *verba dicendi* (verbs of saying), as in "'Muy bien pues, muy bien, el resto cuándo vas a traer?' *nispa*" ("Okay, okay, when will you bring the rest?" *he says*) in sentence 18, and "Si no cancelas, 'Bueno pues tendré que proceder en otra forma, judicialmente,' *nimushasunkitaqmi*" (If you don't pay, "Okay, well, I'll have to proceed in a different manner, legally," *he's telling you*) in sentence 10. The radio announcers used Quechua in this way to align themselves with their listeners—that is, with the agrarian public—in a way that set their voices apart from the Spanish messages.

In addition, I called Quechua a moral metalanguage above because the announcers also used the Quechua agrarian voice to add moral commentary to the Spanish messages. For instance, when the radio announcer interrupted the Spanish text to ask, "Qunqarapurankichu imachá pasakunpas imanaqtin?" (Did you forget, or what happened?) in Quechua (sentence 9), he articulated the moral responsibility that farmers have to pay their debts. Broadcasts on Radio Quillabamba were full of Quechua asides like this one, offering a moral commentary on the Spanish text from the perspective of the Andean agrarian public.

Thus, in 2009–12, discourse broadcast over Radio Quillabamba served important functions in the day-to-day social dynamics of coffee production: arranging transportation, transmitting coded information, mediating the collection of debts within the informal financing system of the frontier, and even articulating the moral principles of the agrarian society. Importantly, this omnipresent feature of the local frontier soundscape was one way in which Matsigenkas were exposed to the discourses and moral ideologies of colono society (for instance, regarding debt), as well as its humor. It was thus an important communicative context in which Matsigenkas engaged with the Spanish and Quechua languages, which were closely linked to the discourses of agrarian sociality and morality that they presented (indeed, it was an interesting experience to listen to Radio Quillabamba alongside Matsigenkas who were just joining the agrarian economy and society). This was one facet of the ideological, moral, and economic terrain on which colonos and Matsigenkas encountered each other in multilingual interactions on the multiethnic coffee frontier in 2009–12.[6]

However, this function of Radio Quillabamba will not likely last long. Cell phone coverage has been quickly expanding through the valley since 2012, providing a more attractive communicative medium to many farmers than the public message program (though some creditors will surely miss the opportunity to publicly shame their debtors). At the same time, as Internet connectivity has become more widely available, social media have emerged as an increasingly important form of communication. Between 2014 and 2017 most of my Matsigenka and colono friends joined Facebook, which has opened a rich new dimension of communicative practice in their lives. However, as newcomers to the Internet, they are vulnerable to the kinds of scams and fake news that circulate there. At the time this book went to press, some Matsigenka friends were sharing stories about alien abductions and an imminent invasion by the Chilean military, as well as conspiracy theories regarding the faked suicide of former Peruvian president Alan García. In 2019, I tried to help a Matsigenka friend after she turned over several months' income to someone who claimed to represent the vast estate of a deceased West African prince who had chosen her to be the sole beneficiary (this is a dark side of the Internet indeed). Following how both the beneficial and pernicious dimensions of social media are interwoven into the ongoing social turmoil of the Alto Urubamba frontier in the coming years will be an interesting experience indeed.

Market Day

The final context of coffee-related language use during my fieldwork in 2011–12 that I discuss in this chapter is the actual interactions in which coffee and money changed hands in Yokiri. (Such interactions vary widely across the region and are much more routinized in other places, particularly within cooperativas; this description is limited to the particular relationship between Yokiri and Edison during my fieldwork.) One might have supposed that these moments of exchange were the most consequential instances of language use related to the sale of coffee, since it was at this time that Edison finally revealed the price he intended to offer for the Yokiriños' product on a given trip. However, these interactions were notably anticlimactic and avoided indexical invocations of the bargaining discourse genre that is so prevalent in the region. Edison and the Yokiriños avoided this discourse genre because bargaining, at its core, is an adversarial interaction that requires that one or the other party be willing to walk away from the sale. These parties were too vulnerable to each other, because of just how much they each stood to lose if their precarious relationship collapsed, to allow such a possibility to be aired. In place of bargaining, they engaged in a range of interactional practices that foregrounded their solidarity, displaced the adversarial nature of their relationship, and dispelled the possibility of dangerous open conflict.

The sound of a clanking, honking diesel truck grinding its way up the steep road to Yokiri can be heard from more than a kilometer away. At the first distant grunt of the engine, Yokiriños would freeze in place and speculate excitedly about who was arriving and what they might be bringing. Since in some seasons during 2011–12 the trucks (or any vehicle at all) arrived in Yokiri as infrequently as once every two weeks, the sound of a creaking engine would halt all school activities and bring the schoolchildren, and even the teachers, running to the road.

When a visit by Edison and Gladys had been scheduled, many Yokiriño farmers showed up near the school early in the day to await their arrival. Others, particularly those who lived hours away, came later, carrying their coffee to the school on the back of a donkey or a mule. People who lived close to the road rushed to intercept the truck at the nearest bend when they heard it approaching, in order to avoid a long and exhausting trek to the school.

Over the course of the morning, people converged on the school area from different directions, some leading mules or donkeys, others sweating and struggling under the weight of the hundred-pound sacks of coffee on their backs.

They greeted their fellow Yokiriños as they always did: with a brief, weak clasp of the hand or fingers, usually without making eye contact, quietly muttering a Spanish *buenos días* (good morning), Matsigenka *kutagitetanai* (good morning), or Matsigenka *pigantaga?* (lit. "are you the same?"). After some quiet conversation, people found a bit of shade in which to sit in upturned wheelbarrows and chew coca, smoke cigarettes, drink from large bottles of *shitea* (homemade yuca beer), and take small sips from plastic Coca-Cola bottles filled with sugarcane liquor. This was one of the few times during the month when community and family members saw each other, and they used the opportunity to socialize.

When the truck finally came around the bend, rattling and coughing to a halt in the dirt next to the school, Gladys and Edison were greeted with laughing, joking, and inquiries about their family members. Some Yokiriños addressed them in Quechua, which keyed a frame of camaraderie and foregrounded their shared orientation to—and coequality within—the agrarian society. The first order of business was to buy large bottles of warm beer from Gladys, which she sold from crates in the back of the truck at a slight markup. Gladys also filled special orders of crates of beer for Yokiriño entrepreneurs who operated beer "stores" in their homes, selling bottles to their community-mates at a further markup above Gladys's price (sometimes those people even sold their doubly marked-up beer on the spot once Gladys's own supply had run out on market day). Some Yokiriños bought beer on credit, which Gladys recorded in a notebook, and which might be paid off later in the day after the coffee sale. Usually, groups of two to four men or women approached the truck to buy one bottle of beer at a time, inviting their kin to sit or stand in a gender-segregated group and pass around a small plastic cup. The atmosphere around Edison and Gladys's truck often resembled a party—even at ten or eleven in the morning—and sometimes, after a few bottles of beer had been passed around, Edison turned on the truck's radio so that the assembled group could dance *huaynos* and *cumbias*.

Despite this party-like atmosphere, the question of coffee prices hung heavy in the air. This was, after all, an adversarial encounter in which Edison would eventually reveal how much he intended to pay for the farmers' coffee. His goal, as a merchant unconnected to a locally organized *cooperativa*, was to buy coffee from farmers for as little money as possible and sell it to the distributors in Quillabamba for as much as possible. He kept the difference, minus whatever he spent on the trip. The drop in coffee prices in 2011 had squeezed everyone along the commodity chain, and the relationship between Yokiri and Edison had reached a breaking point. However, at this late point in the season, with so much invested on all sides, nobody could afford to walk away. Farmers traded tense glances and nervous laughter as they drank and danced on the dusty roadside.

Laughing, joking, and drinking played a central role in dispelling this tension. Indeed, drinking is an important social practice in the rural Andean region, serving such functions as creating a space for community and ceremonial action (Allen 1988; Isbell 1978), allowing the airing of grievances (Harvey 1991), and forging an Indigenous ethnic identity (Butler 2006). Part of being accepted into the social world of the Alto Urubamba coffee frontier is being able to participate in the light ribbing that goes back and forth during a drinking session, mostly in Quechua. One must be able to gently mock other merchants and farmers (both present and absent) without being overly malicious, and be able to "take a joke" without taking offense. When I was still adapting to this kind of interactional event early in my residence in Yokiri, people occasionally pulled me aside after joking sessions to make sure I hadn't been offended and to reassure me that good-natured mocking was part of how they expressed affection. I became an increasingly frequent target of this affection as people grew more familiar with me and saw that I could "take a joke"; I sought to reaffirm our bonds by laughing heartily at such mockery and attempting, however clumsily, to respond in Quechua with some light ribbing of my own. Striking an appropriate tone in such interactions—one that is both lightly transgressive and gently affectionate—is a communicative skill of great nuance, and I am grateful to the Yokiriños for their patience and good humor as I tried my hardest to respond in kind.

An example of such an exchange is given in transcript 13, in Quechua, between me (NQE) and a farmer in Yokiri. This common joke references Sophia, who was my girlfriend at the time and is now my wife, and who was the subject of much curiosity during and after her visit to Yokiri in 2011.

Transcript 13

MAN: Imatan musquranki?

NQE: Mana imatapas musquranichu. Qanrí, imatan musquranki?

MAN: Sofiata!

[*Very hearty laughter among all assembled.*]

MAN: What did you dream about [last night]?

NQE: I didn't dream about anything. And you, what did you dream about?

MAN: Sophia!

[*Very hearty laughter among all assembled.*]

Once the amicable tone of the interaction had been established during moments like these, women began to approach the truck and buy goods from Gladys: tomatoes, pasta, sugar, salt, bread, cheese, fish, onions, coca, and live chicks and ducklings, as well as durable manufactured items including flashlights, bullets, soap, and matches. Generally, it was the women who bought the market goods from Gladys and the men who sold the coffee to Edison; this followed a broader gendered division in which women were responsible for the home while men worked in the fields. Notably, Gladys's business of selling manufactured goods and Edison's business of buying coffee were kept strictly separate. Women who incurred debt with Gladys might pay it off using the money their husbands received from Edison the same day, but they were not expected to. This was beneficial to Yokiriños who did not have much money to spend, but these debts also gave Gladys and Edison leverage over them.

When Edison finally declared his price, it was often strikingly nonchalant, as in one Spanish interaction in October 2011:

Transcript 14

FARMER [*leaning against the truck*]: ¿A cuánto está el café ahora?

EDISON [*in the back of the truck, leaning back for a carton of eggs*]: Está a trescientos cincuenta.

FARMER [*leaning against the truck*]: What's coffee at right now?

EDISON [*in the back of the truck, leaning back for a carton of eggs*]: It's at three hundred and fifty.

Edison cited the figure casually, and the farmer received the information with the same cool indifference, though the atmosphere around the truck changed abruptly as all the bystanders listened in discreetly. The farmers then weighed their coffee with Edison, one by one, on a scale hung from the side of his truck, then received their money and took their leave.

This interaction was most significant for what it was not: bargaining. In many other commercial interactions that Yokiriños and people across the region engage in, the announcement of a price would mark the beginning of a bargaining session, an easily recognized interactional genre that is often highly conventionalized and metapragmatically regimented (Keane 2008). In fact, Edison often bargained with Yokiriños for goods other than coffee, sometimes even on the same days when he visited to buy coffee. For instance, in July 2011

Edison and a Matsigenka woman engaged in a bargaining session on the road over roughly one hundred pounds of yuca before he arrived at the place where the rest of the farmers were waiting with their coffee. Edison and the woman went back and forth for several minutes, haggling over the price and adjusting the quantity of yuca in the pickup truck bed. Edison leveraged other events outside of the bargaining session to bring down the price, including the fact that he had just given her a ride to Huillcapampa to return an empty beer crate. This interaction was intense and openly oppositional, but it was also cordial, and each party appeared to genuinely enjoy the sport of bargaining (for other ethnographic descriptions of the bargaining genre, see French 2000; Orr 2007; Kharraki 2001; Seligmann 1993).

The difference between these two episodes was that neither side had much riding on the hundred pounds of yuca, while the precarious agreement between Edison, Gladys, and the Yokiriños was freighted with the possibility of financial catastrophe for both parties. That is, the ultimate basis of leverage in bargaining interactions—a credible threat to "take one's business elsewhere"—was simply too dangerous to assert in this fragile relationship. To avoid this danger, both sides suppressed the indexes of the bargaining genre, what Briggs and Bauman (1992, 149) call "manipulating generic intertextuality." That is, the remarkably un-bargaining-like interaction described above involved the deliberate nonin-vocation of the bargaining speech event type (Silverstein 2005). The parties thus effectively disavowed the oppositional nature of the transaction and avoided putting pressure on the precarious relationship.

This generic reframing was accomplished through a number of linguistic strategies. First, on some occasions, Edison presented his coffee price as an objective figure issuing from an external authority—for instance, when he says that coffee "está a trescientos cincuenta" (it's at three-hundred fifty) in transcript 14 above. In fact, the coffee isn't "at" any price, of course; this was simply the lowest price that Edison thought he could get away with offering. This is similar to Brigittine French's observation that market women in Quet-zaltenango, Guatemala, reduce their responsibility for their positions by stating that a product "doesn't go for [that price]" (2000, 164). Similarly, when the coffee in Yokiri had been weighed and Edison had calculated the total price of the sale, he sometimes typed this total into a small calculator to show it to the farmer—that is, he didn't use the calculator to compute the figure, but simply to display the number that he had entered. This act symbolically displaced respon-sibility for the price away from him and into the external realm of objective, disinterested calculation. In place of references to the bargaining genre, Edison, Gladys, and the Yokiriños deployed frequent linguistic indexes of solidarity and even kinship. For instance, some community members crowded their conversations with the ritual kin address terms *compadre* and *comadre* when addressing Edison and Gladys, who had recently baptized their son. These terms were used far more frequently in such moments of interactional anxiety than in other contexts, and their use increased in frequency as the tension mounted.

Conclusion

An important question that one might ask about the agricultural frontier is: How does one become a coffee farmer? The most obvious answers to that question might concern the technical skills of cultivation and processing, which indeed are fundamental to adopting agriculture. However, in this chapter I have explored some of the linguistic and interactional practices that were also an important part of becoming a successful farmer, and of inhabiting the social persona of the farmer. I presented just four of the countless types of interactions that were necessary to this endeavor at the time of my fieldwork in 2009–12: (1) municipal training workshops in which farmers learned agricultural techniques through a technical register of Spanish; (2) tense, combative negotiations in Quechua, in which farmers and merchants struggled for leverage in the upcoming harvest season; (3) personal messages broadcast on Radio Quillabamba in Spanish and Quechua, in which senders circulated information about the logistics of coffee production and took advantage of the medium's structural affordances to conceal information or shame delinquent debtors; and (4) the delicate dance of the moment of sale, in Spanish or Quechua, when farmers and merchants treaded lightly to avert a catastrophic collapse of the relationship. Each of these interactional practices required the ability to speak particular languages, but they also involved different ideologies that linked languages to particular spaces, participant frameworks, and ideas about institutions like the state agricultural development program and the social world of the rural Andes. In this sense, becoming a farmer required adopting nuanced cultural practices regarding language use, which always had broader social, economic, and political implications. Since colonos usually had more experience than Matsigenkas with such discursive practices, these kinds of interactions could be a site at which socioeconomic inequality was generated and reproduced.

These interactions were also the common ground on which Matsigenkas and colonos encountered each other in the multiethnic, multilingual frontier. Coffee production was a context of broader sociocultural integration for Matsigenkas and colonos alike. In the next chapter, I present an interactional context that was constructed in opposition to the integrating nature of coffee production described in this chapter: the asamblea (community meeting). People in such meetings used a very different set of interactional practices precisely to differentiate their communities from—and establish a measure of autonomy in opposition to—the broader rural agrarian society of the Alto Urubamba.

Chapter 5

Speaking as a Comunero

In 2011, I visited a Matsigenka comunidad nativa that I shall call Tsimiato, which was in the midst of a bitter conflict with a neighboring colono. Due to the messiness of the land titling bureaucracy, both parties had been issued documents asserting their ownership of the same piece of land at their border. Rather than leave the land alone until the dispute was settled (as custom dictates), the colono escalated the conflict by clearing part of the land, burning it, and planting coffee bushes in a long, neat row along what he claimed was the boundary. The Matsigenkas of Tsimiato, incensed by this provocation, raised the stakes even further by hiking out to the land late one night and tearing up those plants, which they considered to be on their side of the boundary. As the confrontation threatened to spiral out of control, the municipal authorities were called upon to step in before it turned violent.

Over the course of this conflict, the families of Tsimiato devised a number of legal and extralegal strategies and carefully coordinated their efforts to carry them out. They did this through public oratory and debate during a series of community meetings called *asambleas*, held in a central building called the *salón comunal* (community meeting hall). The asamblea was a "public," in Habermas's (1989) sense: it was conceptualized as a democratic forum for rational discussion, in which each *comunero* (community member) could voice their opinion, irrespective of personal characteristics like gender or family background. As they debated a proper response to their colono neighbor, one man named Diego stood and advocated a confrontational stance, in Spanish: "Compañeros, tenemos que luchar, porque ¡somos una comunidad organizada!" (Friends, we have to fight, because we're an organized community!).

What was striking about this declaration was that the man did not, despite his conviction, have much to do with his fellow community members. Like many Matsigenkas, he lived most of his life according to the sort of family-level social organization discussed in chapter 1: his house lay a nearly forty-five-minute walk away from his closest neighbor; his family grew, hunted, and gathered most of what they ate; and until recently he rarely spent time with non-kin. A few years before, when a different colono family moved to the land just beyond Tsimiato's boundary, relatively close to his home, he began to interact with that family occasionally. However, the only time he actually encountered his fellow community members beyond his own kin group was in the monthly asambleas themselves, and during the occasional *faenas* (community work parties) and other events that they organized during those meetings. Given these distinctly non-community-like practices of everyday sociality, what do we make of this man's passionate invocation of the community—a tenuous unit of social organization in Tsimiato, to say the least—as a locus of social action and obligation?

This chapter examines the ongoing emergence of a sense of community in comunidades nativas on the Alto Urubamba frontier—that is, a nascent commitment to a new unit of social organization that spans kin groups but is differentiated from the surrounding colono society. The advent of "community" has involved the construction of a new domain of morality and social practice, inhering in the political subject of the comunero (community member), who regularly devotes a portion of his or her time, labor, and goods to the collectivity. This incipient distinction between the family and community domains of everyday life draws on a private/public principle of semiotic differentiation (Irvine and Gal 2000; Gal 2005), which provides a new template for interpreting spaces, resources, periods of time and labor, and all manner of social and discursive practices. A comunero's willingness to subordinate his or her private (i.e., family) interests to the public (i.e., community) good was interpreted through the moral idiom of *sacrificio* (sacrifice), while the aggregate measure of the comuneros' commitment to the community's public sphere was described in terms of the community's degree of *organización* (organization)—as when Diego declared Tsimiato to be "una comunidad organizada" (an organized community). In this chapter, I use the Spanish terms *sacrificio* and *organización* instead of their English translations because of these terms' prominence in the local ideological lexicon.

This sense of community was mediated through the use of public speech, mostly in Spanish, in the democratic forum of the asamblea. The asamblea provided a context in which people interacted as comuneros rather than as members of kin groups (in theory if not always in practice). In this manner, the political subject of the comunero emerged when one stood and spoke—as a comunero—in the public discursive arena itself. In particular, the use of a Spanish discourse genre I call "official talk," the associated "official Spanish" register, the performance of sacrificio, and the disavowal of private, kin-level commitments in public interactions (for instance, through the avoidance of kin terms) were important parts of creating a public sphere and, through it, a community. The chapter concludes with a comparison of Yokiri's culture of public discourse with that of a nearby comunidad nativa where community-level social organization had not taken hold during my fieldwork in 2009–12, and where comuneros code-switched between Spanish and Matsigenka in public speech as a way of moving between the family and community domains of social authority.

Like the previous chapter, this chapter demonstrates one way in which Matsigenkas and colonos used language as they navigated their place in the rapidly changing social order of the Alto Urubamba frontier. The previous chapter explored how Matsigenkas and colonos came to participate side by side in a new agrarian economic and social system that had overtaken the landscape of the Alto Urubamba over the last few decades. That participation happened largely in Quechua, and to a lesser extent in Spanish. The communicative phenomena discussed in this chapter served an opposing function: asamblea discourse allowed Matsigenkas to carve out a place for themselves apart from that new agrarian society. This was true at a practical level, since Matsigenka families were able to defend their land and livelihoods by organizing a unified stance with respect to the world beyond their boundaries (as in the case of Tsimiato described above). It was also true at a symbolic level, as they created a sense of belonging to an independent and autonomous "community" through the act of speaking as comuneros in the asamblea. This happened almost exclusively in Spanish, and indeed the asamblea was the only context in which one regularly heard Spanish in some comunidades nativas. In this way, the interethnic encounter between colonos and Matsigenkas—and the expansion of the frontier writ large—was negotiated through discourse, the different spaces in which it occurred, language choice, and day-to-day social practices.

From Families to Communities

As I discussed in chapter 3, the community of Yokiri was formed by the inter-marriage of a handful of families who migrated from a wide variety of places and circumstances across the region beginning in the 1970s. Some came from remote valleys beyond the frontier, while others migrated from the nearby Dominican mission at Chirumbia, the highland province of Paucartambo, and coffee plantations in the Yavero Valley that used enslaved Matsigenkas as laborers. These places were sociolinguistically quite different from one another, and Quechua, Matsigenka, and Spanish were spoken in the community's twenty households in all combinations. Most people born since the community's foundation were trilingual, though the youngest generation appeared to be using Spanish more than their parents and grandparents.

The families of Yokiri, who were mostly unknown to each other before they arrived in the community, came together to claim their land through the legal protections of the comunidades nativas law that allows Indigenous Amazonians to title their land as a corporate body.[1] Since the amount of land they can claim depends on the size of the community's population, the first families of Yokiri recruited other Matsigenkas across the valley to help them claim as much land as possible. In this sense, the families' legal designation as a comunidad nativa preceded their formation as a "community" in the social organizational sense (see Killick 2008a for a similar process among Ashéninkas in central Peru). Until recently, social activities were largely limited to kin groups, who visited each other frequently, hunted together, shared meat, and aided each other in *ayni* (Quechua for "reciprocal labor"). They seldom engaged in such activities with non-kin in Yokiri—in fact, most had never even seen the houses of their non-kin neighbors, even though they had inhabited the same hillside for decades. (More than once, Yokiriños asked me what the houses of their non-kin neighbors looked like.) This disposition toward family-level autonomy and lack of engagement with non-kin community members is reflected in Yokiri's dispersed settlement pattern, shown in map 5. Homes are marked by squares on this map and numbered according to their membership in one of the two

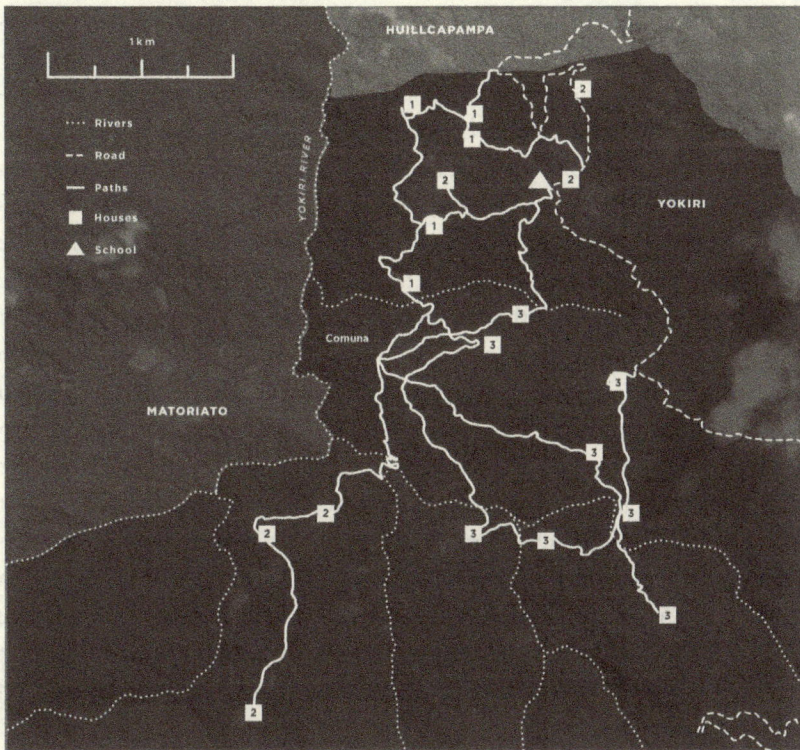

MAP 5 Yokiri. Map data: Google, DigitalGlobe, Instituto del Bien Común. IBC-SICNA. Enero 2017, incluye información levantada en gabinete, AIDESEP-CIPTA, GEF PNUD, GOREL y PFS. Author's GPS data also used. All landscape labels added by the author.

major kin groups (1 and 2), or 3 if they are outside of the community's two major kin groups.

Consistent with the strong tendency toward kin commitments in Yokiri, the community's footpaths (indicated with solid lines in map 5) link homes of kin-affiliated households but avoid the homes of non-kin. This can be seen in the houses of kin group 1 at the top of the map, which were connected to each other but did not connect to households from kin group 2.[2]

The introduction of the comunidad nativa political structure since the mid-1970s has led some Matsigenkas to engage in sustained (though limited) social commitments beyond their families for the first time. This social organizational template is modeled on the nucleated *comunidades campesinas* (peasant villages)

of the Andean highlands, a structure that was foreign to many Amazonians'
principles of social organization (Veber 1998, 394; Rosengren 2003, 230; Killick 2008a), though some Yokiriño families had experience with such arrangements in the highlands and in the nearby Dominican mission at Chirumbia.
Many of these principles are prescribed by the legal structure itself: members
of comunidades nativas own their land and certain goods collectively, petition the government as a corporate body, recognize an *estatuto* (bylaws) for the
administration of the community and its resources, elect a *presidente* (president,
also known as a *jefe*) and other positions of leadership, and deliberate issues of
community concern in the asamblea. Community members are also required to
participate in faenas, regular work parties in which all of the community's men
(and sometimes its women, during a busy harvest) put aside work in their own
plots to invest a full day's labor on a communal project such as repairing the
road or maintaining a community agricultural plot. The novel political subject
of the comunero—organized around the moral virtue of sacrificio—is incul-
cated through these new responsibilities and privileges. A community in which
comuneros are willing to sacrifice their private interests for the benefit of the
collectivity is considered to have a high degree of organización, a quality that
is highly valued as the foundation of political modernity, upward mobility, and
national integration.

The attempt to institute this governing system in the Alto Urubamba has
met with mixed success, as other anthropologists have observed (Rosengren
1987, 2003; A. W. Johnson 2003). In most of the communities I visited in
2009–12, the jefe and the other *dirigentes* wielded little influence over the other
comuneros, and only a small proportion of the residents attended asambleas,
faenas, and other activities involving coordination beyond the kin group. Once,
when I brought a large box of medical supplies to a comunidad nativa, the
comuneros divided up the contents among the families—antidiarrheal pills for
one, gauze and bandages for another—rather than hold them in common so
that anyone could use them when a particular ailment arose. Most important
decisions in such communities were made in private conversations elsewhere
rather than in the asamblea (for a similar case in Piro communities, see Gow
1991, 206–11). In some communities the only attendees at communal events
were members of the jefe's family, suggesting that the comunidad nativa governing structure had simply been absorbed into the kinship-based social organization (Veber 1998, 401). The unwillingness to participate in community-level
activities is perhaps the most widely noted fact in ethnographic accounts of

Matsigenka social organization.[3] Allen Johnson offers the following description of the community of Shimaa in the 1970s: "It is extremely difficult to motivate them to participate in group activities: they listen to exhortative speeches attentively with mild expressions and then generally walk away and refuse to join in, whether the project is to maintain the central clearing of the community or to attend Maestro's Columbus Day celebration. They are most reluctant to be led" (2003, 2).

But while the comunidad nativa system had not taken hold in some parts of the Alto Urubamba in those decades, the situation in some places during my fieldwork in 2009–12 was notably different, including in Yokiri: attendance at asambleas and faenas was nearly perfect, and when a person did not turn up, comuneros from across the kin groups expressed concern for the person's well-being and, often, irritation at their absence. When a man failed to appear at a faena, his absence was recorded by the *secretario* (secretary) and reported in the next asamblea, where he was made to either justify his absence, pay a fine, or arrange to make up his day's labor in communal work (indeed, it was common to see a lone man working off his debt in the communal coffee plantation in the days after such asambleas). Yokiri's high degree of organización, which was noted with admiration by neighboring colonos and the municipality's agricultural extension agents, was a point of great pride among Yokiriños concerned with the widely held stereotype of Matsigenkas as antisocial and opposed to socioeconomic development. Observing Yokiri's determined implementation of community-level social organization, one neighboring Andean man remarked to me in Spanish with surprise: "¡Los nativos son casi más organizados que nosotros!" (The natives are almost more organized than we are!).

The Creation of a Private/Public Distinction

Yokiri's notable community-level organización was accomplished through the establishment and careful maintenance of a distinction between private (family) and public (community) domains of social life. The private/public dichotomy was a principle of semiotic differentiation (Irvine and Gal 2000) that ran through daily life in Yokiri and gave meaning to all manner of experiences and cultural practices, as described by Susan Gal: "The ideology of public/private divides spaces, moralities, types of people, activities, and linguistic practices into opposed categories" (2005, 24; see also Gal 2002). For instance, certain spaces in Yokiri were conceived as public—e.g., the salón comunal and the *comuna* (communal coffee plantation)—and defined in opposition to the private spaces of the homes and family plots. Private and public spaces were normatively associated with different regimes of morality and social commitment: discourse and work in public spaces were organized around the virtues of sacrificio and community-level organización (which are themselves connected to ideas about modernity, participation in the agricultural economy, and the Peruvian nation), while social and cultural practices in private spaces were based in obligations to kinspeople. I argue below that these spaces and domains were also connected to ideologies of language, in which Spanish was deemed fit for public discourse, Quechua was associated with commercial relationships on the agricultural frontier, and both Matsigenka and Quechua were used for private communication in domestic contexts (depending on the sociolinguistic background of each family). As in so many societies (Rosaldo 1974; Landes 1998), the private/public dichotomy was also a gendered distinction in Yokiri, and men tended to engage in community-level activities to a greater degree than women. For instance, men usually represented their households in the public labor of faenas while women stayed home to look after the children, attend to domestic tasks, and cultivate garden crops. However, women sometimes also participated in faenas as cooks, which was considered the most domestic (i.e., private) form of public labor. In this manner, the gendered private/public distinction was subject to a recursive projection (Irvine and Gal 2000) within the domain of public labor itself (Gal 2005, 26–28). The distinction between private and public spaces in Yokiri was also projected outward in the opposition between community and noncommunity: just as Yokiriños waited patiently on the trailhead rather than approach the private domestic spaces of non-kin, outside visitors to Yokiri's asamblea were usually made to wait on the roadside (sometimes all day) before being invited inside to what was, by virtue of their status as non-Yokiriños, a private event.

The Asamblea: Creating Community Through Public Discourse

In 2011–12, Yokiri held an asamblea every month, with more frequent meetings as circumstances required. Normally, only comuneros were welcome to attend, though occasionally municipal officials, coffee merchants, schoolteachers, and neighboring colonos were invited to discuss particular issues. The primary social function of the asamblea was to institute community-level social organization through the careful differentiation of the private and public domains; indeed, the event was largely dedicated to the negotiation and policing of that boundary. This policing also went on in other contexts such as faenas, celebrations, and countless other supra-kin interactions—and indeed, institutionalized forums such as the asamblea are not the only site where politics plays out (F. R. Myers and Brenneis 1984, 3). However, Yokiriños understood the asamblea to be the most important and salient expression of communityhood. As I mentioned earlier, the asamblea was structured according to the language ideology of the "public," in Habermas's (1989) sense of a forum, equally accessible to all community members, in which "groups of private individuals gather to discuss matters of common political concern . . . on the basis of reason rather than the relative status of the interactants" (Gal and Woolard 2001, 5). To be a comunero was to have—in theory—an equal stake in the determination of community policies regardless of personal characteristics such as gender, seniority, and kin-group affiliation, and to have the right and responsibility, according to article 7 of Yokiri's bylaws, to *intervenir con voz y voto* (intervene with voice and vote) in community decisions (Comunidad Nativa de Yoquiri 1990).[4]

However, public spheres are always, of course, ideological and idealized constructs (Gal and Woolard 2001, 6), and in practice they can have the paradoxical effect of reproducing and institutionalizing relations of inequality (Fraser 1990). Personal characteristics can never be fully removed from the public self, and despite the ideological construction of the asamblea in terms of universal participation, not every Yokiriño had equal access to political participation. Men spoke more frequently than women and occupied most of the positions of community leadership. The oldest community members, who did not speak Spanish well, were also at a disadvantage in the arena of public discourse, and young members often didn't feel comfortable asserting themselves among their elders. Additionally, some descendants of Andean colonos were occasionally challenged as illegitimate participants within the context of the comunidad nativa, a structure that was created to serve Indigenous Amazonians. As a result, despite the great amount of discursive work that went into realizing the universalist ideology of the public, in practice the comuneros did not all have equal presence in the asamblea.

Asamblea discourse itself was a central mechanism for constituting what Warner (1992, 377) calls a "public subjectivity"—in this case, that of the comunero. Because the asamblea is, in its essence, a framework for engagements between non-kin community members, the very act of attending the event both presupposed and entailed (Silverstein 2003) the subjective experience of belonging to an aggregate of people called a "community." In other words, the political subject of the comunero was created through participation in the public event itself (Warner 2005, 77–78): consciousness of community belonging was enacted as private individuals made the long trek from their widely dispersed homes to deliberate over collective concerns in the public space as comuneros. For this reason, the often intense conflicts that took place in Yokiri's asamblea were not evidence of a failure of the community's public sphere but rather of its success. Members of other comunidades nativas with little tradition of public participation simply did not attend such events.

The regimentation of the asamblea around the ideology of the public could be seen in the physical arrangement of the space of the salón comunal itself in Yokiri. The comuneros sat on low wood-plank benches around the periphery of the room, giving everyone equal access to the floor, rather than in rows of pew-like benches facing a podium, as in other communities. People generally sat wherever they could find a space and made little attempt to segregate themselves by kin group. The egalitarian structure of the public forum also manifested in gestures toward gender equality: as the comuneros took their seats, the elected leaders moved about the room loosely enforcing a policy of alternating male-female seating order. This was a deliberate departure from most other contexts in Yokiri, in which men and women tended to gather in gender-segregated groups, and from meetings in other comunidades nativas in the region, in which men and women tended to sit apart from one another (see, for example, Baksh 1984, 417–18; Beier 2010, 384). However, as I mentioned above, the gendered disparity in participation remained significant. The *dirigentes* (elected leaders), who usually donned the green or tan municipal employee vests that served as highly visible signs of power, authority, and access to influential outsiders, sat behind a large wooden table on one side of the room. Significantly, in 2011–12 the salón comunal doubled as a classroom for the school—one of the primary institutions through which the community interacted with the world beyond its borders—and the walls were decorated with multiplication tables, portraits of Peruvian heroes, a large handwritten poster displaying the lyrics of the Peruvian *himno nacional* (national anthem), and other signifiers of modernity and national belonging.

Spanish as the Language of Public Life

The predominant language of the asamblea, and of Yokiri's public life in general, was Spanish. A representative example of public Spanish discourse comes from a speech in 2012 in which the presidente attempted to recruit his fellow comuneros to attend a meeting in the nearby settlement of Huillcapampa, so that they could entreat the municipal government to move forward with plans to build a new health post on their side of the Yavero River. As in most instances of public discourse, the presidente used the "official talk" discourse genre (described below) and invoked the principles of democratic participation as well as the ideology of community-level commitment. Note that this speaker adopts the same impassioned tone as Diego, the speaker from Tsimiato above, and uses the same turn of phrase, *somos una comunidad organizada* (we are an organized community).

Transcript 15

Hay que bajar también hombres y mujeres porque es necesario.$_1$ Lo iban a poner a este lado, pero los otros lo quieren al otro lado.$_2$ Entonces incluso quiero–¿cómo dice?–estaban pensando tener un voto.$_3$ Entonces tenemos que ir todos, o sea como ya como–tenemos que bajar todos, compañeros.$_4$ ¡Somos una comunidad organizada, y tenemos que bajar y hacer sentir nuestro derecho!$_5$ ¿Ya?$_6$ Eso sería todo, compañeros.$_7$

Both the men and the women have to go down [to Huillcapampa] because it's necessary.$_1$ They were going to put [the health post] on this side [of the river], but the others want it on the other side.$_2$ So I also want–what's it called?–they were thinking of holding a vote.$_3$ So we all have to go, I mean since–we all have to go down there, my friends.$_4$ We are an organized community, and we have to go down [there] and make our rights heard!$_5$ Okay?$_6$ That would be all, my friends.$_7$

While such public Spanish discourse was very common in the asamblea, the use of Matsigenka and Quechua was rare and was usually seen as inappropriate. This was not an explicit policy but rather an unspoken feeling among the community members. This division of linguistic practices partook of the same ideological principle of private/public differentiation that organized other domains of social practice in Yokiri: only Spanish was considered fit for community-level discourse, while Matsigenka and Quechua were generally reserved for private discourse among kin (though, as discussed in chapter 4, Quechua and Spanish were also associated with commercial and social interactions with neighboring Andean colonos and coffee merchants). Two ideological features of Spanish qualified it as suitable for public discourse in Yokiri: First, since its arrival in the region was understood to be relatively recent and thus not associated with any subset of the community as an ethnically marked "mother tongue," it was seen as impartial and consistent with the participatory ideology of the Habermasian public. Second, the use of Spanish (and the "official talk" discourse genre in particular) created indexical associations with public political institutions across the region and beyond, and thereby asserted the type of authority exercised in those institutions. These two ideological dimensions of Spanish as a language of public discourse are discussed in turn (below, then in the section called "Official Talk").

First, Spanish was understood to be a new feature of the linguistic panorama and, consequently, unconnected to claims of historically rooted ethnic affiliation. This was different from Matsigenka and Quechua, which were associated with either side of a deep historical conflict between Indigenous Matsigenka people and Andean colonos (the history, of course, is far more complex than this dichotomy suggests—these are local ideological formulations rather than empirically delimitable "groups"). While in the Andes Spanish is associated with centuries of violence and oppression, chapters 1–3 of this book have shown that some Matsigenkas had a longer and more intimate historical experience of domination by Quechua speakers. It was this (relative) freedom from partial and exclusionary associations that made Spanish fit for public discourse in a community that conceived of itself as multiethnic: because Spanish was no one's, it could be everyone's. This is an important element of the ideological construct of the public: rational and transparent debate must be conducted in a neutral and universally accessible language, lest private and partial interests jeopardize its integrity. Such ideologies of language were common, for instance, among some English-speaking voters in California in the 1980s who feared that Spanish-English bilingual ballots would introduce divisive partiality into what is meant to be an open and transparent democratic process (Woolard 1989). Similarly, national standardization movements often seek to institutionalize a public language that is seen as ethnically unmarked or "unnative" (Errington 2000, 206), and thus ostensibly disinterested and free from private, partial, ethnic, or regional commitments. That is, these languages can serve the purposes of national integration insofar as they belong to "everyone-because-no-one-in-particular" (Gal 2001, 33; see also Warner 1990).

Yokiri's Spanish-only culture of public speech was different from that of the neighboring Andean colono communities, where everyone spoke and understood Quechua, and where a handful of the older residents did not speak much Spanish. In these communities, Quechua and Spanish were both acceptable in public speech because they both served the function of (nearly) universal accessibility and because neither language was associated with a particular ethnic subset of the community. For this reason, speeches given in Quechua and Spanish in the nearby Andean settlement of Estrella during the visit of the municipal authorities in 2012 were considered perfectly acceptable. In transcript 16, from a meeting in Estrella, a man code-switched between Spanish and Quechua discourse in a plea for a road (Quechua discourse is underlined):

Transcript 16

Señor alcalde, señores regidores, compañeros, muy buenos días. <u>Wakin</u> compañer<u>uykuna</u> comenta<u>nku</u>, <u>manan kanchu</u> carretera. <u>Manan kan</u>–o sea, ruta–a veces vienen comentarios, ¿no? <u>Anchayta munayku</u>, señor alcalde.

Mr. Mayor, council members, my friends [i.e., other community members], good morning. <u>Some</u> of <u>my</u> friend<u>s</u> have commented, <u>there's no</u> road. <u>There's no</u>–I mean, road–sometimes people make comments, no? <u>That's what we want</u>, Mr. Mayor.

But while this use of Quechua public speech was acceptable and unremarkable in neighboring Andean settler communities, in Yokiri it would have been considered a provocative transgression of the community's public discursive space, regardless of the fact that most Yokiriños understood Quechua. Such incidents were not unknown in Yokiri, however: tensions mounted in one asamblea when a comunero with close ties to the rural agrarian society and economy asserted his superior knowledge of agriculture by embedding a brief Quechua statement about cash cropping in a larger exhortative speech in Spanish. (This incident was too sensitive for me to record.) It was incendiary for two reasons: First, not all of the comuneros understood Quechua, so it violated the public accessibility requirement. Second, the man's use of Quechua laid bare the truth that, while Quechua was widely spoken among the comuneros, it was also associated with an invasive economic and social system that Yokiriños regarded with great ambivalence. And insofar as the comunidad nativa system itself was established to protect Indigenous Amazonians from the encroachment of Andean colonos, the presence of Quechua in Yokiri—and particularly in the asamblea, the heart of the community's political identity—was a reminder of the painful recent history of Andean colonization.

On the other hand, the use of Matsigenka also violated the asamblea's principle of universal participation, since some Yokiriños did not understand Matsigenka as well as the others. Thus, even though the community was ideologically and legally constructed around the ethnic category of "Matsigenka," competence in the Matsigenka language was too thinly distributed for it to serve the Habermasian function of universally accessible public discourse in the asamblea. The transgression of this boundary, however, could also serve as a potent pragmatic strategy: if the use of Quechua in the public space of the asamblea represented a challenge to Yokiri's legitimacy as an Indigenous Amazonian community, the use of Matsigenka could assert Matsigenka ethnicity as a necessary criterion of belonging (and thus implicitly challenge the legitimacy of comuneros who counted Andean colonos among their parents and grandparents). These ideological complexities of Yokiri's culture of public discourse were the product of the community's particular history and were therefore different from those of both the neighboring Andean settlements and other Matsigenka communities across the region (such as the one discussed below).

Official Talk

In addition to its ideological construction as a neutral, nonpartisan language, Spanish—in particular the discourse genre of "official talk" and the closely connected register of "official Spanish"—also served the functions of public asamblea discourse through its indexical associations with such discursive contexts outside of Yokiri. Meetings across the country, from the neighboring Andean colono communities to the floor of the Peruvian Congress, were conducted in the genre of "official talk," and Yokiriños entextualized this genre in order to invoke and assert the mode of authority exercised in such contexts. This effect was heightened by the community leaders' municipal employee vests and the countless other signifiers of officialdom and Peruvianness draping the schoolroom walls, which served to minimize the indexical distance (a notion described by Briggs and Bauman [1992]) between the asamblea and the widely recognized "official public meeting" event type (Silverstein 2005). The institutionalization of Spanish as the language of democratic debate and bureaucratic procedure was taken further by its codification in the community's bylaws, according to which "every act must be recorded *in Spanish* in an authorized notebook, [and] the president, the secretary of the communal assembly, and no fewer than five other people must sign the acts" (Comunidad Nativa de Yoquiri 1990, 6; translation and emphasis mine). This sort of textual regime, in Jane Hill's words, "index[es] rationality over emotional commitment" (2001, 91). In these ways, the use of the official Spanish register and the invocation of the official talk genre helped establish the community public by creating interdiscursive links between Yokiri's asamblea and other such institutions across Peru.

Official talk in Yokiri was a particularly monologic discourse genre, normally performed while standing, in which a single speaker held the floor for a period that could range from less than a minute to more than twenty minutes. Speakers usually began their speech with an opening formula in which they acknowledged their fellow comuneros, and in some cases the presidente and other members of the directors' council, as addressees. When prominent non–community members visited Yokiri, speakers often named them as well. A typical example of such an opening formula, given in transcript 17, comes from a 2011 asamblea in which a woman rose to give a report on her recent trip to the education ministry (such opening formulas can also be seen in transcripts 19, 20, and 23 below). Notably, this speaker was the presidente's mother, but she refers to her son here as *señor jefe de la comunidad* (Mr. President of the Community), a common strategy for downplaying private kin associations (discussed below).

Transcript 17

Ante todos, compañeros, comuneros y comuneras, señor jefe de la comunidad, tengan muy buenos días.

Before all of you, my friends, [male and female] community members, Mr. President of the Community, good morning.

The speeches were normally brief and succinct, and they were addressed to the asamblea as a group rather than to specific individuals—what Warner (1992, 378) calls "impersonal reference," a central feature of public discourse around the world. Most speeches ended with a statement of conclusion or thanks, as in "Eso sería todo, compañeros" (That would be all, my friends) in transcript 15 above, or in one woman's closing of a 2011 speech in transcript 18 below (other examples can be found at the end of transcripts 19 and 23). Some of these speeches were followed by light applause.

Transcript 18

Esa sería mi palabra, muchas gracias a todos.

That's my word [i.e., my message], thank you very much to everyone.

With few exceptions, official talk in Yokiri was conducted in Spanish, with virtually no code-switching to Matsigenka or Quechua (Yokiri is unlike other Matsigenka communities in this respect, as I discuss below). The "official Spanish" register was immediately recognizable by people across the region and included features and constructions not normally used in other interactional contexts, such as the indirect first person construction *mi persona* (my person), used in phrases such as *éste es un regalo de mi persona para la comunidad* (this is a gift from my person [i.e., me] for the community). Public speeches also often featured the address term *compañeros* (as in transcripts 15, 16, 17, and 19), which can be glossed as "my friends" or "my companions," and which created a sense of egalitarian solidarity with other comuneros. Speakers also maintained their audience's attention by punctuating their speech with brief interrogative constructions, which added a sense of dialogism into otherwise overwhelmingly monologic stretches of discourse. These consisted of tag questions that the speaker posed and then immediately answered—see sentences 4–6 of transcript 19 below, in which the speaker says, "Tal vez no lo hemos hecho hasta hoy, ¿no? ¿Por qué? Por los motivos de que siempre hemos estado pues en dificultades" (Perhaps we haven't done it until today, no? Why? Because we have always had difficulties). Other times, these questions simply consisted of a brief *¿no?* (no?) or *¿no es así?* (isn't that right?), as in transcript 20 below.

The use of such features of Spanish official talk positioned the asamblea in the context of other public forums across Peru. It is therefore worth pointing out the most salient local model of the genre, which was produced by the municipal officials and functionaries who visited Yokiri periodically, and who were the immediate exemplars of the sort of democratic political modernity enacted in asambleas. For instance, in 2012 a local regidor (councilperson) stood and gave a long speech during the laying of the first stone for Yokiri's new municipally funded salón comunal, excerpted in transcript 19. He deployed many of the features described above—monologic participant structure, opening and closing formulas (sentences 1 and 7–8, respectively), frequent use of the address term *compañeros* (sentences 1 and 7), and brief interrogative constructions (sentences 1, 3, 4, 5, and 7) that introduced a sense of dialogism—in the service of modern political themes such as infrastructure development and engagement between the community and the local government.

Transcript 19

Bien, este, compañero regidor, ingeniero jefe del obra, el arquitecto Alex, al jefe de personal que nos ha acompañado hoy día–¿no?–Mario.$_1$ Y compañeros de esta comunidad de Yokiri.$_2$ En verdad para mí es realmente un día significativo–¿no?–estar junto a ustedes.$_3$ Tal vez no lo hemos hecho hasta hoy, ¿no?$_4$ ¿Por qué?$_5$ Por los motivos de que siempre hemos estado pues en dificultades.$_6$ . . . Bien, compañeros, con todo esto dicho, yo pues agradezco por escucharme, y también felicitarles–¿no?–a todos ustedes por estar hoy día.$_7$ Muchas gracias.$_8$

Okay, um, my friend the [fellow] councilman, the engineer, leader of the project, the architect Alex, [and] the team leader who has accompanied us today–no?–Mario.$_1$ And my friends in this community of Yokiri.$_2$ Truly, for me this is a really significant day–no?–being together with you.$_3$ Perhaps we haven't done it until today, no?$_4$ Why?$_5$ Because we have always had difficulties.$_6$ . . . Okay, my friends, with all of this said, I thank [you] for listening to me, and [I] also congratulate you–no?–to all of you for being [here] today.$_7$ Thank you very much.$_8$

Such instances of Spanish official talk by influential and politically prominent outsiders represented important models for public speech in Yokiri.

Performing Sacrificio and Policing the Private/Public Boundary

As a practical matter, the primary social function of the asamblea was to coordinate community action and mediate relationships among members of different kin groups (the planning of faenas, the organization of community celebrations, the making of decisions about the community's stance toward neighboring colonos, the distribution of public goods, interactions with the state, etc.). These things became more important as Yokiri's interactions with the world beyond its boundaries became more intense and sustained. Nearly all such concerns were organized around encouraging each family's commitment to the collectivity (i.e., the fulfillment of their duties as comuneros) and ensuring that each family benefited equally from community membership.

The asamblea, then, can be seen as an extended litigation of the boundary between the private (kin) and public (community) domains, and in particular as a context for enacting and monitoring the moral virtue of sacrificio described above. Indeed, the performance of sacrificio, in which comuneros recounted the hardships they endured on behalf of the community, was a major discursive theme in the asamblea. An example of such a performance is a speech delivered by a woman who had been appointed as the community's radio operator because of the proximity of her home to the antenna, and who listened to the transmissions and took messages every morning and evening. In 2011 she stood before the asamblea and described the great burden this public responsibility put on her—also saying, crucially, that she had borne this sacrificio without complaint or expectation of anything in return. This sort of unhesitating generosity was understood as a virtuous act within the moral context of community social organization. Dirigentes also frequently recounted their sacrificios in the idiom of *sufrimiento* (suffering)—for instance, in one asamblea a presidente said, "Yo he sufrido mucho por esta comunidad" (I have suffered greatly for this community). These invocations of sacrificio and sufrimiento drew on the moral ideologies of public action and served an important role in building commitment to the collectivity.[5]

The most spectacular performance of sacrificio I witnessed in Yokiri was during the planning of the festivities for the community's patron saint, Santa Rosa de Lima. The comuneros contributed material supplies for such events, and the two major kin groups of Yokiri used them as an opportunity to outdo each other with lavish acts of public sacrifice. In this asamblea, in which a few municipal officials were present, members of each household stood and publicly stated what they would contribute to the next year's celebrations. Hernán, a prominent member of one of the two main kin groups, keyed the genre of official talk by beginning with an opening formula similar to those discussed above, and by using features such as the honorific second-person forms. In transcript 20 he pledges to donate a bull (*torete*) to be slaughtered for the next year's celebration and uses his act of selflessness to imply that the municipal official is guilty of stinginess.

Transcript 20

SECRETARY: Procediendo el compromiso, vamos a ceder los micrófonos al compañero Hernán.[1]

[*passes microphone to Hernán*]

HERNÁN [*inaudible, joking confidently with his kin, laughing*]: Bueno, este, compañeros, este [inaudible] de Santa Rosita este lo que están aquí tengan todos muy buenas tardes.[2] Yo como mi voto de Santa Rosita de Lima, yo–como me estoy escuchando todo cómo se llama este, los que están presentes–¿no?–ya creo que ya [ha puesto] un torete, ¿no?[3] Y a mí, [inaudible] no me quedo atrás compañeros, y yo también voy a hacer, cómo se llama, voy a, cómo se llama, ya estoy–o sea que todos se achican–¿no?–a pesar que tienen plata a pesar que aquél cómo se llama mi amigo Hernán Díaz, ¿no?[4] A pesar que trabaje en municipio se ha achicado, ¿no?[5] Pero yo no voy a achicar, ¡yo voy a poner un torete![6]

COMMUNITY: ¡Bravo![7]

[*loud applause*]

SECRETARY: Moving along with the pledges, let's yield the microphone to our friend Hernán.[1]

[*passes microphone to Hernán*]

HERNÁN [*inaudible, joking confidently with his kin, laughing*]: Well, my friends, the [attendees] of [the festival] of Santa Rosita de Lima that are here, good afternoon to all of you.[2] I, as my pledge to Santa Rosita de Lima, I–since I've been listening to everyone present–no?–I think someone [pledged] a bull, no?[3] And me, [inaudible] I'm not going to be left behind, my friends, and I'm also going to make, what's it called, I'm going to, what's it called, I'm–I mean, everyone has been stingy–no?–even if they have money, even though he, what's his name, my friend [the municipal official] Hernán Díaz, no?[4] Even though he works for the government, he is stingy, no?[5] But I'm not going to be stingy, I'm going to contribute a bull![6]

COMMUNITY: Bravo![7]

[*loud applause*]

The contribution of a bull, which could cost more than 1,000 soles (around 350 dollars at the time), was a major act in Yokiri. The speaker's dramatic display of sacrificio and his defiant and confrontational tone positioned him and his kin

FIGURE 22 Bringing a bull to be eaten during a community festival in Yokiri, 2011. Photograph by the author.

group as a dominant force in the community and an exemplar of virtue in the moral context of the community public.

"No Tengo Ni Mamá Ni Papá": The Suppression of Kin Allegiances

Since the moral space of the asamblea was organized around the subordination of private interests to those of the community, the expression of kin allegiances in the asamblea context was hazardous. For this reason, another major theme in the asamblea was performing the separateness of family and community commitments. However, one of the fundamental structural tensions within the tiny community of Yokiri was that the presidente and the other dirigentes—the people responsible for enforcing the prioritization of community action over kin-based allegiances—were, of course, themselves members of kin groups with their own interests and agendas. The leaders made great efforts to avoid the appearance of impropriety by foregrounding the separateness of their public and private commitments. This was accomplished through innumerable acts of semiotic differentiation, including the use of Spanish official talk to assert the kin-neutral nature of the asamblea, and the discursive disavowal of kinship commitments. For example, while in most contexts Yokiriños referred to their kinspeople almost exclusively with kin terms, in the asamblea they used the same honorific constructions that they used for non-kin (such as the woman in transcript 17 above, who addresses her son, the president of the community, as "señor jefe de la comunidad," or "Mr. President of the Community"). On another occasion, shown in the following transcript, the presidente listed the names of several community members and only used the honorific title *señor* (Mr.) for his own father, Aníbal (underlined):

Transcript 21

. . . cuarto, Julián; quinto, Santiago; como sexto tenemos al <u>señor Aníbal</u>; séptimo Mario. . . .

. . . fourth, Julián; fifth, Santiago; as the sixth we have <u>Mr. Aníbal</u>; seventh, Mario. . . .

These acts of semiotic differentiation entailed a public space populated by comuneros rather than kinsmen, and reassured members of the other kin groups that the elected officials could be trusted to act in the interest of the collectivity rather than of their families.

An example of the delicate negotiation of kin and community commitments was a conflict between Yokiri's two major kin groups that developed in 2012. The foreman of a municipal construction crew working in Yokiri needed a cook for his workers, and prominent women from each of the community's two major kin groups declared their interest in being hired. It fell to the asamblea and the presidente to choose which of the women would get the prestigious and remunerative job. However, one of the nominees was the presidente's kin, which presented a clear conflict of interest. This dispute went unresolved for several days, and eventually led to an unusually frank public discussion about the management of private and public commitments. During the meeting the presidente made a long and emotional plea on behalf of community organización, and he reaffirmed the boundary between private and public spheres by promising to leave his own kin-level commitments out of community matters. In his words: "En la asamblea, no tengo ni mamá ni papá" (In the asamblea, I have neither a mother nor a father)—that is, in the public space of the community forum, there are no kinsmen, only comuneros.

Yokiri's Public Discourse in Comparative Perspective

The role of public discourse in Yokiri's enactment of community-level social organization becomes particularly clear when it is compared with corresponding practices in other comunidades nativas of the Alto Urubamba. The next example comes from a larger and more remote community that had just begun to interact regularly with outsiders over the previous several years. At that point, the public/private semiotic principle had not been firmly established as a framework for sorting the domains of community and family commitments, dividing spaces and sociolinguistic practices, and enforcing the new type of morality—characterized by sacrificio and the suppression of kin allegiances—associated with the public political subject of the comunero.

For the community's 2011 anniversary, the dirigentes planned an ambitious multiday celebration featuring a soccer tournament, speeches, drinking, feasting, and dancing. Municipal officials and other local dignitaries were invited, and the comuneros were expected to bring *masato* (yuca beer) for the guests and carry on the merriment for as long as they could last. The celebrations appeared to be successful during the first afternoon, but when the party moved indoors for speeches, dancing, and the distribution of soccer jerseys, the crowd began to thin. The remaining comuneros sat with their kin and talked among themselves in Matsigenka instead of listening to the speeches, and the dirigentes had to shout over the din to make themselves heard. Eventually, once the jerseys had been distributed, the remaining comuneros began to file out of the salón comunal and walk home early. The dirigentes were embarrassed by this because they felt it reflected poorly on their leadership and the community's organización. As the comuneros rose to leave, a panicked leader made the following plaintive appeal (Spanish in plain text, Matsigenka underlined):

Transcript 22

Señores comuneros, por favor, <u>gara piaigai, tera ontsonkatempa</u>, por favor,[1] . . .
Suplico a cada uno de ustedes, quedan invitados para poder iniciar este aniversario
que concierne con nuestro [X] años de vida institucional,[2]

Fellow community members, please, <u>don't leave, it's not over [yet]</u>, please.$_1$ . . . I beg each of you, you are invited so that we can begin this anniversary regarding our [X] years of institutional life.$_2$

This plea for participation illustrates the fragile nature of the community political structure, as well as some of the discursive strategies that leaders deploy in its defense. For instance, the speaker explicitly invokes the moral domain of the community public by addressing the attendees as comuneros (sentence 1) and by referring repeatedly to the institutional structure that unites them. He also frames his discourse as public by deploying Spanish official talk, as indicated by the opening formula "señores comuneros, por favor" (fellow community members, please). Recognizing that his addressees are unmoved by his entreaties, however, he switches to Matsigenka to make a personal and intimate appeal outside of the frame of public discourse: "Gara piaigai, tera ontsonkatempa" (Don't leave, it's not over [yet]). In this utterance, code-switching serves as a contextualization cue (Gumperz 1982) signaling the alteration between two "voices" (Bakhtin 1981), each connected to distinct ideologies and moral regimes (J. H. Hill 1995). Through Spanish he inhabits the position of the official leader whose authority lies in a powerful but foreign system of public value, while through Matsigenka he steps outside of this position to speak as a kinsman, friend, and neighbor who, along with his audience, also regards this system from the outside.

Such discursive practices were common in this community, and many dirigentes code-switched between Spanish and Matsigenka to assert both modes of authority. For instance, during the same evening a few current and former dirigentes delivered speeches to the remaining comuneros. They felt frustrated and embarrassed by the event, and some used their speeches to exhort their fellow community members to take community involvement more seriously. To make this point, a former leader recounted the difficulties of the land titling process to illustrate the sacrificio and sufrimiento that he had endured on behalf of the community (transcript 23). As in transcript 22 above, this speech is characterized by frequent Spanish-Matsigenka code-switching as the speaker moves between the two modes of social authority (Spanish in plain type, Matsigenka underlined).

Transcript 23

Eh, buenas noches señores, señores directivos y todos, muy buenas noches, ¿no?$_{1...}$
En el año [X] sale el título de propiedad de [community name].$_2$ <u>Ovashi otima-</u>

nunganira aka.[3] De repente viroegi yoga ikyari kimoiganagitsi te pineaigena.[4] Naroegi nantavageigake maani, aunque no será mucho.[5] Maika nanuventakero ashi comunidad, a lo menos debemos felicitar a [name], que ha luchado bastante, iniaventakera ashi comunidad ompeganakempara–ontimakera ampatoitakempara agaigakerora gipatsiegite.[6] Ganiri yagapitsahaigiro yoga virakocha.[7] . . . Oga otimakera maika como día como veinticuatro nokogavetake irinake presidente de la comunidad [inaudible] y con toda la nueva junta directiva nonei aryori maika shineventaigakemparo shatekaigakempara aka maganiro todos los comuneros, pogavoaigakera sekatsi ashi shitea.[8] Sin embargo noneavetaro maika ontirika pikisaigaka onti kisaigankicha yonta tera impokaige ahorita.[9] Pairatake mameri.[10] Kantaka ontinirika tata oita yovetsikaiganake, noneakero naro tera onkametite.[11] Estoy triste.[12] Lamentablemente la nueva junta directiva ikogaigavetaka irovetsikakerora kameti, pero tyani kañoigankitsi?[13] Viroegita kañoigankitsi, comuneros.[14] Tenika patsipereigero viro pero sí naroegi natsipereaventaigakero para que salga la titulación oka de siete mil hectáreas y otra titulación de la ampliación.[15] Nashi novetsikaigakerira naroegi nantaigavetakarira, viroegi jóvenes te pogogeeronika–viro pineirokari okavagetaka kogapage.[16] Pisureiganaka pogutera shitea, y ¡no!.[17] Noneakero naro te onkametite.[18] Antari maika sureigakemparomera es una celebración conmemorativo patoigakempara maganiro ariangi gaveakoigakerora nuestra comunidad otimakera.[19] Hemos tenido título, game otimi título, tya gaigakero timaigakera?[20] Matsi ari timake karaseigake inkisaigapaakae inti virakocha.[21] Eso sería mi única recomendación, gracias.[22]

Um, good evening sirs, directors, and everyone, very good evening, no?[1] . . . In the year [X] we got the property title for the community of [community name].[2] That's why it's here.[3] Perhaps you young ones don't know who I am.[4] We [elders] did some work, even if it wasn't much.[5] We traveled [to complete the titling] for the community, at least we should congratulate [name], who has fought a lot, he has conversed [i.e., made the official arrangements] so that the community would become–so that there would be, so that we could get together and get our land.[6] So that the colonists don't take it away.[7] . . . Now on a day like the twenty-fourth, I wanted the president of the community [inaudible] to be here with all of the new directors' council, [and] I thought that we were going to celebrate it, and that [the building] would be full of all, all the community members, [and] that they would bring yuca for masato.[8] Regardless, from my perspective it seems that the ones who didn't come now are annoyed and angry now.[9] Nobody is here.[10] It seems that they're doing something wrong, from my point of view that's not good.[11] I am sad.$_{12}$ Unfortunately the new directors' council <u>wanted to have a good [cele-bration]</u>, but <u>who are the guilty ones?</u>$_{13}$ <u>You are the guilty ones</u>, comuneros.$_{14}$ <u>You haven't suffered</u>, but <u>we [exclusive]</u> have <u>suffered</u> in order to obtain the title, <u>um,</u> to seven thousand hectares and the other title to the territorial extension.$_{15}$ <u>What we did during our tenure, what we were doing, you</u> young people <u>don't know—you must think it just happened by itself.</u>$_{16}$ <u>You thought about bringing masato</u>, but no!$_{17}$ <u>From my point of view it's not good.</u>$_{18}$ <u>We would have thought that since</u> it's a commemorative celebration, <u>everyone would have come together, for the effort and the achievement to make</u> our community <u>exist.</u>$_{19}$ We got the title, [because] <u>if there weren't a title, where would we find to live?</u>$_{20}$ <u>If we hadn't lived and made our agricultural plots here, the colonists would have pushed us out.</u>$_{21}$ That's my only recommendation, thank you.$_{22}$

In this emotional speech, the former dirigente blamed the assembled community members for what he viewed as a disappointing anniversary celebration (e.g., in sentence 14, "Viroegita kañoigankitsi, comuneros," or "You are the guilty ones, comuneros"), which he attributed to their unwillingness to meet the obligations of the comunero. The speaker relates this message through the careful management of voice and authority, in particular through his code-switching practices. First, he invokes the public authority of the community by framing his remarks as a performance of public official talk, as in the opening (sentence 1) and closing (sentence 22) formulas described above. He also uses Spanish to highlight concepts linked to the comunidad nativa social structure—for instance, "es una celebración conmemorativo" (it's a commemorative celebration; sentence 19) and "hemos tenido título" (we got the title; sentence 20).[6] The speech also makes frequent references to sufrimiento and sacrificio (e.g., "Tenika patsipereigero viro pero sí naroegi natsipereaventaigakero," or "You haven't suffered, but we [exclusive] have suffered"; sentence 15) that invoke the morality of the community public.

As above, the speaker switches frequently between Matsigenka and Spanish to maintain a foot in both domains of authority. For instance, in some cases he frames his utterances as official talk through the use of Spanish discourse markers and then continues his utterance in Matsigenka to appeal to his audience in a more personal manner. In sentence 4, for example, he establishes his utterance as official talk with a loud Spanish *de repente* (perhaps), then follows this with Matsigenka discourse (Spanish emphasized): "*De repente* viroegi yoga ikyari kimoiganagitsi te pineaigana" (*Perhaps* you young ones don't know who I am).

Similarly, in sentence 9 the speaker keys the frame of official talk by shouting the Spanish discourse marker *sin embargo* (regardless, nevertheless) over the din before making a personal and emotional appeal to his audience in Matsigenka: "*Sin embargo*, noneavetaro maika ontirika pikisaigaka onti kisaigankicha yonta tera impokaige *ahorita*" (*Regardless*, from my perspective it seems that you're angry, and the ones who are angry didn't come *now*).

A similar discursive strategy was the pairing of a Spanish utterance that reconfirmed the speaker's position of official authority with a Matsigenka utterance that aligned the speaker personally with his or her audience. For instance, in both sentences 2–3 and sentence 20 above, the speaker assumes the official voice to introduce the subject of land titling and then switches to Matsigenka to reflect upon the importance of that subject from the perspective of his kinspeople and fellow comuneros in the audience (Matsigenka italicized here). In the first case, he says, "En el año [X] sale el titulo de propiedad de [community name]. *Ovashi otimanunganira aka*" (In the year [X] we got the property title for the community of [community name]. *That's why it's here*). In the second: "Hemos tenido título, *game otimi* título, *tya gaigakero timaigakera?*" (We got the title, *[because] if there weren't* a title, *where would we find to live?*).

This discursive strategy allowed the leader to assert the legitimacy of the comunidad nativa's fragile community structure while also aligning himself with an audience that was not yet fully committed to it. In a sense, he came as close as possible to speaking both languages at once, as a way of keeping a foot in each domain of authority. By contrast with this community, community-level social organization in Yokiri was taken for granted by the time of my fieldwork, and the distinction between private and public social, moral, and discursive spaces had been carefully delineated. For this reason, code-switching was rare in the asamblea. But in the comunidad nativa just examined, public code-switching practices were tied to the incipient nature of the private/public boundary and the still-contested nature of the community as a unit of social organization.

Conclusion

In the Alto Urubamba and other regions of Peruvian Amazonia, the legal structure of the comunidad nativa had existed for nearly forty years by the time of my fieldwork in 2009–12. The principles of community-level social organization that it prescribes were quite foreign to the Matsigenkas' traditional dispersed and atomistic kinship-based pattern. However, at that point, the majority of the residents of many communities had been born after the comunidades nativas law, and they had begun to embrace its social organizational principles. In Yokiri, the creation of a community from a handful of dispersed families was achieved by cleaving off a new domain of social life from that of the kin group, through the introduction of a semiotic distinction between public and private commitments. The creation of the public political subject of the comunero—defined in opposition to the family member and morally obligated to people beyond the private world of kin relations—was created and maintained in myriad social and discursive practices. For Yokiriños, the most important of these was the Habermasian forum of the asamblea, where public subjectivity was created and enacted through discursive features such as the nearly exclusive use of Spanish, the use of the "official talk" discourse genre and the "official Spanish" register, the performance of *sacrificio* (sacrifice), and the disavowal of family commitments. While other studies have examined the social, political, ecological, and historical dimensions of the adoption of the comunidad nativa system in Peruvian Amazonia, the discursive and linguistic features of this process as it is enacted and negotiated at the micro level of interaction are also important for understanding how this new framework of social organization is taking hold.

During my fieldwork, community social organization was one of the primary mechanisms through which Matsigenkas across the Alto Urubamba worked to establish a place for themselves amid the rapidly changing frontier society. While people in communities like Yokiri spent much of their time producing coffee and engaging in the agrarian economy that had come to surround them—speaking Quechua with merchants and neighboring colonos, attending workshops, and the like—they established a place for themselves apart from that society as communities. Asamblea discourse was a way of managing the encroachment of the frontier society and engaging with it on their terms—for instance, when the comuneros of Tsimiato at the beginning of this chapter put aside their kin commitments and developed a unified, community-wide stance to oppose the colono at their border. The incorporation of Matsigenkas into colono society should thus not be thought of in terms of "assimilation" or "acculturation," but rather in terms of a dynamic interplay between integration and resistance that emerged in particular moments, spaces, and, above all, acts of speaking.

Chapter 6

Speaking About the Land

Across the Yavero Valley from Yokiri there is a small river called Yogeato, locally spelled Yoyato, which means both "Rainbow River" and "Rainbow Demon River" (*yoge*, "rainbow, demon"; *-ato*, "water, river"). It is a beautiful, cool, blue-tinted torrent that winds beneath a canopy of trees through one of the remotest and most densely forested parts of the valley. The Yogeato River forms one boundary of the Santuario Nacional Megantoni protected area (see map 2), so it is subject to stringent environmental restrictions, as well as much technical and legal discussion in Spanish among local officials and environmental advocates in the region's musty, paper-strewn municipal offices. During my fieldwork, newly arriving colonos talked excitedly over bottles of beer in dirt-floored frontier bars, in Quechua, about the cheap, high-quality land still available in the Yogeato Valley; Yokiriños also spoke about the valley in their homes, in Matsigenka, invoking it as a place where their ancestors had once sought refuge from the slave raids of the early-twentieth-century rubber industry. At the same time, nearby Matsigenkas warned their children, in Matsigenka, that the Yogeato River was the home of a malevolent *yoge* (rainbow demon), whose multicolored cushma gown gives it the outward form of rainbows and ferruginous soils, and which curses anyone who sees it with skin rashes, miscarriages, or violent, fatal diarrhea (Baer 1994, 110; Renard-Casevitz and Dollfus 1988, 16; Ferrero 1966, 343; Vargas Pereira and Vargas Pereira 2013, 233).[1]

I found it remarkable that a single place like the Yogeato River could mean so many things to so many people, and that it could be bound up in so many different ways of talking and thinking about the landscape. Even more remarkable was that the very same individuals talked about the Yogeato River in these different ways between one conversation and the next. That is, it was not the case that Matsigenkas talked about the land in one way, colonos in another, and agents of the state in a third, for instance, but rather that particular ways of speaking about the land were associated with particular types of interactions and activities, which often crosscut ethnicity and background. Landscape discourses inhered in particular moments, situations, and purposes—connected, in turn, to particular languages and registers—not just in people (though people engaged in those situations to varying degrees, and with varying degrees of comfort and authority, as we saw in chapter 4). Thus, over the course of my fieldwork, I came to understand that the changing landscape was intimately connected to changing ways of talking about the landscape, and that Matsigenkas and colonos encountered each other as much on this linguistic terrain as on the physical terrain of the valley. In this view, the ideological contours of daily multilingual practice, the changing uses of the land, and the local interethnic encounter were inseparable.

Landscape discourses have played a prominent role in various parts of this book so far. In chapter 4, I described how Matsigenkas and colonos alike had come to use techno-scientific language about soil quality, fertilizers, elevation, and sun exposure, usually in Spanish, and particularly in municipal training workshops. These discourses focused on the material and chemical properties of the land and how to manipulate and control them to produce coffee that would command the highest possible price—thereby bringing a particular consumerist future within the reach of novice colono and Matsigenka farmers. Meanwhile, at the beginning of chapter 5, I discussed how members of a comunidad nativa and a neighboring colono engaged in an escalating land conflict, and how they each used legal and extralegal strategies to assert their claims. These strategies drew on the discourse of land as a bounded possession—in Spanish—and played out through impassioned asamblea speeches about autonomy, conversations with surveyors while poring over maps, the consultation of land deeds in the provincial capital, and the careful counting and recording of measured paces between landscape features. These interactions were oriented toward aspirations to political autonomy and self-sufficiency. In this chapter, I describe how such discourses of the land sat alongside others—in particular, Matsigenkas' long, detailed stories about what kinds of agentive beings inhabit the landscape (e.g., the yoge mentioned above) and about how the actions and moral transgressions of ancient humans gave rise to the world as it is today.

I argue that all of these acts of speaking about the landscape, and innumerable others as well, are indexically associated with different spaces, relationships, land use practices, ideas of history, types of morality, languages, registers, discourse genres, and even ontologies of the animate world. In a place like the Alto Urubamba frontier, where the grueling daily work of making a place for oneself in the tumultuous emerging economy requires constant, hands-on interpretation of the landscape, people move between such discourses from one conversation to the next. A story in Matsigenka about a dangerous monkey demon that jealously guards a nearby forest grove might be interrupted to plan the next day's weeding or fertilizing in Spanish, and then resumed; a discussion in Spanish about how to buy a parcel of land in a far-flung corner of the valley might turn into a mytho-historical speculation, in Quechua, on the Inka archaeological footprint in the forest. These are not just switches between topics and languages; they are also switches between conceptualizations of the landscape, each of which sits within broader ideas about economic activity, history, and even the kinds of things that exist in the world. Seen this way, the local culture of language use is intimately linked to the varied daily experience of the landscape itself. An important corollary of this connection is that as the landscape is transformed, so too are the ways in which people speak about it—and vice versa, since so much of the work of becoming a farmer is, in fact, linguistic work, as I argued in chapter 4.

This chapter is about some of the different ways people in the Alto Urubamba talked about the landscape amid the social, economic, and environmental turmoil of frontier expansion, and how these ways of speaking were embedded in broader conceptualizations of the world. Discourse about the landscape in the Alto Urubamba is so vast and varied that a comprehensive description would fill a bookcase; in this chapter, I limit my discussion to just two moments of landscape-language connection. In the first part of the chapter, I examine five cases of how Yokiriños talked about the elusive etymology of the toponym Yokiri. This is such a narrow aspect of language and landscape that it might seem almost trivial. However, the discourses that people invoked to reflect on the origin of this opaque toponym reveal a great deal about how they conceptualized the landscape of the Yokiri Valley and their own place in the emerging frontier society. The second part of the chapter turns to a proposal, made by a Yokiriño man, to build a road through the community to open new sections of the Yokiri Valley to intensive coffee production. This would have brought

Yokiri's farmers up the slopes of a mountain named Tampianironi and into contact with a dangerous wind demon that lives there—a key figure in the stories of Yokiri's etymological origin presented in the first part of this chapter—and which is widely believed to strike down trespassers on its territory. Interestingly, this danger was not raised in the discussion of the new road; instead, the proposal was turned down simply because the comuneros wished to invest the money elsewhere. In other words, this demon provoked fear in Yokiriños as they talked in Matsigenka about the landscape in mythical terms by the hearthside, but not in the public space of Spanish asamblea oratory about infrastructure and economic development. This disjuncture shows that different conceptualizations of the landscape operated in different interactional contexts in Yokiri, each of which was linked to different places, histories, institutions, and ideologies of language. In the changing social and environmental world of the Alto Urubamba frontier, this multiplicity of landscape discourses was a fact of everyday life and was not necessarily considered to be contradictory.

Language, Landscape, and Equivocation

One dimension of the relationship that some Matsigenkas conducted with the landscape of Yokiri is consistent with the principles of perspectivism, a kind of ontological system that has been described by anthropologists in various forms across the Indigenous societies of Amazonia. For these Yokiriños, many of the animals, plants, and other entities that populate the world were humans or deities during earlier "presocial times" (Santos-Granero 2004, 98). These beings adopted their current forms through the process of "cosmological transformism" (Viveiros de Castro 1998, 471), and their human subjectivity, consciousness, and agency persist even in these new forms (Rosengren 2006). These inner human essences are sometimes referred to in the Amazonianist literature as the "doubles" or "spirit rulers" of the animals, plants, and other beings (see, e.g., A. W. Johnson 2003). This was the case, for instance, with the murderous human-like yoge that inhabited the Yogeato River, and which revealed itself to humans by its multicolored garment, in the form of rainbows or shimmery ferruginous soils. The presence of such entities makes interactions between humans and other beings in the landscape into moments of intersubjectivity, communication, and sociality (Descola 1994). For instance, Allen Johnson observes about Matsigenka hunting practices: "When the hunter encounters a male howler monkey in the forest, he is encountering the powerful spirit ruler, the *seripigari* (shaman) of the origin folktale, made manifest in the body of this particular animal" (2003, 205; see also, e.g., Shepard 2002). In Matsigenka cosmology, these beings mostly exert a malevolent influence on humans and can be a great source of danger.

Significantly, these primordial beings and their ancient activities are often closely associated with specific places in the landscape. For instance, a place called Komempiniku, where the Kiteni and Koshireni Rivers nearly meet as they join the Urubamba, is thought to be where Kashiri (the moon deity) used wood from the *komempi* tree to create a huge weir before teaching humans how to fish (Renard-Casevitz and Dollfus 1988, 11). The ruins of this great weir still sit at the bottom of the Urubamba River, creating a dangerous rapid that caused problems for commercial boat pilots before the river port moved downriver to Tintinikiato and Ivochote in the 1980s. Here, Matsigenka mythology and landscape are inseparable. Fernando Santos-Granero (2004, 94) describes a similar phenomenon among other speakers of Arawak languages in the Peruvian Amazon, where such "emplaced myths" serve to "confer meaning to particular landmarks," though he also describes ritual practices associated with those myths that do not have an analogue in Yokiri (see also Santos-Granero 1998; Santos-Granero also shows how more recent historical events have continued to contribute to the mythic Yanesha' landscape of central Peru over the last few centuries). As we will see in the next section, this is precisely how some Yokiriños explained the origin of Yokiri's landscape: they linked a toponym (Yokiri) with particular events in ancient times, in which nonhuman actors visited violence upon human interactants.

In Yokiri and other communities on the Alto Urubamba coffee frontier, this way of talking about the landscape and its history mostly occurred during my fieldwork in 2009–12 in myth narrations. These narrations were a rarefied kind of monologic interactional genre, almost always performed in the home, in which one of the community's elders recounted the origins of particular animals, plants, and places before an audience of kin members. These narrations could last for hours at a time and were almost always performed in a purist variety of Matsigenka that admitted little code-switching and lexical borrowing from Spanish (and even less from Quechua). As such, these narrations were ideologized as culturally exemplary models of Matsigenka speech (cf. Kroskrity 1998), even though they were rare and quite unrepresentative of the mixed speech practices that predominated in nearly every other interactional context.

These performances were characterized by a particular set of enregistered discourse features (Agha 2005) that were indexically associated with the mythic discourse genre, including dramatic pitch contours, special voices, and a distinctive kind of narrative rhythm created through interclausal recapitulative linkage constructions, which I describe below (see also Emlen 2019). They also made frequent use of *ideophones*, which imitate the sensory experience of the things they represent, like bird calls or the sound of thunder. That is, they are "depictive" in the sense that they "are uttered not for the purpose of referring but with the intention of simulating a sensory perception" (Nuckolls et al. 2016, 96). Ideophones were used in all kinds of storytelling in Yokiri, including mythic and personal narratives, and they added a degree of drama and engagement to the performances. By using these kinds of discursive features, Yokiriños could frame their speech as an instance of mythic speech and thereby invoke all of the ontological and moral associations of Matsigenka cosmology.

The kinds of ontological principles discussed above are widespread in Indigenous Amazonian societies, and the theoretical tradition of perspectivism has received a great deal of attention among anthropologists over the last couple of decades. One insight related to this matter that is offered by a place like Yokiri is how these landscape conceptualizations might be complicated when their adherents come from different backgrounds and participate in the surrounding Andean agrarian society, and in other national discourses and institutions, to differing degrees (and at different moments). What happens when—as we will see in this chapter—people talk about the very same parts of the landscape in dramatically different terms from one household to the next and from one interaction to the next? This problem of co-present ontological principles is raised by Marisol de la Cadena (2010, 2015), who points out that what one person might see as a mountain in the southern Peruvian Andes, another might see as an animate being. This kind of ontological disjuncture—how the same "thing" might be seen to have a different essence or nature from different ontological perspectives—is what de la Cadena and Eduardo Viveiros de Castro call "equivocation": "referential alterity between homonymic concepts" (Viveiros de Castro 2004, 5). That is, a single mountain like Ausangate might in fact be "more than one but less than two entities"—subject to interpretation through multiple ontological frames (de la Cadena 2010, 351).

The simple observation that I wish to make on this subject is that when we focus on language use in Yokiri, it becomes clear that such equivocations exist not just between people with different ontological outlooks, but also among the same people between one kind of interactional context and the next. In such a view, neither ontological frame necessarily encompasses the totality of experience. That is, one ontological casting of the landscape might be articulated during Matsigenka-language myth narrations in the home, and another might be invoked in conversations about infrastructure and economic development, in Spanish, during an asamblea in the public meeting hall—crucially, *by the very same people*. Such an approach places ontological equivocation in the varied interactional and linguistic contexts of everyday life, which become inseparable from the local sociolinguistic dynamics of the multiethnic frontier.

Etymology, History, and Politics

During my time in the Alto Urubamba, I found that toponym etymologies— stories about how places got their names—were an important nexus between language, ontology, landscape, history, and politics. Indeed, to speak about the land and how it got its names in any society is to invoke a particular understanding of history that plays out in everyday conversation (Basso 1996). Matsigenka speakers in the Alto Urubamba gave long and detailed explanations of how particular places got their names, which were often anchored in cosmological discourses about the origin of the world and its inhabitants. Andean migrants, for their part, renamed the landscape as they inhabited it, giving settlements in the nearby Yavero Valley names like Túpac Amaru (the name of the last Inka ruler), Nueva Luz (meaning "New Light," a settlement formed by Evangelicals and given a name celebrating the establishment of a Godly community in the forest), and Penetración (or "Penetration," invoking the discourse of triumphant colonization in the forest). These toponyms, which each invoked different ideas about history and the landscape, sat uncomfortably alongside Matsigenka toponyms, which called up an entirely different world of beings and history (to those who knew their story).

Toponymy is political, to be sure. During the second Iraq war, the American military created its own street map of Baghdad, overlaying the original with names like "California Street" and "Coors Street"; simultaneously, the newly empowered Iraqi Shi'a community replaced some city place names associated with Saddam Hussein's fallen Sunni regime (Rose-Redwood, Alderman, and Azaryahu 2010). Basque nationalists painted over Spanish versions of toponyms on road signs, asserting a particular ethnolinguistic politics of place (Raento and

Watson 2000). Everywhere, to name a place is to assert a particular interpretation of it and to claim authority over it. Sometimes place names in the Alto Urubamba threw the ethnic politics of the valley into similarly sharp relief, albeit in more subtle and less public ways. Colonos stumbled over Matsigenka words, to the snickers of Matsigenka speakers, betraying their status as newcomers in a foreign landscape. Some Matsigenka speakers even asserted their own prior claim to the landscape by declaring that local Quechua toponyms were translations of earlier Matsigenka ones. For instance, one Matsigenka man in a heavily colonized part of the valley told me that the Quellomayo River—"Yellow River" in Quechua—was originally called by the Matsigenka name Kiteriari, of the same meaning (see below). A prominent Matsigenka leader, similarly, proclaimed in a public speech in the provincial capital of Quillabamba that the Quechua toponym Quillabamba (Plain of the Moon)—the political and economic heart of Andean colonization in the Alto Urubamba—named a place that had previously been called Ivampane Kashiri (Plain of the Moon) in Matsigenka (see below).[2]

	Quechua	Matsigenka	
a:	*Quellomayo*	*Kiteriari*	
	q'illu mayu	*kiteri-ari*	
	yellow river	yellow-RIVER	
	"Yellow River"	"Yellow River"	
b:	*Quillabamba*	*Ivampane Kashiri*	
	killa pampa	*i-pampa-ne*	*kashiri*
	moon plain	3M-plain-ALIEN.POSS	moon
	"Plain of the Moon"	"Plain of the Moon"	

In this way, some Matsigenkas asserted a layer of history in the landscape that lay below, and prior to, the region's Andean colonization. The implication was that Matsigenkas had a claim to historical legitimacy in the landscape that newly arriving Quechua speakers did not. That neither of the etymological stories above would be endorsed by a lexicographer does not diminish their efficacy as potent political statements about belonging and legitimacy in the tense multiethnic, multilingual frontier society of the Alto Urubamba.

It was in this context of politicized etymology that I asked people what I thought to be a straightforward question: "What does the name Yokiri mean?" To my surprise, nearly everyone I asked had a different answer to that question. This was because Yokiri does not, in fact, have an obvious interpretation in Matsigenka—indeed, it might not even originate in Matsigenka, as I discuss below—which freed the toponym from the etymological constraints of most literal, transparent Matsigenka toponyms. Yokiri was thus, relative to other toponyms, something of a blank etymological canvas, affording interpretations that made explicit markedly different perspectives on the relationship between history, people, and landscape in the region. At stake in the various explanations that I collected were whose ancestors lived in this place in generations past, who had the authority to speak about matters of history and myth, and even what kinds of beings inhabit the landscape and exert agency in the world. In the following sections, I discuss five instances in which people discussed the etymology of Yokiri during my fieldwork there in 2011–12, how these etymological discourses appeared in different interactional contexts, and how they drew on particular conceptualizations of the landscape and its history.

In Yokiri, as everywhere, naming and discussing the landscape was a central part of inhabiting it and making it intelligible. This was true in a practical sense, as Yokiriños tended to orient themselves in geographical space in relation to streams, rivers, hills, forested areas, and other salient landscape features, which were encoded in place names (Shepard et al. 2001). As I discussed in chapter 2, Matsigenka place names are usually morphologically transparent. For instance, the Tsimiato River (*tsimi*, "clay lick," + -*ato*, "water, river") is near a clay lick that attracts birds; Tairishi (*tairi*, a tree species of genus *Erythrina*, + -*shi*, "grove") is an area of forest in Yokiri populated by *tairi* trees; and the Toturoato River (*toturo*, a species of snail, + -*ato*, "water, river") is where some Yokiriños went to collect small *toturo* snails. Some of these names were known up and down the lower Yavero Valley, while others were very local and unknown beyond individual families.

However, as discussed above, invoking an animal, plant, or particular landscape feature in a toponym is rarely a matter of simply referring to a feature of what might be called, from a Western perspective, the "natural world." For instance, some Matsigenka speakers encounter the Yogeato River discussed above not just in terms of its reference to the rainbow as a meteorological phenomenon but also with reference to the spirit that takes the rainbow's form. These referents can be just as real and noteworthy as the salt licks and forest groves for which other places are named; toponymy serves as a vast map of ancient events and spiritual danger inscribed on the landscape (for those who know how to interpret it). For other Yokiriños (particularly the younger generation and those who came from the Andes), these are "just names," or they are purely geographical in their reference. Some Yokiriños who grew up in the nearby Dominican mission of Chirumbia also told me that these beings referred to by place names existed, but that being baptized protected the people from their malevolent agency, illustrating the variation in landscape experiences even within the small community of Yokiri.

Yokiri, however, presents an etymological conundrum. Despite being the most important toponym in the Yokiri Valley—around which the community's political identity is formed—it does not follow the transparent template by which most Matsigenka toponyms are formed. In fact, it may not even come from Matsigenka but rather from one of the unknown languages that preceded the valley's three contemporary languages (see chapter 2).[3] However, the very opacity of the toponym affords the assertion of a certain specialist knowledge of origins, the drawing of a line of legitimacy between Matsigenkas and colonos, as well as a finer-grained distinction about which families and individuals *know the real story*. That is, anyone who understands Matsigenka knows why the river running by the clay lick is called Tsimiato, but to know the significance of an inscrutable toponym like Yokiri is to know something very special indeed. The five etymological discourses that follow deal with this inscrutability in different ways and frame it within particular conceptualizations of the landscape, its history, and the distribution of knowledge in the frontier society.

Etymological Discourse 1: Newcomers, Culture Loss, and Landscape History as Specialist Knowledge

The first etymological discourse to be discussed here was the most common during my fieldwork: the profession of ignorance regarding a toponym's origin and referral to a more qualified cultural authority. At the current nexus of language, history, and landscape, cultural knowledge about the land is in decline as the forest becomes farmland and the younger generations turn their attention away from the concerns of their grandparents. In the heterogeneous social context of the agricultural frontier, where Andean colonos live side by side with Matsigenkas from a wide range of circumstances and where young people tend to pursue interests other than traditional Matsigenka culture, such knowledge is thought to be unevenly distributed. This is true of the distinction between colonos and Matsigenkas: one colono in the frontier settlement of Ivochote wondered in Spanish about that settlement's name, "¿Qué será en su idioma de ellos?" (What might that mean in their language?). His use of *ellos* (them), here, reflects the dim awareness that many Andean colonos have of their Matsigenka neighbors and the language that they speak.

However, some Yokiriños themselves professed ignorance of even the most transparent toponyms and deferred to older community members with greater knowledge of the region's history. Thus the attribution of cultural authority was subject to a recursive set of oppositions (Irvine and Gal 2000): residents of the broader region referred etymological queries to Matsigenkas, Matsigenkas referred them to the families with the greatest knowledge of history, and these families referred them to their oldest members, until, eventually, a handful of maximally authoritative people were willing to make a pronouncement on the subject. Etymological knowledge, in other words, marked a boundary of expert authority that was projected at multiple levels outside and inside of places like Yokiri. Thus, this way of speaking about the landscape was embedded in a broader discourse relating to the intergenerational loss of cultural knowledge about the environment—a conceptualization of Matsigenka culture in decline amid Andean colonization and ecological change.

Etymological Discourse 2: The Unknowability of the Past After an Age of Disruption and Trauma

Andrés, an elderly, monolingual Matsigenka-speaking Yokiriño (likely born in the early 1940s), was one of Yokiri's foremost cultural authorities during my fieldwork. He was very knowledgeable about local history, and we often spent long afternoons talking about the region as it was before, during, and after the arrival of Andean colonos. Unlike families that migrated from more distant valleys, his parents and grandparents had circulated through the area surrounding Yokiri since at least the late nineteenth or early twentieth century, and he had been raised with an intimate understanding of the regional landscape and its history both through personal experience and through the accounts of his elders. The many hours of recordings that I made with Andrés are a precious record of the lower Yavero Valley's history. On the advice of other Yokiriños,

I asked Andrés about the etymology of Yokiri one day as we walked near his house discussing the names of various places in and around the community. I was surprised when he expressed skepticism, in Matsigenka, about the mere possibility of its interpretation:

Transcript 24

Yoga shaenka Efraín ikanti, "Tera.",₁ Ikanti, "Tatarika pairani okantagani ovairo Yokiri?,₂ Tyaka okanta pairani anta timatsi?",₃ Ikantake, "Tera, ikantaigiro koga-page, impatyo gotasanoigatsirira tata oitarika opaitaka Yokiri.",₄

My grandfather Efraín said, "No.",₁ He said, "Who knows what the name 'Yokiri' might have meant?₂ Who knows what was there before?",₃ He said, "No, they [i.e., those with etymological theories] are just talking for no reason, it depends on the ones who knew whatever 'Yokiri' meant.",₄

This was not a referral to a more qualified authority, as above, but rather a declaration of the unknowability of the past: "Tyaka okanta pairani anta timatsi?" (Who knows what was there before?). Andrés's father and grandfather both grew up during the terrible violence of the nineteenth- and early-twentieth-century rubber industry, when Matsigenkas were killed, forced into slavery, or displaced back and forth across remote parts of the Alto Urubamba. Many of his grandfather's family members were killed or separated during that time, and Andrés himself experienced the aftershocks of this violence as he migrated long distances during his childhood around the 1940s. Andrés's statement regarding the etymology of Yokiri demonstrates an acute awareness of the dislocations and disruptions of this period—he experiences an alienation from the landscape that younger Yokiriños do not. In this etymological discourse, historical knowledge about the distant past has been ruptured.

Etymological Discourse 3:
Mythic Origins (Yavero Version)

Despite this verdict from Andrés, a number of etymological interpretations regarding Yokiri circulated widely in the community among other people. As it happens, Yokiri does, in fact, have a meaning in Matsigenka: as a verbal construction, it means "he left him behind" or "he abandoned him."

Yokiri.
i–ok–i–ri
3M-leave.behind-REAL-3M
"He left him behind"

The next two interpretations of Yokiri, those of Mario and Héctor, draw on this analysis of the word. Before considering them, though, it is important to point out that while *yokiri* is indeed a word with this meaning in Matsigenka, it is an unlikely candidate for a toponym, for two reasons. First, Matsigenka speakers, as far as I know, generally do not use verbal constructions as the basis of place names, instead favoring the ubiquitous [noun + landscape suffix(es)] formula discussed earlier. Second, the phrase is syntactically awkward. A more natural construction would employ the perfective suffix *-ak* (*yokakeri*), which would indicate a completed action, or the translocative perfective *-aki* (*yokakitiri*, "he left him behind, in another place"), perhaps in combination with the relativizer *-ra* to form a relative clause (e.g., *yokakerira*, "[the place] where he left him behind"). Indeed, these three constructions were used in Mario's and Héctor's etymological accounts given below in transcripts 25 and 26. For both of these reasons, it is most likely that Yokiri's etymology, from the historical perspective of a lexicographer, does not originate in this verbal construction.

The first origin story of Yokiri comes from Mario, a Matsigenka man who was born farther up the Yavero Valley in the 1960s and migrated downriver to Yokiri in the 1980s. Because Mario had lived in the Yavero Valley for most of his life, he, like Andrés, was considered particularly knowledgeable in matters of local history and culture. But because his parents were born in the faraway Camisea watershed, his knowledge came mostly from his own experience in the valley since the 1960s and from conversations with his Matsigenka neighbors (many of whom also migrated from distant valleys during the twentieth century). He also had a profound knowledge of the vast intertextual network of Matsigenka folklore and mythology, and during our long conversations he often moved back and forth between what non-Matsigenkas might consider historical and mythological discourses (as in his narration below), but which for many Matsigenkas form a more integrated view of the past. During one of our conversations in 2012, I asked Mario about some of the nearby place names. He reported that he didn't know the explanations for many of them, since his family had moved there relatively recently, but he offered a story, which he attributed to his mother, regarding the origin of Yokiri (transcript 25). His account, in Matsigenka, draws on the "he left him behind" interpretation of Yokiri described above. According to it, two brothers traveled down the Yavero River, naming its tributaries and seeking wives. They stopped at the Yokiri River and hiked up into a dangerous part of the valley: the slopes of a mountain called Tampianironi, where a demon associated with thunder and wind kills any trespassers. One man was killed, and the other "left him behind." Spanish elements are underlined in the text.

Transcript 25

MARIO: Hehe ogari pashini nonkenkiake.$_1$ Nonkenkiake pashini ahora Yokiri Yokiri antes pero–okamantana ina pairani yokiri.$_2$ Pairani matsigenka pairani pairani ikantaigi matsigenka ikanta Yokiri.$_3$ Hehe okamantana ina okanti Yokiri Yokiri pairani.$_4$ Hehe iponia matsigenka katonko hehe.$_5$ Aryo ipokaigake ikogaira itsinanetsite oga irirenti mameri itsinanetsite dice.$_6$ [inaudible] Yaviro okya shigaatanankicha dice.$_7$ Hehe iponiaka katonko ipaitapaakero nia iriro matsigenka pe.$_8$ Kara patiro niateni ipaitanakerora, hehe maputonoari posante ipaitanakerora.$_9$ Okya inkenakerora matsigenka okari inkenakero koa, ironkuatanakempa iriatakeme a Huamangaku.$_{10}$

NQE: Ah, ¿Huamanga?$_{11}$

MARIO: Huamanga, ¿dónde quedará ese Huamanga también?$_{12}$

NQE: ¿Ayacucho?$_{13}$

MARIO: Por Ayacucho será.$_{14}$ Entonces oga onta ikenanakero oga yoga irirenti ikenanake shintipoaku, en balsa pe.$_{15}$ Anta yokiro otsitiaku.$_{16}$ Ineapaake pirinitake osuraritsite pe ikantiro ikantiro, "Matsi ige?"$_{17}$ "Ainyo yoka [inaudible] meronki, frutas, hehe."$_{18}$ Parece oga parece capulí, meronki.$_{19}$ Okantiri, "Ainyo yataguitakotake inkuakera meronki."$_{20}$ Hehe okemi samani kantake igiashiaku "saatirin."$_{21}$ Ikantiro maika, "Ogaka pikisanakeri ige pe."$_{22}$ [inaudible] "n, ganakeri choeni."$_{23}$ Aryo kantaka ikantaigi opaitaka ikanki yokanakeri irirenti Yokiriku, aha, eso okamantanakena pe "Yokiriku."$_{24}$ Así pues.$_{25}$ Yokanakeri irirenti okanti así okamantanakena.$_{26}$ Okamantanakena ashi yokanakeri irirenti.$_{27}$

MARIO: Yes, I'm going to tell another one.$_1$ I'm going to tell another one now about Yokiri, Yokiri, before but–my mother told me about Yokiri.$_2$ Long ago, people used to call it Yokiri.$_3$ Yes, my mother told me [it was called] Yokiri before.$_4$ Yes, people came from up the [Yavero] river, that's right.$_5$ That's right, they came to look for women, [because] one man's brother didn't have a wife, they say.₆ [inaudible] they had fled down the Yavero River, they say.₇ Yes, they came from upriver and named the river in Matsigenka, yeah.₈ They gave names to the rivers, yes, Maputonoari, they gave names to various other ones.₉ [Those] people were going to pass by Yokiri, they were going to pass it by and go around it on the way to Huamanga.₁₀

NQE: Oh, Huamanga?₁₁

MARIO: Huamanga, where might that Huamanga be?₁₂

NQE: Ayacucho?₁₃

MARIO: It must be around Ayacucho.₁₄ So his brother went by on a raft, on a raft.₁₅ He left it there at the mouth of the [Yokiri] river.₁₆ He found his [brother's] wife sitting there, right, and he said to her, "What about my brother?"₁₇ "He [inaudible] went to collect *meronki*, fruits, yes" [she said].₁₈ It looks, um, like a capulí fruit, meronki.₁₉ She said, "He went up there to pick meronki fruits."₂₀ Yes, she heard from up the valley "saatirin" [distant thunder sound].₂₁ He said to her, "You must be making my brother angry, yeah."₂₂ [inaudible] "I'm going to leave him behind."₂₃ So they've always called it, they said, "He left his brother [*yokanakeri*] in Yokiri," that's what [my mother] told me, yeah, "in Yokiri."₂₄ That's right.₂₅ He left his brother behind, that's what [my mother] told me.₂₆ She told me, "He left his brother behind."₂₇

This explanation was, unmistakably, a performance of myth narration. As discussed above, this discourse genre was used by older Matsigenka speakers in Yokiri when they articulated the principles of cosmological transformism—how the beings in the world came to take their current forms. Thus Mario placed the etymology of Yokiri in the ancient time of origins by deploying the enregistered linguistic features associated with the myth narration discourse genre. These features include frequent recapitulative linkages between clauses, which establish a narrative rhythm distinctive to Matsigenka myth performances in and around Yokiri (Emlen 2019). Here a verbal construction is uttered, followed by a pause, and then the construction is repeated (sometimes with modifications) and linked immediately to a new clause. An example of this clausal recapitulation construction is seen in sentences 1–2 of transcript 25 (reference clauses and their recapitulations are boldfaced, the length of the pause is indicated between brackets, and Spanish elements are underlined, as above):

Hehe ogari pashini **nonkenkiake**. [1.3 seconds] **Nonkenkiake** pashini ahora Yokiri Yokiri antes pero–okamantana ina pairani yokiri.

(Yes, **I'm going to tell another one**. [1.3 seconds] **I'm going to tell another one**
now about Yokiri, Yokiri, before but–my mother told me about Yokiri.)

Another example comes from sentence 5, when Mario says that the people
had come from upstream, and then sentence 8, when he returns to that subject
and recapitulates the clause after a 2.1-second pause following sentence 7.

Hehe iponia matsigenka katonko hehe. . . . [inaudible] Yaviro okya shigaatanankicha dice. [2.1 seconds] **Hehe iponiaka katonko** ipaitapaakero nia iriro matsigenka pe.

(**Yes, people came from up the [Yavero] river**, that's right. . . . [inaudible] they
had fled down the Yavero River, they say. [2.1 seconds] **Yes, they came from
upriver** and named the river in Matsigenka, yeah.)

By using this distinctive clause-linking structure, Mario frames his discourse
as mythic speech. As such, he invokes the whole social and moral world of
Matsigenka cosmology that comes along with that discourse genre. Another
linguistic feature he uses in this way is ideophones: iconic or sound-symbolic
words that represent their referents through a relation of resemblance (Nuckolls
1996). These also appear in other types of narratives (for instance, stories about
personal experiences), and they give the stories a sense of excitement and veri-
similitude. They are especially common in the myth narration discourse genre,
particularly as expressions of danger and foreboding. This is the case in sentence
21, when Mario imitates the ominous sound of distant thunder with the ideophone *saatirin*, associated in Yokiri with the dangerous Tampianironi mountain.

As Mario uses such formal linguistic features to frame his speech as an
instance of myth performance, he also invokes the emotional and moral world
of Matsigenka myth. Matsigenka myths often follow a distinctive "emotion
schema" (Izquierdo and Johnson 2007), in which anger is seen as a dangerous
and destabilizing force (Rosengren 2000). One man in his account accuses his
brother's wife of angering his brother, provoking the danger marked by the thunder sound *saatirin* and leading to the brother's abandonment. Thus, by drawing
on the discourse of myth narration to account for the etymological origin of
Yokiri, Mario places those events within the world of Matsigenka mythology
and its moral and emotional principles. This is one way in which mythic events
and cosmological notions were invoked in contemporary discourse in Yokiri.

A final feature of note in Mario's etymological account is the way it unfolds geographically: according to him, the founders of Yokiri came from farther up the Yavero River, just as he did in the 1980s. In other words, Mario's account of Yokiri's origin retraces the path of his own arrival in the valley. Map 6 shows Mario's migratory route to Yokiri. Significantly, in transcript 26 below, a speaker named Héctor also links his own family's arrival in Yokiri, from a different direction, with the mythological founding of the valley. In this way, Mario and Héctor both blend the mythological past with their own personal pasts and create a link from those events to the present. Associating the community's origin with their own family histories is also a political statement—if only an implicit one—in a community divided along lines of kin affiliation (see chapter 3).

Etymological Discourse 4: Mythic Origins (Otingamía Version)

The next account of the etymological origin of Yokiri, in transcript 26, comes from Héctor, who was born in Otingamía, a valley to the south of Yokiri, in the early 1970s (for more on geography and migration around Yokiri, see chapter 3). He migrated across the Artillería Pass as the Andean colonization of Chapo-Boyero and Otingamía forced his family to seek new land. Héctor is the son of Andrés, the man who expressed skepticism about etymological explanations above in transcript 24. Héctor told me his story about the etymology of Yokiri one evening in his house during a discussion of local history. This version, which is much longer and more elaborate than Mario's in transcript 25, also draws on the "he left him behind" interpretation of Yokiri. In it, an injured monkey lures a hunter onto the dangerous slopes of the nearby Tampianironi, where he is killed by the same wind demon that is referenced obliquely by the thunder sound in Mario's version. This was also a performance of myth narration, employing recapitulative linkage constructions, as above, as well as ideophones (an element of all kinds of storytelling in Yokiri). However, in this account Yokiri was not named by people floating on rafts down the Yavero Valley, as in Mario's version, but by people who crossed overland over the top of the Yokiri Valley from Otingamía through the Artillería Pass—precisely where Héctor came from. These places are illustrated in map 6 on the facing page. Spanish elements are underlined in this transcript.

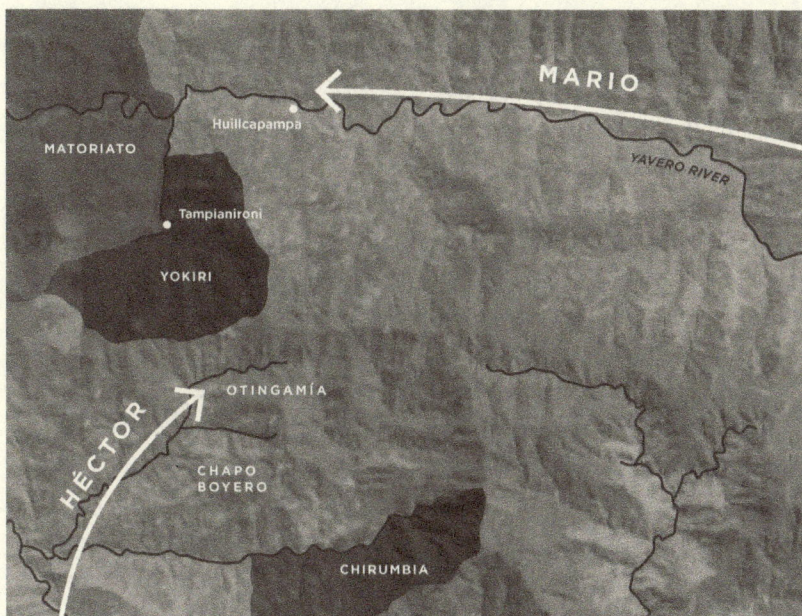

MAP 6 Landscape of Yokiri. Map data: Google, Landsat, DigitalGlobe, Instituto del Bien Común. IBC-SICNA. Enero 2017, incluye información levantada en gabinete, AIDESEP-CIPTA, GEF PNUD, GOREL y PFS. Author's GPS data also used. All landscape labels added by the author.

Transcript 26

Kara itsamaitapai shainka, impo isureiganaka irirori "tsame impatyompa shonkaigera intatonikya.$_1$ Shonkaigera intatonikya."$_2$ Impo ishonkaigapaakero oga tya opaita opaitara ikya tesakona oga oga ompegempa tekyaenka ompaitempa Yokiri.$_3$ Ishonkaigapaakaro, ishonkaigapaakaro pitepageni tsonkavakoaka inake matsigenka ishonkaigakaro otinkamiaku.$_4$ Ikenaigapai nikoriko [*pointing to Artillería Pass*].$_5$ Onti ipampiaigapai oga iravo tya ipaita yoga ikantaigiri pairani ikantaigiri . . .

My grandfather worked there [in Otingamía], then they thought, "Let's go, what will it be like when we go to the other side [of the hill, to Yokiri]?$_1$ Let's cross to the other side."$_2$ Then they crossed here to, what's it called, it was just, it wasn't yet called Yokiri.$_3$ They crossed over, they crossed over, four or five Matsigenkas, they crossed over in Otingamía.$_4$ They came from up there [*pointing to Artillería Pass*].$_5$ They followed on the path of, what's it called . . . of the bear.$_6$ Our parents, yes.$_7$

oso.[6] Apaegi ehe.[7] Iriro ipokaigapai ishonkaigaka ineaigapaakeri kipatsi omaarane kipatsi aka pue.[8] Imaarane kipatsi.[9] Pero pairani ina oneavetaroni.[10] Maika ishonkaigapaakaro ishonkaiga-paakaro oka Tairishiku maika itimakera yoga yoga Juan Carlos.[11] Opaita maika Tairishi.[12] Ishonkaigaka, nero ipokai aikiro yogonkeigapaa pairani ineaveigaro pairani aka aikiro yogonkeigapaakaro oga pairani ineaveigaro aikiro ineaiga-paakero aikiro, akya ishonkagani aka.[13] Nero.[14] Yamaigakeri tya opaita shaenka itimavetaka anta oga Yokiriku otsitiaku.[15] Aikiro ipokai ponyarona, ishigaa.[16] . . . Pashini ipokaigapai ink-antaige pairani yoga kovintsaigatsirira y oga ishonkaigakarora anta, ikanti opaita Kanaishiato.[17] Ishonkaigakaro ikovintsavageigira pairani yagi inoshiki ikanti chakopi omaarane oga ikovint-saigira pairani pue, shintoripage magat-iropage ikovintsaigira.[18] Ipokaigake iita ipaita irapitene Jorge ipaigakena oga onkante maika Jorge, pairani ikan-tagani Jorge.[19] Pairani—matsigenka pe.[20] Nero ipokaigapai ipokaigapai oka ehe.[21] Ineaigakero oka [*gestures to the hills across the valley*] opaitara Tampianironi.[22] Tampianironi.[23] Oga piatimatake piatake ontampiatanake tirinkari puede ogakempira pue iro.[24] Pa iaigake piteni yoga inkovintsav-ageigera, inkovintsavageigera piteni.[25] Iaigake iaigake pine kovintsavageigera chakopiku patiro yogaigiri.[26] Ehe, pine.[27]

They came and crossed over, they found a lot of land here, that's right.[8] A lot of land.[9] But before, my mother already knew about [the Yokiri Valley].[10] So they crossed over, they crossed over in Tairishi, where Juan Carlos lives now.[11] Now it's called Tairishi.[12] They crossed over and came here, and the ones that had known it before also came, they had seen it before and they also crossed over and came here.[13] That's right.[14] They brought, what's he called, my grandfather, and he lived at the mouth of the Yokiri River.[15] The colonos also came, and [the Matsigenkas] fled [from them].[16] . . . Others used to come to hunt, and the ones that crossed over there, they called it Kanaishiato.[17] They crossed over, and they hunted by taking out a big arrow, I mean they really hunted, wild pigs, they hunted every-thing.[18] They came, and there was a man named Jorge who gave us—his name was Jorge.[19] Long ago—he was a Mat-sigenka, that's right.[20] Yes, they came, they came.[21] They saw this [*gestures to the hills across the valley*] and called it Tampianironi.[22] Tampianironi.[23] When you go, if it's windy [and it's] thunder-ing, it can kill you, yeah.[24] Long ago, two men went to hunt there, two went to hunt.[25] They went to hunt, they could kill [monkeys] with just one arrow.[26] Yes, you see?[27] They chased [a monkey] and hit him, but one man said, "Don't follow [the monkey]."[28] [But] the other

Iaigi ipatimaigi pashini yagake ikanti, "Gara pipatimatanake."$_{28}$ Tera inkematsateri irapitene, ikanti, "Naro naro naro nokovintsatakera naro novegotiakeri komaginaro," oka, pine.$_{29}$ Iatake iatake tyarika tyarika yamanakerira komaginaro anta.$_{30}$ Ikemi pairani—naro nogoigi tatarika tatarika tya opaita gakempi ikanti pairani yashireake tsuvani *tipe*.$_{31}$ Ikanti "Tatarika gakeri."$_{32}$ Isonkavati isonkavageta mameri.$_{33}$ Tera iripokae, ehe.$_{34}$ Itsaroganake irapitene, yoga tentanakarira itsaroganake.$_{35}$ Ikanti, "Tyari tyari tyari," atanake shavini anta.$_{36}$

Ikanti, "Tatarika otimake irirokya pegakeri yoga tya opaita sankenari."$_{37}$ Ineapaakero tya yavotaraasetagakeri tya opaita yoga matsontsori ikanti, "Irirota gakeri."$_{38}$ Itsaroganake ipokai yagapanitiri komaginaro ipokai.$_{39}$ Ikanti maika, "Nopegakitirityo maika nopegakitirityo nokakitiri inkenishiku."$_{40}$ Ipokai yamakitiri oga komaginaro piteni ikanti ipokai pankotsiku okanti, "Matsi yoga pogisantanakarira?"$_{41}$ Ikanti yapishigopirea ikanti—pairani otimake shitea onkante maika oga onti oga tya opaita oga onti pao pairani oga pao, okanti, "Matsi inti irapitene?"$_{42}$ Ikanti, "Nopegakitiri nokakitiri anta inkenishiku.$_{43}$ Nokakitiri nokakitiri nokakitiri.$_{44}$ Maika tya ompaitakempa kara oga tya opaita niateni?$_{45}$ Aryo ompaitempa 'nokirira, nokirira, nokirira.'$_{46}$ Y̱ pashini yoga inkantaigerira yoga yoga kantaka

man didn't listen to him, and he said, "I, I, when I hunt, I catch lots of monkeys," you see?$_{29}$ He went and went, wherever the [injured] monkey led him.$_{30}$ He heard—we [Matsigenkas] used to think that when something is going to kill you, the *tsuvani* bird [makes the sound] *tipe*.$_{31}$ He said, "I wonder what happened to him."$_{32}$ He whistled and whistled [to him], [but] he wasn't there.$_{33}$ He didn't come back.$_{34}$ The other one was afraid, the one who accompanied him was afraid.$_{35}$ He said, "What, what, what," it was getting late.$_{36}$

He said, "What happened, perhaps he turned into a jaguar."$_{37}$ He saw where the jaguar had opened up a path [in the forest], and he said, "He ate him."$_{38}$ He was afraid, he came, he got the monkey and came back.$_{39}$ He said, "Now I've lost him, I've lost him and left him in the forest."$_{40}$ He came and brought the two monkeys, he came to the house and [his wife said], "What about the man you went with?"$_{41}$ He said, resting—they used to have masato, [he must have had] what's it called, a gourd, a gourd [like they used to have] long ago, and she said, "What about the other [man]?"$_{42}$ He said, "I lost him, I left him there in the forest.$_{43}$ I left him behind, I left him behind, I left him behind [*nokakitiri*].$_{44}$ Now what will that river be called?$_{45}$ Well, it will be called 'where I left him behind, where I left him behind, where I left him behind [*nokirira*].'$_{46}$ And

maika tovaini opitenkani aka ah inti
ompaitempa 'yokirira yokirira.'"₄₇
Aryo opaitaka maika "yokirira."₄₈
Yokiri, yokakitirira yoga tya ipaita o̱
sea–yoga yogisantanakarira yokakitiri
tera intentaeri pankotsiku.₄₉ Maika
aryoka impo okutagitanake oga kantaka maika kutagiteri okutagitanake
iaigake inkogaigakiterira inkogaiga-
kiterira.₅₀ Ikogaigavetakari omaarane
mapu kara oga tya opaita aityo maika
oga mapu.₅₁ Kanyoma matsontsori
kaontaka pankotsi iaveiga tyarika
yoganakero ichakore kantanatsi onti
inti ineaigapai igonta.₅₂ Ikanti "inti
gakagakari yoga iri sankenari," pairani
ikantagani "sankenari" yoga matsontsori "sankenari" aryo.₅₃ Ikantake–
sonkavatanatsi.₅₄ Sonkavatanatsi
tya ipaita yoga ipegakerira.₅₅ Nero.₅₆
Omagisantagiteanaka, ikanti, "Aryo
maika aryo ompaitakempa maika, oka
Yokiri."₅₇ Oga inkenishi magatiro onti
opaita Yokiri.₅₈ Yokakitirira yoga tya
ipaita yogisantanakari yokakitiri.₅₉
Nero.₆₀ Nero maika ishonkaigapaaka–
aryo opaitaka yoga ikantaigirira maika
hasta maika maika okantaka okantaka
opaitakara Yokiri.₆₁ Intagati maika
nonkantakempira.₆₂

other people who say it, and as long
as we stay here, it's going to be called
'where he left him behind, where he left
him behind [*yokirira*].'"₄₇ Like that, it's
now called "where he left him behind."₄₈
Yokiri, where he left him behind, I̱
mean–the man who went with him and
left him and did not accompany him
back home.₄₉ Then the next day, in the
daytime, the next day in the daytime
they went looking for him, looking
for him.₅₀ They looked for him in vain,
and there was a large rock, what's it
called, there was a rock.₅₁ It looked like
a jaguar, it looked like a house, and
when they left, they saw his footprint
where he had left his arrow.₅₂ He said,
"The striped one [i.e., jaguar] ate him,"
they used to call the jaguar "the striped
one."₅₃ He said–he kept on whistling
[to him].₅₄ He kept on whistling, what's
his name, the man who lost him.₅₅ There
you have it.₅₆ He was forgetting, so
he said, "That's how this place will be
called now, Yokiri."₅₇ [Now] all the forest [here] is called Yokiri.₅₈ The one that
left him behind, what's it called, the one
who accompanied him left him behind
[*yokakitiri*].₅₉ You see?₆₀ Crossing over
here–it's called, it's what they call it,
until now it has been called Yokiri.₆₁
That's all I'm going to tell you now.₆₂

Like Mario's account in transcript 25, Héctor's also draws on the enregistered
features of Matsigenka myth performance in his account of Yokiri's etymology.
He uses the same recapitulative linkages that are so characteristic of the mythic
discourse genre, as in sentences 50–51:

. . . iaigake **inkogaigakiterira inkogaigakiterira**. [2.4 seconds] **Ikogaigavetakari** omaarane mapu kara. . . .

(. . . they went **looking for him, looking for him**. [2.4 seconds] **They looked for him in vain**, [and there was] a large rock. . . .)

He also uses the ideophone *tipe* in sentence 31, the call of the *tsuvani* bird (Spanish *chicua*, a species of cuckoo). The call of this bird is considered a bad omen in Matsigenka society and in other Indigenous Amazonian societies in Peru. Héctor uses it to signal the cruel fate that is about to befall the man as he climbs toward the dangerous mountain Tampianironi, though we don't hear the sound of thunder itself in this account.

These discourse features invoke the ontological and cosmological principles of Matsigenka landscape history and establish the origin of the toponym Yokiri in the mythic past. This way of speaking about the landscape creates a close connection between Matsigenka migration and the naming of the valley. Significantly, the protagonists in Héctor's version migrated to the Yokiri Valley from Otingamía, over the Artillería Pass, the very same place where Héctor himself came from (see map 6). More specifically, these ancestors first came over from Otingamía to hunt and plant crops in Yokiri before moving there permanently, just as in the story. Thus, like Mario, Héctor uses his etymology of Yokiri to assert a link between the universe of Matsigenka mythology and morality and his own family's arrival there.

Etymological Discourse 5: State Neglect

A final account of the etymology of Yokiri came from a community leader during a speech at the community's twenty-third anniversary celebration in 2011. This was the first year that municipal officials had attended Yokiri's anniversary, and the leader took the opportunity to make a plea, in Spanish, for the municipal government's support in development and infrastructure projects. Lamenting the absence of officials at previous anniversary celebrations, he translated *Yokiri* with the Spanish term *abandono* (neglect), alluding to the "he left him behind" interpretation discussed above. This speech drew on the discursive conventions of public speech described in chapter 5, including a brief opening and closing formula and tag questions like *¿no?*

Transcript 27

Porque son veintitres años que estamos pasando, y lo hemos pasado solos.$_1$ Nunca hemos tenido la presencia de una autoridad.$_2$ Y el otro quiero decir, ¿no?, que la palabra Yokiri significa "abandono."$_3$ ¿No?$_4$ Tiene una historia, pero—que es algo triste, ¿no?$_5$

Because we've reached twenty-three years, and we've reached it alone.$_1$ We have never had the presence of a [government] official.$_2$ And the other thing I want to say, no?, is that the word Yokiri means "neglect."$_3$ No?$_4$ It has a history, but—which is a bit sad, no?$_5$

Here the community leader gives only a Spanish translation of the term, "neglect," which positions the notion of "he left him behind" in the context of a longer history of government disregard for Yokiri and Matsigenka people. In this way, he articulates the etymological account in a different interactional context from the examples above, using a different discourse genre, and with different social and political implications. We might call this fifth etymological story the discourse of state neglect.

In the five etymological discourses presented above, when people talked about the etymology of the toponym Yokiri, they articulated different conceptualizations of the landscape, its inhabitants, and its history. These included: (1) a vision of the frontier society in which Andean colonization since the 1950s has ruptured the transmission of knowledge about the landscape, leaving just a handful of elders with authority in such matters; (2) a discourse of alienation from the landscape, in which the terrors and displacements of the nineteenth- and early-twentieth-century rubber industry have rendered the history of the landscape unknowable; (3 and 4) cosmological renderings of the landscape, performed with the enregistered features of the myth narration discourse genre, in which each speaker associates the ancient populating of the Yokiri Valley with their own migratory history; and (5) a Spanish discourse of state neglect, performed with the enregistered features of the public speech discourse genre, framing the "he left him behind" interpretation of *yokiri* in the context of the community's contemporary struggle to find support from the government.

These were just a few ways of talking about the landscape that became relevant in discussions of Yokiri's etymology. In the next section, I discuss an issue that arose in 2012 regarding the same part of the Yokiri Valley described by

Mario (transcript 25) and Héctor (transcript 26), but which was discussed in very different terms.

The Road to Tampianironi

Tampianironi, the dangerous mountain that Héctor and Mario both brought up in their accounts of Yokiri's origin, towers high above the Yokiri Valley. Much of it sits across the border in the neighboring comunidad nativa of Matoriato, but at around 2,100 meters (7,000 feet) in elevation, it is visible from almost everywhere in Yokiri and is one of the most discussed landscape features in the area. Tampianironi, as viewed from Yokiri's *comuna* (communal agricultural plot), is shown in figure 23. I snapped this photograph at a rare moment when it was not shrouded in mist. The mountain is also indicated on map 6 earlier in this chapter.

As one might expect from Mario's and Héctor's harrowing accounts of the men killed and "left behind" on Tampianironi's slopes, few Yokiriños have ever ventured there. As Héctor explains in transcript 26, the mountain is home to a powerful and malevolent demon that takes the outward form of wind (*tampia* means "wind" in Matsigenka), or of a small *tampianiro* monkey. If someone climbs this mountain, it gets very windy, thunder roars, and then the demon kills them for trespassing on its territory. As Héctor explains (from sentence 24 in transcript 26; Spanish elements are italicized): "Oga piatimatake piatake ontampiatanake tirinkari *puede* ogakempira *pue* iro" (When you go, when it's windy [and it's] thundering, it *can* kill you, *yeah*).

FIGURE 23 Tampianironi. Viewed across the Yokiri River from Yokiri's communal agricultural plantation, 2012. Photograph by the author.

Given the widespread acknowledgment of Tampianironi as a dangerous place, I was surprised when, in early 2012, the mountain came up in a very different context: an asamblea debate, in Spanish, about whether or not to petition the municipal government to build a road that would eventually extend to the lower slopes of the mountain. Yokiri was entitled to a state-directed infrastructural project, funded by royalties from the Camisea natural gas project, and this was one of the options. The primary advocate of this option in Yokiri proposed that this road project could be developed in conjunction with the neighboring comunidad nativa of Matoriato, and it would link Yokiri's comuna with the main road. This would mean that merchants like Edison (see chapter 4) would be able to drive their trucks straight to the comuna, instead of the arrangement that was in effect in 2011–12, in which hundred-pound sacks of coffee and achiote were carried by mule, or even on the comuneros' own backs, for as long as an hour to the school area. Yokiri would be able to substantially increase its agricultural production as a result. The road would also eventually continue farther into the Yokiri Valley, where it would open new forested areas on the slopes of Tampianironi to agricultural development—impossible at the time, given how far the area was from the nearest road.

I was not able to record this debate, but it had the same characteristics of asamblea discourse described in chapter 5. The proposal's primary proponent stood before his fellow comuneros in the salón comunal and bracketed his speech between formal opening and closing formulas. He used the "official Spanish" register that I described in chapter 5 and held the floor for some ten minutes. He used these characteristics to frame his speech as "official talk" and invoke the moral and institutional world of the community's public space, as well as other democratic forums across Peru.

At the time, the Tampianironi road proposal was short-lived—I only heard it debated during one asamblea in 2012, though it was later approved and construction began in 2019. I was struck that the comuneros in attendance—including Mario and Héctor, who both listened attentively—had even considered this proposal. What about the wind and the thunder? What about the certain death that awaited anyone who trod the mountain's slopes?

Based on my conversations with the comuneros, I came to understand that the omission of the spiritual dangers of Tampianironi from this infrastructural debate—the allowance of this ontological "equivocation," in the words of Eduardo Viveiros de Castro (2004) and Marisol de la Cadena (2010)—was connected to the ideological regimentation of the community's discursive life.

The comuneros had different expectations of what kinds of factors "count" as legitimate political concerns in particular contexts. In other words, discussing the dangers of the wind demon would have been quite out of place in an official meeting—particularly in Spanish—about agriculture and state infrastructure projects. Such considerations belonged to a different sphere of history and experience, and they were discussed in different spaces, languages, and discourse genres. Most people were careful in their interactions with such spirits and demons during hunting trips and other forays into the forest, but in adopting the democratic political forum of the community meeting, they also adopted an ideology of what kinds of actors and discourses were relevant, or not, in that context. The social, economic, and ontological universes invoked in those dramatically different landscape discourses were articulated in distinct kinds of interactions, and through distinct language ideologies.

Conclusion

As the forests of the Alto Urubamba Valley are transformed into farmland, the people who live there have come to speak about the landscape in innumerable new ways. At some moments, and in some interactional contexts, the land was described as the domain of intersubjective relations with other-than-human entities. This was the case with some Yokiriños (particularly among the older generations) who drew on the discourse genre of myth narration, and thus on the historical and moral principles with which it is indexically associated, to articulate a particular vision of the landscape's past. At other moments, the landscape was cast as a resource to be exploited for commercial gain. We saw this in the discussion of the Tampianironi road, which would have opened new parts of the mountain to coffee cultivation and, possibly, exposed Yokiriños to the malevolent agency of a dangerous spirit. This debate took place in the very different interactional context of Spanish asamblea discourse. Discussions of the etymology of the name Yokiri also drew on other discourses, such as the loss of cultural information about the environment, historical trauma following the murderous rubber industry of the early twentieth century, and a history of state neglect toward Matsigenka people.

To a great extent, such discourses depended on the background of the participants in the interactions; however, some were also articulated by the very same people in different contexts. In other words, in the Alto Urubamba this kind of ontological equivocation marked a line not just between people or ethnic groups, but also between different domains of experience and social practice, which were rooted in particular types of interactions and ideologies of language. For this reason, they could coexist without being contradictory—as I wrote earlier, none of them encompassed the totality of experience.

These links between language and landscape offer a picture of how the practices of multilingualism and the changing socioeconomic and environmental situation in the Alto Urubamba were interconnected. As people in the valley used the land differently, they spoke about it differently. The reverse was also true, since a major part of becoming a coffee farmer was learning to speak as a coffee farmer (chapter 4). Viewed this way, the patterns of multilingual discourse and the expansion of the frontier across the landscape were inseparable.

Conclusion

"The Air Was Totally Still"

In April 2012, I heard Matsigenka speakers use ideophones of a different kind. These were not the ominous *saatirin* of distant thunder or the foreboding *tipe* of the *tsuvani* cuckoo bird that I described in chapter 6. Instead, these were the sounds of a more immediate danger: *pugararara* and *prrrrrr*, the sounds of machine gun fire; *puririri*, the roar of explosives; *monkiree*, a military helicopter flying low overhead; *tan, tang, tak, tsak*, and *takung*, various kinds of gunshots; and *tsing*, the sound of bullets whistling through the air.

These ideophones were used by members of the Matsigenka community of Inkaare during their stay in a makeshift refugee camp in the provincial capital of Quillabamba. A battle between the Peruvian military and a group of narco-terrorists had broken out in their forests after thirty-six employees of the Camisea natural gas project were kidnapped and brought there. The people of Inkaare, terrorized and fearing for their lives amid the violence, were evacuated to the COMARU (Matsigenka Council of the Urubamba River) headquarters in Quillabamba until it was safe for them to return. By the time the fighting ended, the narco-terrorists had freed all of the hostages, five police and soldiers had been killed, the community's footpaths had been planted with land mines, the nearby town of Kiteni had been transformed into a sprawling military garrison, and the people of Inkaare were waiting anxiously to learn what had become of their community and their homes.

One woman from Inkaare, whom I will call Angélica, told my colleague Julio Korinti Piñarreal, in Matsigenka, about her experience of the battle (transcript 28). A military helicopter took her by surprise as she worked in her gardens, and, like many of her fellow comuneros, she thought the soldiers were going to kill her. Spanish is underlined in the following transcripts.

Transcript 28

Hehe nokemakiti impo nopitantavake impogini maika pa arapaakemera helicóptero intagaro okenapaake savi.₁ Okenapaake savi akya avisanake maika opoimatanake "monkiree" okantavagetaketyo hehe nonei tata oitari?₂ Noka atashitake aryo nogotake nonkante [inaudible].₃ Oga impo okomutagaka nokanti okantapaaketyo tovaini okantapaake otinkamienkatake akya avisanake opoimatanake "pugararara."₄ Nani nopitake nantavagetake onani oga okenagematanake nantavagetai.₅ Nonei aryo yaraigake nokantake aryoroka–noka aryoroka irogutaigena.₆

Yes, then I heard it, I was sitting and the helicopter came flying low.₁ It came down low and went by, and it made a sound, "monkiree," yes, I saw it, what might it have been?₂ I thought, "It's [the military]," how would I know [inaudible]?₃ Then it was [surprising], a lot of them came, smoke was rising [from the gunfire], passing by making the noise "pugararara."₄ Okay, I just kept working, they kept on passing by, but I just kept on working.₅ I saw them fly over and I thought, perhaps–I thought, perhaps they're going to kill us.₆

Another man from Inkaare, Roberto, told Julio about his own terrifying experience when the soldiers arrived at his home (transcript 29). He reported that they mistook him for a narco-terrorist and shot at him. He was separated from his family and hid in the forest until the soldiers moved on.

Transcript 29

Maanikya nokianake nokemisantake kemisantakena, ipegagetaka tya.₁ Itonkavake avotsiku "tan" koa nokemisantimatirityo avotsiku kara "tan" yobombatakerora kara "tang."₂ Okantagematake "puririri" okaontaka pine itonkaigiro imperitaku pine carretera.₃ . . . Asa kantaka nokemisantakera nokaontakara nokaragetakera otapisetakera nokatigaka nokemisantake nokanti, "Impatyo nohina otonkenkaniroka notomi itonkenkaniroka."₄ Pairaenkagitevagetake.₅

I quietly entered [a little hole] and stayed very quiet, and they went away somewhere.₁ He was shooting on the path—"tan!"—and soon I heard them on the path, "tan!" where they were <u>bomb</u>ing, "tang!"$_2$ It made the sound "puririri," just like when they detonate the rock on the <u>road</u>.$_3$ . . . So I stayed quiet at the edges of the forest, hiding and being quiet, and I thought, "Perhaps my wife has been shot, perhaps my son has been shot."$_4$ The air was totally still.$_5$

Thankfully, nobody from the community of Inkaare was killed, and after a few months in Quillabamba—once the land mines had been cleared—they were able to return to their homes.

I chose to close this book with a Matsigenka perspective on this terrifying incident to emphasize once again the human stakes of frontier expansion in the upper Amazon today. The chaos and violence of the cocaine trade is one of the many challenges that the current generations of Matsigenka people, as well as their colono neighbors, are facing for the first time. This is one of the many hard new realities of the Alto Urubamba frontier.

Indeed, nearly every aspect of life in the Alto Urubamba today is, in one way or another, new. The cool, damp cloud forests of a decade ago have become a warm, dusty, landslide-prone patchwork of agricultural plantations and cow pastures—bringing relative prosperity to tens of thousands of farmers while decimating the edge of one of the earth's last great forests. Natural gas pipelines have been dug underneath Matsigenka communities, providing energy to people across the world and in other parts of Peru, while benefiting the communities themselves relatively little. New roads are cut through the forest using revenues from the gas project, bringing health care and schools, but also furthering a destructive cycle of deforestation and providing a transportation network for violent cocaine smugglers. Hardworking people make an honest living in a thriving new economy, while hustlers and con men conspire with corrupt politicians in get-rich-quick schemes that leave streams clogged with poisonous chemicals. All of these things have come to exist together in a frontier that is saturated with cash, but where the rule of law remains a distant abstraction.

The most vulnerable inhabitants of the valley have suffered the worst consequences of these changes. This includes Matsigenkas in particular, who are bystanders to much of the turmoil, as we saw in the harrowing testimonies of Angélica (transcript 28) and Roberto (transcript 29). But while much of this book has focused on the struggles of Matsigenka people, we must also be sensitive to the experiences of Andean migrants, many of whom might rightly be called climate refugees and who have fled poverty and racism in the highlands to seek a better life for their families in the lowlands. They, too, are buffeted by the winds of global geopolitics—particularly now, as the changing climate has made an already precarious life in the high Andes even more uncertain. Many of the abuses on the Alto Urubamba frontier are visited upon young Quechua-speaking seasonal laborers and upon colono smallholders who are threatened by cocaine producers.

In this book, I have described how people from across the region tried to find their place in this new society which, during my fieldwork in 2009–12, was churning across the landscape at a frenetic and uncontrolled pace. This society was *new* in the sense that it was emerging in a landscape where no intensive commercial agriculture had been conducted before, and in the sense that it brought together people who lived lives radically different from those of their parents and grandparents. Some were the children of Quechua speakers who grew up as pastoralists and farmers high in the frigid Andes; others were the children of Matsigenka speakers who lived entirely off hunting, fishing, and horticulture in the tropical forests. Many counted people from both of these backgrounds among their forebears. What they had in common was that they encountered each other as newcomers in a nascent and unfamiliar agricultural society. This was the *society of beginners* that I have referred to throughout this book.

I approached this society through the lens of language. The first half of the book explored the social organization of multilingualism among Matsigenka, Quechua, and Spanish in the emerging frontier milieu. I argued that the Alto Urubamba is *just one world*—that is, that Indigenous Amazonians and Andeans were connected in a single unbroken network extending from the remotest corners of the tropical forest to the rural agropastoral communities of the high Andes and beyond. The three languages were spoken in all combinations by the people in this network, while in communities like Yokiri, each household had its own multilingual history formed within the upheaval of frontier expansion.

I also showed how this multilingual network was mediated by kinship ties forged through widespread interethnic marriage on the agricultural frontier. Most Andeans who migrated to the Amazonian frontier were young Quechua-speaking men, and when they started families with Matsigenka women on the frontier, Matsigenka men were forced, in turn, to travel into the more remote tributaries in search of spouses. This created an asymmetrically gendered flow of languages and people, mediated by kinship: men moved down the Urubamba River and into the remote tributaries, bringing Quechua with them, while Matsigenka-speaking women moved out of the remote areas and upriver toward the highlands. In the multilingual, multiethnic society generated by this dynamic, who "counted" as Matsigenka or Andean could be quite fluid, perspectival, and contextual. The trilingual children of interethnic unions might be treated as Matsigenkas while visiting colono communities, and as colonos while visiting Matsigenka communities. At the same time, census counts and bilingual education programs sorted them on one side or the other of a binary institutional division, giving the illusion of separateness.

By considering such binary discourses through an ethnographic view of the frontier's ethnic and linguistic fluidity in this book, I intend to pose a critique of the discourse of Andean-Amazonian division that predominates in scholarly and popular conceptualizations of western South America. This dominant notion treats the two macrogeographical regions (implicitly, for the most part) as each having an essential coherence and as being naturally distinct from one another. This division is extended to the Indigenous people who live in those regions, constructing Amazonians and Andeans separately, in relation to two distinct "racialized imaginative geographies" (Radcliffe and Westwood 1996, 118). This language of twoness persists even when connections between those people and regions are recognized—framed most often as clashes or as exceptional forms of continuity across a boundary between coherent wholes. I have tried to move beyond this discourse of division and exceptionality by writing a book that is both an Andean and an Amazonian ethnography, focused on the unity rather than the separateness of those worlds.

In the second half of the book, I examined a few important contexts of language use to show how people from various backgrounds used Matsigenka, Quechua, and Spanish as they forged a place for themselves in the tumultuous social world of the agricultural frontier in 2009–12. By focusing on the day-to-day details of interaction—frontier life, as it is experienced on the ground—I offered an alternative to the notion of a clash between Andean and Amazonian groups of people. Indeed, in the richness of their social and linguistic lives, people in the Alto Urubamba moved between various roles and identities within the frontier social world. At some moments they adopted the social persona of the coffee farmer, which was associated with a range of enregistered linguistic and cultural practices: joking in Quechua over bottles of beer on the roadside, sitting side by side with other farmers in a Spanish training workshop and talking about soil chemistry, or laughing along to the Quechua verbal dramas on Radio Quillabamba as members of an agrarian public (chapter 4). At other moments, members of comunidades nativas spoke Spanish in asambleas, adopting the social persona of the comunero (community member) as they pushed back against the agrarian society that was closing in around them (chapter 5). Discussions about a single hillside in mythic Matsigenka discourse and in technical Spanish discourse were based on different conceptualizations of history and even on different ideas of what kinds of beings exist in the world (chapter 6). Languages were thus associated with particular spaces, economic practices, kinds of moral obligation, and visions of the landscape, all of which could be quite different from one context of interaction to the next. Most importantly, individuals moved among these various associations over the course of their daily lives. Seen this way, the multiethnic frontier encounter in the Alto Urubamba was not a clash between groups, but rather an experience negotiated through the complexities of everyday social relationships and interactions.

This book is also about the social dynamics of coffee production, frontier expansion, and deforestation. This focus came as something of a surprise to me as I conducted my research: I first traveled to the Alto Urubamba to learn about multilingualism and knew nothing about these other things before my arrival. However, I quickly realized that by documenting the day-to-day facts of language use, I was also writing an ethnography of the emerging coffee industry and its environmental effects. This is because there was no distinction between the world in which people moved between their three languages and the world in which people spent their days transforming the forest into farmland. That is, as people participated in Spanish agricultural training workshops, negotiated in Quechua over prices and terms, and sent radio transmissions to relay logistical information or publicly shame delinquent debtors in Spanish and Quechua, they were doing the daily business of frontier expansion and coffee production just as much as when they cleared land and put seeds in the soil. In terms of academic disciplines, multilingualism and agricultural frontier expansion seem like radically different topics, studied by linguists and linguistic anthropologists on the one hand and by environmental scientists, agronomists, and development economists on the other. These domains of scholarly literature rarely overlap. However, following the holistic theoretical and methodological tradition of linguistic anthropology (Mannheim 2018a), I show in this book that the coffee economy and the frontier society are built up, in part, through communicative acts. Conversely, the Alto Urubamba's culture of multilingualism must be understood in the day-to-day contexts in which it is used, which are all connected to the extraordinary environmental and economic changes in the valley. Thus this book is an ethnography both of multilingualism and of the coffee industry's expansion into the rain forest, which are one and the same.

A final contribution that I hope to have made with this book has to do with the historical linguistic dynamics of western South America. After I finished my PhD, I joined an interdisciplinary group of linguists, archaeologists, and geneticists at Leiden University and at the University of Tübingen who were interested in the ancient movement of people, languages, and goods around South America. As I began collaborating with these colleagues, I thought about how the patterns I observed in the Alto Urubamba might be reflected in other regions and at greater time depths. Indeed, converging evidence from recent interdisciplinary research in South America suggests that particular parts of the Andean highlands and the Amazonian lowlands have been closely interconnected at various points in history, much as we find in the Alto Urubamba today. First, linguistic typological features, including phonology (Michael, Chang, and Stark 2014) and morphosyntax (van Gijn 2014), have been shown to follow a gradual transition between the two regions, such that it is more productive to speak of a broad east-west linguistic division in South America than an Andean-Amazonian one in particular (Krasnoukhova 2012; Birchall 2014; Epps and Michael 2017). Second, some populations from the Andean highlands and the Amazonian lowlands have undergone substantial gene flow throughout history, suggesting a relatively integrated population history at some parts of the highland-lowland transitional zone (Corella et al. 2007; Di Corcia et al. 2017). Finally, historical research indicates that Andean-Amazonian interaction in many places was more intense in the past than it is today (A. C. Taylor 1999; Saignes 1985; Santos-Granero 1985). Together, these interdisciplinary perspectives offer a rich way forward in understanding the prehistoric dynamics of western South America.

The most relevant comparison in this regard comes from Yanesha' (discussed in chapter 2), an Arawak language of the eastern foothills of central Peru that was heavily influenced by the neighboring Yaru variety of Quechua from the nearby highlands (Adelaar 2006; Wise 1976). Yanesha' borrowed some Yaru Quechua grammatical suffixes and a great number of lexical items, many of which involve emotion and sensation. These effects predate the period of Inka imperial expansion—and Yaru Quechua was not an imperial language—all of which suggests a period of language contact based in relatively nonhegemonic social relationships among neighbors (like we find in the Alto Urubamba) rather than in a hierarchical relationship between conquerors and subjects. These patterns of intensive language contact are consistent with the findings of C. Barbieri et al. (2014), who find substantial Andean influence in the genomes of Yanesha' speakers today. Notably, this Andean influence exhibits a male sex bias, consistent with Andean men traveling to the lowlands and having children with Yanesha'-speaking women. These are precisely the same kinds of gendered social dynamics that we see among Matsigenkas and Quechua-speaking Andean migrants in the Alto Urubamba from the mid-twentieth century onward.

If this is the case, then paying attention to historical and contemporary social relations in the Alto Urubamba may help us interpret the kinds of broad-scale genetic and linguistic typological patterns identified by scholars of South America in recent years. It is clear that some places and people—for instance, the ancestors of today's Yanesha' speakers—have been involved in intensive bursts of Andean-Amazonian contact, but in many cases it is difficult to fill out the details of what those relationships might have been like. The interplay between language, gender, kinship, migration, geography, resources, and labor that we find in the Alto Urubamba may help us interpret historical cases like the Yanesha'-Quechua relationship in central Peru. For this reason, I presented a linguistic history of the Alto Urubamba in chapter 2, with the hope that it might contribute to a broader perspective on the interregional history of western South America.

Indeed, as we have seen in this book, the traces and echoes of this interregional history are everywhere in the Alto Urubamba. One need look no further than the military confrontation in Inkaare described above: nearly five centuries earlier, the very same patch of forest was thrust onto the global stage when the Inkas fled Cusco during the European invasion and operated a capital-in-exile at Espíritu Pampa for more than thirty years. The ruins of Espíritu Pampa are just a few kilometers from Inkaare (see map 4), and Roberto and Angélica traveled there frequently as children during hunting and gathering trips. The intrusion of global geopolitics into their forests on that terrifying April morning in 2012 was, thus, but the most recent episode in a long history of such entanglements in the Alto Urubamba.

Antonio, the Matsigenka friend I mentioned at the beginning of this book, certainly sees it this way. He knows the stories of how his parents and grand-parents, and his more distant ancestors before them, struggled to find a place for themselves in the tumultuous and ever-changing social world of the Alto Urubamba. When he looks out across the valley at the snowy Andean peaks to the south, and across the misty Amazon plain to the north, he contemplates the many things that have happened in this landscape, and the things that are yet to come.

Notes

Introduction

1. Following the recommendation of the Native American Journalists Association, the term *Indigenous* is capitalized throughout this book, as is the term *Native* when it refers to heritage or ethnic category.
2. Thanks to Frank Salomon for suggesting this formulation.
3. I thank an anonymous reviewer for suggesting this connection to the literature on historical settlement frontiers.
4. Many Matsigenka people remain outside of regular contact with colonos in places like Manu National Park, which was created to block colonization from the Andes. Bunce and McElreath (2018, 2017) have studied interethnic interactions between Matsigenkas in Manu National Park and colonos outside of it. However, that situation is somewhat different from the Alto Urubamba, where colonos and Matsigenkas live much more closely integrated lives, and where widespread interethnic marriage has made those social categories more complicated.
5. I'm grateful to Joshua Shapero for pointing out the use of this term in animal husbandry in Peru.
6. The influential Peruvian geographer Javier Pulgar Vidal (1967) made a finer distinction between eight natural regions. The terms *montaña* and *ceja de selva* are also sometimes used to describe the hilly upper Amazon.
7. It is not a coincidence that the very same area was also a *zona roja* for much of the sixteenth century, when the Inka nobility eluded the Spanish and kept up a forty-year assault on the colonial regime from their inaccessible forest redoubt of Espíritu Pampa (see chapter 2 and map 3).

Chapter 1

1. Ironically, the Camisea project was first marketed as an environmentally responsible "roadless" project (Tollefson 2011), linked to the outside world only through pipelines and river and air traffic. However, while the gas project did not build roads, royalties from the project supported road construction. Those roads have wrought environmental devastation on a much larger scale than the immediate effects of the project itself (Shepard 2012a). In this context, the comment from one of the project's advisors about the small area around the main Las Malvinas plant—"This is far from an idyllic forest, but what I see is something that is contained" (Tollefson 2011, 23)—is out of touch with the project's broader impacts.

2. Some colonos in the region who interact frequently with Matsigenkas have taken to referring to themselves as *gente blanca* as well, as a point of pride.

3. *tovaiganankitsirira*
   tova-ig-an-ankits-i-rira
   be.many-PL-ABL-SUBJ.FOC-REAL-REL
   "the ones who are becoming many"

4. People in some districts of La Convención boycotted the national census that was conducted in 2017. This was due to a conflict between the provinces of La Convención and Calca over parts of the Alto Urubamba. For this reason, I take the 2017 census in this area to be unreliable, and I use data from 2007 instead. Thus this discussion does not refer to the district of Megantoni, which was created in 2016.

5. Upper valley districts in the 2007 census include Huayopata, Maranura, Ocobamba, Santa Teresa, and Vilcabamba. Lower valley districts include Echarate, Kimbiri, Pichari, and Quellouno. The city of Quillabamba is counted as the Santa Ana district.

6. In 2007, the population density of the rural highland provinces of Cusco was 100.4 people per km²; in La Convención, the population density was only 5.5 people per km².

7. A long-standing anxiety in Matsigenka society is that colono men will come and take away the women (see, e.g., Tennant 1958, 100).

8. Note that the comunidades nativas in Peru frequently face the question of how to handle colonos residing in their midst (see, e.g., Gray 1998, 182); however, situations such as this in which the categories of "colono" and "Indigenous" are negotiable and contestable can be considerably more complex.

9. A common English translation of *campesino* is "peasant"; however, this English term has gone out of vogue since the twentieth century and has taken on something of a negative connotation. For this reason, I have chosen to simply translate *campesino* as "farmer."

Chapter 2

1. For a comparable discussion of Asháninka history on the Amazonian frontier of central Peru, see Brown and Fernández (1992).

2. For more on the classification of the Kampan Arawak languages, see Michael (2011). Note that Yine, a more distantly related Arawak language spoken far-

ther down the Urubamba Valley, may have been spoken in the region before this time.

3.   Wilkinson (2018) posits a relationship of trade in tropical bird feathers between the highland Wari polity and speakers of Arawak languages on the eastern Andean slopes during the Middle Horizon (ca. 600–1000 AD). It is not likely that Arawak languages had arrived as far as the Urubamba and Apurímac Valleys at that early time, but trade at that time may indeed have involved Arawak languages in the Amazon plain more indirectly.

4.   For more on the classification of the Quechuan languages, see Adelaar and Muysken (2004); Cerrón-Palomino (1987); Mannheim (1991); Parker (1963); and Torero (1964).

5.   The sources of the historical toponyms listed here are, respectively, Rostworowski (1963, 224); de Ocampo ([1610] 1907, 239); Hemming (1970, 476–7); Oricaín ([1790] 1906, 350); Marcoy (1875); Samanez Ocampo (1907, 354); and Maúrtua (1906, 284).

6.   Travelers in the Alto Urubamba also record Quechua toponyms far beyond the colonization zone of their day, suggesting an earlier history of Quechua expansion through the region (e.g., in the Yavero Valley; see Hassel 1907).

7.   It may be possible to build a corpus of these unidentified toponyms and to look for phonological or morphological patterns suggestive of historical relationships to other languages in the region.

8.   Alejandro Camino (1977, 124n1) notes the ethnonym *Manariegui*, which appears to comprise the common term *Manarí* and the Matsigenka nominal plural suffix *-egi*. This would constitute evidence that some Manaríes spoke Matsigenka (or at least a closely related Arawak language). However, I have been unable to find more information about when and where this term was attested.

9.   Guaman Poma de Ayala writes about such a punishment for rape: "And if the woman forced the man, they sentenced the woman to death and the man to whipping and banishment to the forest, to the Chunchos Indians, never more to be seen" (1615/1616, 307 [309]; Y ci lo forsó la muger al hombre, le sentencia a la muger a muerte y al hombre a los asotes y destierro a la montaña a los yndios Chunchos para nunca más pareser; see also Bertazoni Martins 2007; Steele 2015, 132). Translation mine.

10.   The Dominicans also availed themselves of Matsigenka labor on their plantations through similar arrangements, leading some to describe Chirumbia and Koribeni as "hacienda-missions" (Fioravanti 1974, 55)—an accusation that the Dominicans vigorously dispute (Encinas Martín, Perez Casados, and Alonso Ordieres 2008, 70–82).

11.   Renard-Casevitz, Saignes, and Taylor (1988, 148) attribute Arawak origin to the term *apitire*, found in an unnamed document describing the events of Vilcabamba in the colonial period. This term refers to a historical figure's neighbors, and they interpret it as an Arawak term for "los demás" (the others). However, in all contemporary Matsigenka varieties, the relevant form usually appears as *apitene* ("others," feminine form), or *irapitene* (masculine form). Similarly, they interpret the place name Momori, attested in the same period, as being derived

from Matsigenka *mámori* (fish species, genus *Brycon*). However, I am not aware of independent evidence for this place being named after the *mámori* fish. Because of the inexact sound correspondences and indirect semantics of these attributions, I do not count them as evidence that a Kampan language was spoken in the Alto Urubamba during the colonial period (particularly since this would mean pushing back the first attestation by around two hundred years).

12. The Matsigenka toponym Eriapani comprises the noun *eriapa* (shotgun) and the suffix *-ni* (watercourse). After Quechua speakers colonized the area with this name in the mid-nineteenth century, the toponym became Illapani. Interestingly, Matsigenka *eriapa* (shotgun) is itself a loan of Quechua *illapa* (lightning, flash, shotgun). Here it appears that Matsigenka *eriapa* was replaced with Quechua *illapa*—the term from which it was originally borrowed—while retaining the Matsigenka suffix *-ni* (watercourse). Even more interesting is that the word's sense of "shotgun," which was also borrowed from Quechua to Matsigenka, is a Quechua neologism following European contact. This example illustrates the complexity and porousness of the Alto Urubamba's linguistic history.

13. For a detailed description of such terms in the closely related Alto Perené Kampa language, see Mihas (2015).

14. Modern sources include the maps produced by Peru's Instituto Geográfico Nacional (http://www.ign.gob.pe); the maps of the road network from Peru's Ministerio de Transportes y Comunicaciones (www.mtc.gob.pe); SERNANP (www.sernanp .gob.pe); CEDIA (www.cedia.org.pe); the Instituto del Bien Común (www .ibcperu.org); and my own fieldwork. Historical data come from the accounts of voyages through the Alto Urubamba in the nineteenth and early twentieth centuries, which are particularly helpful since they took place before the current wave of Andean colonization displaced many Matsigenka speakers (and toponyms). These include the voyages of Paul Marcoy in 1840–46 (Marcoy 1875, 355–454); of José B. Samanez Ocampo in 1883–84 (Samanez Ocampo 1907, 343–59); of Ramón Zubieta in 1903 (Zubieta 1903, 133–46); and of Georg M. von Hassel in 1904 (Hassel 1907). Note that toponyms are sparsely recorded in protected areas, since most mapping and recording of toponyms takes place during the processes of political administration and infrastructure development.

15. In the Spanish verb *chagompitar* (to tie a baby in a sling), the /t/ is an epenthetic segment used to break up vowel adjacencies in Matsigenka constructions. For instance:

> *otsagomputakeri*
> *o-tsagompu-t-ak-i-ri*
> 3F-tie.baby.in.sling-EP-PF-REAL-3M
> "she tied him up in a sling"

Chapter 3

1. The confluence of these two waves of colonization has created a political situation that is complex for reasons beyond its implications for Matsigenka people.

The colonos from the Urubamba Valley side came from the province of La Convención and established the new district of Quellouno within that province as they populated the area; meanwhile, the colonos from the Yavero Valley came from the province of Calca and established their own new district of Yanatile, which overlaps with Quellouno's borders. This has created an intense territorial dispute. Complicating matters further, the conflict also has a religious dimension, as many of the Calqueños are Evangelical Christians, while most of the Convencianos are Catholic. Each province lays claim to the contested land by building public infrastructure there, and, as a result, some places are home to two schools and health posts belonging to the competing municipalities. This construction race also implicates the Camisea natural gas project in the territorial conflict, since La Convención receives more revenues for infrastructure investment. This conflict has occasionally become violent—several people have been killed and injured in skirmishes, and competing bridges and schools have been burned and damaged. In October 2017, the INEI census workers were blocked by Convencianos from entering parts of the region to conduct the national census, over fears of a new map that would legitimize the claim of the Calqueños (Carrasco 2017). Some people told me they were surprised that such acrimony and violence would emerge over a dispute between provinces, which are, after all, second-level administrative subdivisions in Peru (roughly equivalent to two counties or municipalities battling over land within the same state in the United States). However, the combination of Camisea gas revenues, the recent history of land colonization, and the undertones of religious confrontation have made this a particularly volatile situation. Interestingly, even though this is a conflict among competing groups of colonos, Yokiriños have taken a side: having originated mostly in La Convención, and (perhaps more importantly) considering themselves Catholic, they only recognize the district of Quellouno and reject the district of Yanatile.

2. Andrew Gray reports that as enslaved Asháninkas in central Peru have moved away to claim their own land, the "sudden drainage of the labour force has put severe pressure on the economy of both the old colonists and the new settlers, which is completely dependent on very cheap or free Indian labour" (1998, 210). A similar process has occurred in the Alto Urubamba.

3. Note a methodological problem with population estimates of comunidades nativas, and census data in particular: Matsigenkas are generally only counted as such if they are members of a comunidad nativa, even though there are a great number of people living elsewhere who consider themselves Matsigenkas. This bias is offset to some degree by the inverse error: colonos living within comunidades nativas are counted in Matsigenka population estimates, even though they do not consider themselves ethnically Matsigenka. There are also many people inside and outside of comunidades nativas whose ethnicity is more contingent and contextual (see chapter 1), and whose presence calls into question the utility of these labels as empirical and administrative categories altogether.

4. A similar phenomenon relates to the large territorial extensions that some communities in the Alto Urubamba have managed to title in more remote areas. In some cases, it has turned out that the community members have preferred not to leave the relative comforts of the agricultural frontier, and the territorial extensions have gone unused.

5. I visited this man in a convalescent home for Salesian priests in Lima in 2011. He told me about recruiting these colonos from Lares after the flood, about the journey they took together into the uncolonized forests of the lower Yavero Valley, and about how this expedition was tied up with his own decades-long search for the legendary Inka city of Paititi.

6. The Dominicans abandoned the mission at Chirumbia when the agrarian reform swept through the Urubamba Valley and the missionaries were targeted alongside other large landowners.

7. A similar agricultural lifestyle was also expected of the Matsigenkas living with Evangelical SIL missionaries farther down the Urubamba Valley (Camino 1979, 140–41).

8. One of the biggest problems for the Dominicans has been that many Matsigenkas who have been incorporated into the economic and social norms of colono society no longer wish to be confined to the mission.

9. Otingamía is sometimes called Otinganía.

10. During the filming of this movie, about an abusive rubber trader who operated around the nearby Fitzcarrald Pass (connecting the Urubamba and Madeira watersheds) in the late nineteenth century, "Herzog had to commit some of the same transgressions as the film's protagonist" (Brown 1982, 20). In 2012, the local Dominican missionary priest screened it in comunidades nativas (often onto a bedsheet hung from a roof beam in the salón comunal) during his periodic rounds across the Alto Urubamba. The choice of this film was meant to invoke parallels between the abuses of the rubber industry a century ago and the extractive industries at work in the region today—most notably the Camisea natural gas project.

Chapter 4

A section of this chapter was published, in a slightly different form, in the *Journal of Latin American and Caribbean Anthropology* (Emlen 2017a).

1. I mention China as a salient global example of an emerging coffee market, though China does not currently import much Peruvian coffee. Peru's largest export markets in 2016 were the United States (27 percent), Germany (25 percent), Belgium (10 percent), and Sweden (5 percent) (Bean and Nolte 2017).

2. Arabica coffee in the eastern Andean slopes currently grows best between 500 and 1,500 meters (~1,600 to 4,900 feet) above sea level. However, global warming is pushing suitable coffee land to higher elevations, and Ovalle-Rivera et al. (2015, 7) predict that by the 2050s the suitable coffee zone in the Andean region will move to 1,000–2,800 meters (~3,300–9,200 feet) above sea level. This change is projected to devastate low-elevation coffee industries, where it is impossible to move

uphill—as in Brazil, for instance—and it will drastically reduce the amount of land around the world that is suitable for coffee cultivation. The decline in quantity and quality of Brazilian and Mesoamerican coffee could benefit Andean producers (Ovalle-Rivera et al. 2015, 11), but overall, arabica coffee, the predominant global variety, is in for a difficult few decades.

3.   Coffee rust also destroyed the Sri Lankan and southern Indian coffee industries in the late nineteenth century, which is one reason for the increased popularity of tea in the United Kingdom since that time (Waller, Bigger, and Hillocks 2007, 172).

4.   Two decades later, in 1998, the Cusco-Quillabamba rail link was destroyed after a terrible landslide dammed the Aobamba River. When the dam broke, the lake of water that it had held back flooded the valley and swept the town of Santa Teresa into the river (Thomson 2010; Gade 2016, 10). Locals knew that the receding waters below the landslide meant trouble, and they scrambled to high land; remarkably, only seventeen people were killed. The rail link was never rebuilt, and in 2009–12 a few abandoned train cars still sat rusting at Quillabamba's Pavayoc terminal.

5.   The institutional connection between Radio Quillabamba and COMARU comes from the fact that both emerged from the Dominican missionary sphere in the Alto Urubamba. Note that the term *mavaintini* is a complex notion in Matsigenka culture, referring to mortal humans as viewed by immortal spirits (Snell 2011, 275).

6.   Members of comunidades nativas in the Urubamba Valley used radio transceivers to communicate on one frequency, 4520, usually in Matsigenka. This created an interesting ethnic counterpublic, or at least parallel public, in the sense that it linked people around the valley in a separate, ethnically defined communicative network. The fact that members of widely dispersed comunidades nativas could communicate with each other, mostly in Matsigenka and to the exclusion of colonos, strengthened people's day-to-day consciousness of ethnic belonging. It was also a helpful communicative channel through which relatives could communicate with one another and public demonstrations could be planned in Matsigenka without the knowledge of neighboring colonos or local officials. I plan to address the linguistic and ethnic complexities of this radio ecosystem in further work.

Chapter 5

A version of this chapter was published in *Language in Society* (Emlen 2015).

1.   The full name of this law is the Ley de Comunidades Nativas y de Desarrollo Agrario de la Selva y Ceja de Selva (no. 22175). Thorough introductions can be found in García Hierro, Hvalkof, and Gray (1998) and Chirif and García Hierro (2007), and a description of the process from the perspective of Ashéninka community members is given by Killick (2008a). Tubbeh and Zimmerer (2019) point out that the "ethnoterritorial fix" promised by the law has not always resulted in stable livelihoods among Indigenous Amazonians.

2.   Baksh (1984, 416–28) notes a similar phenomenon in the Matsigenka community of Camaná, where kin groups that came together to form a nucleated settlement

maintained the social and physical division between the hamlets in their new home.

3. Joseph Henrich (2000) demonstrates this principle with a comparative economic experiment conducted with subjects around the world, including the Matsigenka community of Camisea. When asked to share a sum of money with a partner, Matsigenkas shared much less than subjects from other places, and their partners were far more willing to accept a small proportion of that money.

4. Just as the Constitution of the United States is constructed as both authored by and addressed to a depersonalized American public "we" (Warner 1990, 111–12), Yokiri's estatuto (bylaws) is conceived as both issuing from the community's collective will and mandating a framework for its proper execution.

5. Interestingly, these discourses also have a suggestive resonance with the Catholic idioms of sacrifice and suffering. I thank Mercedes Niño-Murcia for this observation.

6. The construction *es una celebración conmemorativo* (it's a commemorative celebration) exhibits a lack of gender concord that is typical of Andean Spanish (Adelaar and Muysken 2004, 598) and of the way Spanish is spoken in Yokiri (Emlen, forthcoming).

Chapter 6

1. Such ideas about rainbows are widespread in native Amazonian societies: see Valadeau et al. (2010) and references therein.

2. Note that the Matsigenka term for "plain" used here, *pampa*, is itself a Quechua loan—the same as in Quilla*bamba*—illustrating the historical complexity of this assertion.

3. The earliest references to the toponym Yokiri that I have found in the historical record come from a 1903 expedition by the Dominican missionary Ramón Zubieta (1903, 144), and Georg M. von Hassel's expedition in 1904 (Hassel 1907, 377). The forebears of some of today's Yokiriños migrated around the area and likely had a passing familiarity with the valley, but historical consciousness regarding the region only reaches back a generation or two beyond the memories of the community's oldest residents.

References

Academia Mayor de la Lengua Quechua. 2005. *Diccionario: Quechua-español-quechua (Qheswa-español-qheswa: Simi taqe)*. Cuzco: Academia Mayor de la Lengua Quechua (Qheswa Simi Hamut'ana Kurak Suntur).

Adelaar, Willem F. H. 2006. "The Quechua Impact in Amuesha, an Arawak Language of the Peruvian Amazon." In *Grammars in Contact*, edited by Alexandra Y. Aikhenvald and R. M. W. Dixon, 290–312. Oxford: Oxford University Press.

Adelaar, Willem F. H. 2008. "Review of *Quechua-Spanish Bilingualism: Interference and Convergence in Functional Categories*." *International Journal of American Linguistics* 74 (2): 265–68.

Adelaar, Willem F. H. 2012. "Cajamarca Quechua and the Expansion of the Huari State." In *Linguistics and Archaeology in the Andes: A Cross-Disciplinary Exploration of Prehistory*, edited by Paul Heggarty and David Beresford-Jones, 197–217. Oxford: Oxford University Press.

Adelaar, Willem F. H., and Pieter Muysken. 2004. *The Languages of the Andes*. Cambridge Language Surveys. Cambridge, UK: Cambridge University Press.

Agha, Asif. 2005. "Voice, Footing, Enregisterment." *Journal of Linguistic Anthropology* 15 (1): 38–59.

Agha, Asif. 2007. *Language and Social Relations*. Cambridge, UK: Cambridge University Press.

Aikhenvald, Alexandra Y. 1999. "The Arawak Language Family." In *The Amazonian Languages*, edited by R. M. W. Dixon and Alexandra Y. Aikhenvald, 65–106. Cambridge, UK: Cambridge University Press.

Albó, Xavier. 1973. *El futuro de los idiomas oprimidos en los Andes*. La Paz: Centro de Investigación y Promoción del Campesinado.

Alconini, Sonia. 2004. "The Southeastern Inka Frontier Against the Chiriguanos: Structure and Dynamics of the Inka Imperial Borderlands." *Latin American Antiquity* 15 (4): 389–418.

Allen, Catherine. 1988. *The Hold Life Has: Coca and Cultural Identity in an Andean Community*. Washington, D.C.: Smithsonian Institution Press.

Altamirano, Teófilo. 1984. *Presencia andina en Lima metropolitana: Un estudio sobre migrantes y clubes de provincianos*. Lima: Pontificia Universidad Católica del Perú, Fondo Editorial.

Álvarez, Enrique. 1932. "Las ruinas de Mosocllacta." *Misiones Dominicanas del Perú* 69:64–69.

Alvarez, Nora L., and Lisa Naughton-Treves. 2003. "Linking National Agrarian Policy to Deforestation in the Peruvian Amazon: A Case Study of Tambopata, 1986–1997." *AMBIO: A Journal of the Human Environment* 32 (4): 269–74.

Anderson, Benedict. (1983) 1991. *Imagined Communities: Reflections on the Origin and Spread of Nationalism*. London: Verso.

Aramburú, Carlos E. 1982. "Expansión de la frontera agraria y demográfica en la selva alta peruana." In *Colonización en la Amazonía*, edited by Carlos E. Aramburú, Eduardo Bedoya Garland, and Jorge Recharte Bullard, 1–39. Lima: Centro de Investigación y Promoción Amazónica.

Aramburú, Carlos E. 1984. "Expansion of the Agrarian and Demographic Frontier in the Peruvian Selva." In *Frontier Expansion in Amazonia*, edited by Marianne Schmink and Charles H. Wood, 153–79. Gainesville: University of Florida Press.

Araujo Salas, Brenda Liz. 2017. "Estudio de la mujer indígena amazónica: Situación y propuestas." In *Mujeres en nuestras misiones: Informe 2017*, 14–88. Lima: Centro Cultural José Pío Aza; CAAAP.

Avineri, Netta. 2012. "Heritage Language Socialization Practices in Secular Yiddish Educational Contexts: The Creation of a Metalinguistic Community." PhD dissertation, University of California, Los Angeles.

Avineri, Netta, and Paul V. Kroskrity. 2014. "On the (Re-)production and Representation of Endangered Language Communities: Social Boundaries and Temporal Borders." *Language & Communication* 38:1–7.

Babel, Anna M. 2018. *Between the Andes and the Amazon: Language and Social Meaning in Bolivia*. Tucson: University of Arizona Press.

Baer, Gerhard. 1994. *Cosmología y shamanismo de los matsiguenga*. Quito: Ediciones Abya-Yala.

Bakhtin, Mikhail M. 1981. "Discourse in the Novel." In *The Dialogic Imagination*, edited by M. M. Bakhtin, 259–75. Austin: University of Texas Press.

Baksh, Michael. 1984. "Cultural Ecology and Change of the Machiguenga Indians of the Peruvian Amazon." PhD dissertation, University of California, Los Angeles.

Barbieri, Allison F., and David L. Carr. 2005. "Gender-Specific Out-Migration, Deforestation and Urbanization in the Ecuadorian Amazon." *Global and Planetary Change* 47 (2–4): 99–110.

Barbieri, Chiara, Paul Heggarty, Daniele Yang Yao, Gianmarco Ferri, Sara De Fanti, Stefania Sarno, Graziella Ciani, Alessio Boattini, Donata Luiselli, and Davide Pettener.

2014. "Between Andes and Amazon: The Genetic Profile of the Arawak-Speaking Yanesha." *American Journal of Physical Anthropology* 155:600–609.

Barclay, Frederica. 2001. "Olvido de una historia: Reflexiones acerca de la historiografía andino-amazónica." *Revista de Indias* 61 (223): 493–511.

Barker, Joshua. 2008. "Playing with Publics: Technology, Talk, and Sociability in Indonesia." *Language and Communication* 28:127–42.

Basso, Keith H. 1996. *Wisdom Sits in Places: Landscape and Language Among the Western Apache.* Albuquerque: University of New Mexico Press.

Bauer, Brian S. 1998. *The Sacred Landscape of the Inca: The Cusco Ceque System.* Austin: University of Texas Press.

Bauer, Brian S., Gabriel E. Cantarutti, and Madeleine Halac-Higashimori. 2016. *Voices from Vilcabamba: Accounts Chronicling the Fall of the Inca Empire.* Boulder: University Press of Colorado.

Bauer, Brian S., Javier Fonseca Santa Cruz, and Miriam Aráoz Silva. 2015. *Vilcabamba and the Archaeology of Inca Resistance.* Los Angeles: Cotsen Institute of Archaeology Press.

Bauman, Richard. 2001. "The Ethnography of Genre in a Mexican Market: Form, Function, Variation." In *Style and Sociolinguistic Variation*, edited by Penelope Eckert and John R. Rickford, 57–77. Cambridge, UK: Cambridge University Press.

Bean, Casey, and Gaspar E. Nolte. 2017. "Peruvian Coffee Production Bouncing Back." USDA Foreign Agricultural Service Global Agricultural Information Network report, May 3, 2017. https://gain.fas.usda.gov/Recent%20GAIN%20Publications/Coffee%20Annual_Lima_Peru_5-3-2017.pdf.

Beier, Christine. 2010. "The Social Life and Sound Patterns of Nanti Ways of Speaking." PhD dissertation, University of Texas, Austin.

Beier, Christine, Lev Michael, and Joel Sherzer. 2002. "Discourse Forms and Processes in Indigenous Lowland South America: An Areal-Typological Perspective." *Annual Review of Anthropology* 31:121–45.

Belaúnde Terry, Fernando. 1965. *Peru's Own Conquest.* Lima: American Studies Press.

Bélisle, Véronique. 2019. "Hallucinogens and Altered States of Consciousness in Cusco, Peru: A Path to Local Power During Wari State Expansion." *Cambridge Archaeological Journal* 29 (3): 1–17.

Beresford-Jones, David G., and Paul Heggarty. 2011. "What Role for Language Prehistory in Redefining Archaeological 'Culture'? A Case Study on New Horizons in the Andes." In *Investigating Archaeological Cultures: Material Culture, Variability, and Transmission*, edited by B. W. Roberts and M. Vander Linden, 355–86. New York: Springer.

Berg, Ulla D. 2017. *Mobile Selves: Race, Migration, and Belonging in Peru and the U.S.* New York: NYU Press.

Bertazoni Martins, Cristiana. 2007. "Antisuyu: An Investigation of Inca Attitudes to Their Western Amazonian Territories." PhD dissertation, Essex University.

Bingham, Hiram. 1914a. "Along the Uncharted Pampaconas." *Harpers Magazine*, August 1914.

Bingham, Hiram. 1914b. "The Ruins of Espiritu Pampa, Peru." *American Anthropologist* 16 (2): 185–99.

Birchall, Joshua. 2014. "Verbal Argument Marking Patterns in South American Languages." In *The Native Languages of South America: Origins, Development, Typology*, edited by Loretta O'Connor and Pieter Muysken, 223–49. Cambridge, UK: Cambridge University Press.

Blanco Galdós, Hugo. 1972. *Tierra o muerte: Luchas campesinas en el Perú.* Mexico City: Siglo Veintiuno.

Boelens, Rutgerd. 2014. "Cultural Politics and the Hydrosocial Cycle: Water, Power and Identity in the Andean Highlands." *Geoforum* 57:234–47.

Bourgois, Philippe. 1995. *In Search of Respect: Selling Crack in El Barrio.* Cambridge, UK: Cambridge University Press.

Bowman, Isaiah. 1912. "The Cañon of the Urubamba." *Bulletin of the American Geographical Society* 44 (12): 881–97.

Bowser, Frederick P. 1974. *The African Slave in Colonial Peru: 1524–1650.* Stanford: Stanford University Press.

Brienen, Roel J. W., Oliver L. Phillips, Ted R. Feldpausch, Emanuel Gloor, Tim R. Baker, Jon Lloyd, Gabriela Lopez-Gonzalez, et al. 2015. "Long-Term Decline of the Amazon Carbon Sink." *Nature* 519:344.

Briggs, Charles, and Richard Bauman. 1992. "Genre, Intertextuality, and Social Power." *Journal of Linguistic Anthropology* 2 (2): 131–72.

Brown, Michael F. 1982. "Art of Darkness." *The Progressive* 46 (8): 20–21.

Brown, Michael F. 2014. *Upriver: The Turbulent Life and Times of an Amazonian People.* Cambridge, Mass.: Harvard University Press.

Brown, Michael F., and Eduardo Fernández. 1991. *War of Shadows: The Struggle for Utopia in the Peruvian Amazon.* Berkeley: University of California Press.

Brown, Michael F., and Eduardo Fernández. 1992. "Tribe and State in a Frontier Mosaic: The Asháninka of Eastern Peru." In *War in the Tribal Zone: Expanding States and Indigenous Warfare*, edited by R. Brian Ferguson and Neil L. Whitehead, 175–98. Santa Fe, N.M.: School of American Research Press.

Brubaker, Rogers. 2004. *Ethnicity Without Groups.* Cambridge, Mass.: Harvard University Press.

Bucholtz, Mary. 1999. "'Why Be Normal?': Language and Identity Practices in a Community of Nerd Girls." *Language in Society* 28 (2): 203–23.

Bucholtz, Mary, and Kira Hall. 2005. "Identity and Interaction: A Sociocultural Linguistic Approach." *Discourse Studies* 7 (4–5): 585–614.

Bües, Christian. 1942. "Contribución a la petropictografía precolombina en el sur del Perú." *Revista del Museo e Instituto Arqueológico* 6 (10–11): 31–38.

Bunce, John A., and Richard McElreath. 2017. "Interethnic Interaction, Strategic Bargaining Power, and the Dynamics of Cultural Norms." *Human Nature* 28 (4): 434–56.

Bunce, John A., and Richard McElreath. 2018. "Sustainability of Minority Culture When Inter-ethnic Interaction Is Profitable." *Nature Human Behaviour* 2 (3): 205.

Butler, Barbara Y. 2006. *Holy Intoxication to Drunken Dissipation: Alcohol Among Quichua Speakers in Otavalo, Ecuador*. Albuquerque: University of New Mexico Press.

Camino, Alejandro. 1977. "Trueque, correrías e intercambios entre los quechuas andinos y los piro y machiguenga de la montaña peruana." *Amazonía Peruana* 1 (2): 123–40.

Camino, Alejandro. 1979. "Sociocultural Change in the Upper Urubamba." In *Peasants, Primitives, and Proletariats: The Struggle for Identity in South America*, edited by D. L. Browman and R. A. Schwartz, 125–47. New York: Mouton Publishers.

Campbell, Jeremy M. 2015. *Conjuring Property: Speculation and Environmental Futures in the Brazilian Amazon*. Seattle: University of Washington Press.

Carranza, Camilo. 2019. "Peruvian Farmers Abandoning Coffee Plantations for Coca Fields." InSight Crime (website). March 7, 2019. https://www.insightcrime.org/news /brief/peru-coffee-farmers-going-coca-fields/.

Carrasco, Ernesto. 2017. "Censo 2017: Paro indefinido contra el censo en el Cusco." *La República*, October 24, 2017. Reportero Ciudadano. http://larepublica.pe/reportero -ciudadano/1135942-censo-2017-paro-indefinido-contra-el-censo-en-el-cusco.

Casevitz, France-Marie. 1972. "Les Matsiguenga." *Journal de la Société des Américanistes* 61:215–53.

Castro Arenas, Mario. 1973. *La rebelión de Juan Santos*. Lima: Editorial Milla Bartres.

Cepek, Michael L. 2018. *Life in Oil: Cofán Survival in the Petroleum Fields of Amazonia*. Austin: University of Texas Press.

Cerrón-Palomino, Rodolfo. 1975. "La 'motosidad' y sus implicancias en la enseñanza de castellano." In *Aportes para la enseñanza del lenguaje*, edited by Martín Quintana Chaupín and Danilo Sánchez Lihón, 125–65. Lima: Retablo de Papel.

Cerrón-Palomino, Rodolfo. 1987. *Lingüística quechua*. Cuzco: Centro de Estudios Rurales Andinos Bartolomé de las Casas.

Cerrón-Palomino, Rodolfo. 2000. *Lingüística aimara*. Cuzco: Centro de Estudios Regionales Andinos Bartolomé de Las Casas.

Chirif, Alberto, and Pedro García Hierro. 2007. *Marcando territorio: Progresos y limitaciones de la titulación de territorios indígenas en la Amazonía*. Copenhagen: IWGIA.

Cobo, Bernabé. (1653) 1890. *Historia del Nuevo Mundo*. Sevilla: Imp. de E. Rasco.

Collins, Jane L. 1984. "The Maintenance of Peasant Coffee Production in a Peruvian Valley." *American Ethnologist* 11 (3): 413–38.

Collins, Jane L. 1985. "Migration and the Life Cycle of Households in Southern Peru." *Urban Anthropology and Studies of Cultural Systems and World Economic Development* 14 (4): 279–99.

Comunidad Nativa de Yoquiri. 1990. *Estatuto de la Comunidad Nativa de Yoquiri*. Archived in the community of Yokiri, La Convención, Peru.

Cook, Noble David. 1981. *Demographic Collapse: Indian Peru, 1520–1620*. Cambridge, UK: Cambridge University Press.

Corella, Alfons, Francesc Bert, Alejandro Pérez-Pérez, Manel Gené, and Daniel Turbón. 2007. "Mitochondrial DNA Diversity of the Amerindian Populations Living in the Andean Piedmont of Bolivia: Chimane, Moseten, Aymara and Quechua." *Annals of Human Biology* 34 (1): 34–55.

Courtwright, David T. 1998. *Violent Land: Single Men and Social Disorder from the Frontier to the Inner City*. Cambridge, Mass.: Harvard University Press.

Covey, R. Alan. 2006. *How the Incas Built Their Heartland: State Formation and the Innovation of Imperial Strategies in the Sacred Valley, Peru*. History, Languages, and Cultures of the Spanish and Portuguese Worlds. Ann Arbor: University of Michigan Press.

Covey, R. Alan, and Donato Amado González. 2008. *Imperial Transformations in Sixteenth-Century Yucay, Peru*. Memoirs of the Museum of Anthropology, vol. 44. Ann Arbor: University of Michigan.

Craig, Wesley W., Jr. 1969. "Peru: The Peasant Movement of La Convención." In *Latin American Peasant Movements*, edited by Henry A. Landsberger, 274–96. Ithaca: Cornell University Press.

Crivello, Gina. 2011. "'Becoming Somebody': Youth Transitions Through Education and Migration in Peru." *Journal of Youth Studies* 14 (4): 395–411.

Cusihuamán Gutiérrez, Antonio. 1976a. *Diccionario quechua: Cuzco-Collao*. 1st ed. Lima: Ministerio de Educación.

Cusihuamán Gutiérrez, Antonio. 1976b. *Gramática quechua: Cuzco-Collao*. Lima: Instituto de Estudios Peruanos.

Decoster, Jean-Jacques, and Margareth Najarro. 2016. "De Tumibamba a Vilcabamba: Los canaris y su ensayo de proyecto colonial." In *Vilcabamba: Entre arqueología, historia y mito*, edited by Jean-Jacques Decoster and Mariusz Ziólkowski, 88–101. Cusco: CBC, U. Varsovia y Centro Tinku.

de la Cadena, Marisol. 2000. *Indigenous Mestizos: The Politics of Race and Culture in Cuzco, Peru, 1919–1991*. Durham, N.C.: Duke University Press.

de la Cadena, Marisol. 2005. "Are Mestizos Hybrids? The Conceptual Politics of Andean Identities." *Journal of Latin American Studies* 37 (2): 259–84.

de la Cadena, Marisol. 2010. "Indigenous Cosmopolitics in the Andes: Conceptual Reflections Beyond 'Politics.'" *Cultural Anthropology* 25 (2): 334–70.

de la Cadena, Marisol. 2015. *Earth Beings*. Durham, N.C.: Duke University Press.

Deloria, Philip Joseph. 2004. *Indians in Unexpected Places*. Lawrence: University Press of Kansas.

Denevan, William M. 1992. *The Native Population of the Americas in 1492*. Madison: University of Wisconsin Press.

de Ocampo, Baltasar. (1610) 1907. *Account of the Province of Vilcapampa and a Narrative of the Execution of the Inca Tupac Amaru*. Translated by Clements Markham. Cambridge: Hakluyt Society.

de Pedro Ricoy, Raquel, Rosaleen Howard, and Luis Andrade Ciudad. 2018. "Walking the Tightrope." *Target* 30 (2): 187–211.

de Quevedo, Cristobal. 1900. "'Exploracion de los indios antis del Cuzco, 1715." *Revista de Archivos y Bibliotecas Nacionales* 4:479–99.

Descola, Philippe. 1994. *In the Society of Nature: A Native Ecology in Amazonia*. Cambridge, UK: Cambridge University Press.

Díaz Martínez, Antonio. 1969. *Ayacucho: Hambre y esperanza*. Ayacucho: Ediciones Guamán Poma.

Di Corcia, Tullia, Cesar Sanchez Mellado, J. Taylor Dávila Francia, Gianmarco Ferri, Stefania Sarno, Donata Luiselli, and Olga Rickards. 2017. "East of the Andes: The Genetic Profile of the Peruvian Amazon Populations." *American Journal of Physical Anthropology* 163 (2): 328–38.

Dillehay, Tom D., Carlos Ocampo, José Saavedra, Andre Oliveira Sawakuchi, Rodrigo M. Vega, Mario Pino, Michael B. Collins, et al. 2015. "New Archaeological Evidence for an Early Human Presence at Monte Verde, Chile." *PLOS ONE* 10 (11): e0141923.

Dudley, Meredith. 2011. "Ethnogenesis at the Interface of the Andes and the Amazon: Re-examining Ethnicity in the Piedmont Region of Apolobamba, Bolivia." In *Ethnicity in Ancient Amazonia: Reconstructing Past Identities from Archaeology, Linguistics, and Ethnohistory*, edited by Alf Hornborg and Jonathan D. Hill, 297–319. Boulder: University Press of Colorado.

Eckert, Penelope, and Sally McConnell-Ginet. 1992. "Think Practically and Look Locally: Language and Gender as Community-Based Practice." *Annual Review of Anthropology* 21:461–90.

Emlen, Nicholas Q. 2015. "Public Discourse and Community Formation in a Trilingual Matsigenka-Quechua-Spanish Frontier Community of Southern Peru." *Language in Society* 44 (5): 679–703.

Emlen, Nicholas Q. 2017a. "Multilingualism in the Andes and Amazonia: A View from In-Between." *Journal of Latin American and Caribbean Anthropology* 22 (3): 556–77.

Emlen, Nicholas Q. 2017b. "Perspectives on the Quechua-Aymara Contact Relationship and the Lexicon and Phonology of Pre-Proto-Aymara." *International Journal of American Linguistics* 83 (2): 307–40.

Emlen, Nicholas Q. 2019. "The Poetics of Recapitulative Linkage in Matsigenka and Mixed Matsigenka-Spanish Myth Narrations." In *Bridging Constructions*, edited by Valérie Guérin, 45–77. Berlin: Language Science Press.

Emlen, Nicholas Q. Forthcoming. "The Many Spanishes of an Andean-Amazonian Crossroads." In *Amazonian Spanish: Language Contact and Evolution*, edited by Stephen Fafulas. Amsterdam: John Benjamins.

Emlen, Nicholas Q., and Willem F. H. Adelaar. 2017. "Proto-Quechua and Proto-Aymara Agropastoral Terms: Reconstruction and Contact Patterns." In *Language Dispersal Beyond Farming*, edited by Martine Robbeets and Alexander Savelyev, 25–45. Amsterdam: John Benjamins.

Emlen, Nicholas Q., and Johannes Dellert. Forthcoming. "On the Polymorphemic Genesis of Some Proto-Quechua Roots." *Diachronica*.

Encinas Martín, Alfredo, Ángel Perez Casado, and Rafael Alonso Ordieres. 2008. *Historia de la provincia de La Convención, tomo II: Historia social y religiosa del siglo XX*. Lima: Centro Cultural José Pío Aza.

Ennis, Georgia. 2019. "Multimodal Chronotopes: Embodying Ancestral Time on Quichua Morning Radio." *Signs and Society* 7 (1): 6–37.

Epps, Patience, and Lev Michael. 2017. "The Areal Linguistics of Amazonia." In *The Cambridge Handbook of Areal Linguistics*, edited by Raymond Hickey, 934–63. Cambridge, UK: Cambridge University Press.

Errington, J. Joseph. 2000. "Indonesian('s) Authority." In *Regimes of Language*, edited by Paul V. Kroskrity, 205–27. Santa Fe: School of American Research Press.

Espinoza Soriano, Waldemar. 1977. "Los cuatro suyos del Cusco: Siglos XV y XVI." *Boletín del Instituto Francés de Estudios Andinos* 6 (3–4): 109–22.

FAO (Food and Agriculture Organization of the United Nations). 2015. *FAO Statistical Pocketbook: Coffee 2015*. Rome: Food and Agriculture Organization of the United Nations.

Faudree, Paja. 2013. *Singing for the Dead: The Politics of Indigenous Revival in Mexico*. Durham, N.C.: Duke University Press.

Fernández Moro, Fray Wenceslao. 1934. "Excursión misionera al valle de Lacco." *Misiones Dominicanas del Perú* 81:67–76.

Ferrero, Andrés. 1966. *Los machiguengas: Tribu selvática del sur-oriente peruano*. Puerto Maldonado, Peru: Instituto de Estudios Tropicales Pío Aza.

Fioravanti, Eduardo. 1974. *Latifundio y sindicalismo agrario en el Perú: El caso de los valles de la Convención y Lares (1958–1964)*. Lima: IEP.

Fioravanti-Molinié, Antoinette. 1975. "Contribution à l'étude des sociétés étagées des Andes: La vallée de Yucay (Pérou)." *Études rurales* 57:35–59.

Fonseca Santa Cruz, Javier, and Brian S. Bauer. 2013. "Dating the Wari Remains at Espíritu Pampa (Vilcabamba, Cusco)." *Andean Past* 11 (1): 12.

Fraser, Nancy. 1990. "Rethinking the Public Sphere: A Contribution to the Critique of Actually Existing Democracy." *Social Text*, no. 25/26, 56–80.

French, Brigittine M. 2000. "The Symbolic Capital of Social Identities: The Genre of Bargaining in an Urban Guatemalan Market." *Journal of Linguistic Anthropology* 10 (2): 155–89.

French, Brigittine M. 2010. *Maya Ethnolinguistic Identity: Violence, Cultural Rights, and Modernity in Highland Guatemala*. Tucson: University of Arizona Press.

Gabai, Rafael Varón. 1997. *Francisco Pizarro and His Brothers: The Illusion of Power in Sixteenth-Century Peru*. Norman: University of Oklahoma Press.

Gade, Daniel W. 1972. "Comercio y colonización en la zona de contacto entre la sierra y las tierras bajas del valle del Urubamba en el Perú." *Actas y memorias del XXXIX Congreso Internacional de Americanistas*, vol. 4, 207–21. Lima: Instituto de Estudios Peruanos.

Gade, Daniel W. 1975. *Plants, Man and the Land in the Vilcanota Valley of Peru*. The Hague: W. Junk.

Gade, Daniel W. 1979. "Inca and Colonial Settlement, Coca Cultivation and Endemic Disease in the Tropical Forest." *Journal of Historical Geography* 5 (3): 263–79.

Gade, Daniel W. 2016. *Spell of the Urubamba: Anthropogeographical Essays on an Andean Valley in Space and Time*. New York: Springer.

Gal, Susan. 2001. "Linguistic Theories and National Images in Nineteenth-Century Hungary." In *Languages and Publics: The Making of Authority*, edited by Susan Gal and Kathryn A. Woolard, 30–45. Manchester, UK: St. Jerome Publishing.

Gal, Susan. 2002. "A Semiotics of the Public/Private Distinction." *Differences* 13 (1): 77–95.

Gal, Susan. 2005. "Language Ideologies Compared: Metaphors of Public/Private." *Journal of Linguistic Anthropology* 15:23–37.

Gal, Susan, and Kathryn A. Woolard. 2001. "Constructing Languages and Publics: Authority and Representation." In *Languages and Publics: The Making of Authority*, edited by Susan Gal and Kathryn A. Woolard, 1–12. Manchester, UK: St. Jerome Publishing.

García Hierro, Pedro, Søren Hvalkof, and Andrew Gray, eds. 1998. *Liberation Through Land Rights in the Peruvian Amazon*. Copenhagen: IWGIA.

Goffman, Erving. 1964. "The Neglected Situation." *American Anthropologist* 66 (6, part 2): 133–36.

Goffman, Erving. 1979. "Footing." *Semiotica* 25 (1–2): 1–29.

Goffman, Erving. 1983. "The Interaction Order: American Sociological Association, 1982 Presidential Address." *American Sociological Review* 48 (1): 1–17.

Goldstein, Ruth. 2014. "Consent and Its Discontents: On the Traffic in Words and Women." *Latin American Policy* 5 (2): 236–50.

Goldstein, Ruth. 2015. "The Triangular Traffic in Women, Plants, and Gold: Along the Interoceanic Road in Brazil, Peru, and Bolivia." PhD dissertation, University of California, Berkeley.

González Holguín, Diego. 1608. *Vocabulario de la lengua general de todo el Perú llamada lengua qquichua o del Inca*. Lima: Francisco del Canto.

Gow, Peter. 1991. *Of Mixed Blood: Kinship and History in Peruvian Amazonia*. Oxford: Clarendon Press.

Gray, Andrew. 1998. "Demarcating Development: Titling Indigenous Territories in Peru." In *Liberation Through Land Rights in the Peruvian Amazon*, edited by Pedro García Hierro, Søren Hvalkof, and Andrew Gray, 163–215. Copenhagen: IWGIA.

Greene, Shane. 2007. "Entre lo Indio, lo Negro, y lo Incaico: The Spatial Hierarchies of Difference in Multicultural Peru." *The Journal of Latin American and Caribbean Anthropology* 12 (2): 441–74.

Greene, Shane. 2009. *Customizing Indigeneity: Paths to a Visionary Politics in Peru*. Stanford: Stanford University Press.

Grillo Arbulú, María Teresa, and Tucker Sharon. 2012. "Peru's Amazonian Imaginary: Marginality, Territory and National Integration." In *Environment and Citizenship in Latin America: Natures, Subjects and Struggles*, edited by Alex Latta and Hannah Wittman, 112–28. New York: Berghahn Books.

Guaman Poma de Ayala, Felipe. 1615/1616. *Nueva corónica y buen gobierno*. GKS 2232 4°, Det Kongelige Bibliotek, Copenhagen. Facsimile available at http://www.kb.dk/permalink/2006/poma/info/en/frontpage.htm.

Gumperz, John Joseph. 1968. "The Speech Community." In *International Encyclopedia of the Social Sciences*, vol. 9, edited by D. L. Sills, 381–86. New York: Macmillan and Free Press.

Gumperz, John Joseph. 1982. *Discourse Strategies*. Cambridge, UK: Cambridge University Press.

Gumperz, John Joseph, and Robert Wilson. 1971. "Convergence and Creolization: A Case from the Indo-Aryan/Dravidian Border in India." In *Pidginization and Creolization of Languages*, edited by Dell H. Hymes, 151–67. Cambridge, UK: Cambridge University Press.

Haas, Randall, Ioana C. Stefanescu, Alexander Garcia-Putnam, Mark S. Aldenderfer, Mark T. Clementz, Melissa S. Murphy, Carlos Viviano Llave, and James T. Watson. 2017. "Humans Permanently Occupied the Andean Highlands by at Least 7 Ka." *Royal Society Open Science* 4 (6): 170331.

Habermas, Jürgen. 1989. *The Structural Transformation of the Public Sphere: An Inquiry into a Category of Bourgeois Society*. Cambridge, Mass.: MIT Press.

Hansen, Matthew C., Peter V. Potapov, Rebecca Moore, Matthew Hancher, Svetlana Turubanova, Alexandra Tyukavina, David Thau, et al. 2013. "High-Resolution Global Maps of 21st-Century Forest Cover Change." *Science* 342 (6160): 850–53.

Harris, Olivia. 1978. "Kinship and the Vertical Economy of the Laymi Ayllu, Norte de Potosí." In *Actes du XLII Congrès International des Américanistes*, vol. 4, 165–77. Paris: Société des Américanistes.

Harvey, Penelope M. 1991. "Drunken Speech and the Construction of Meaning: Bilingual Competence in the Southern Peruvian Andes." *Language in Society* 20 (1): 1–36.

Hassel, Georg M. von. 1907. *Últimas exploraciones ordenadas por la junta de vías fluviales a los ríos Ucayali, Madre de Diós, Paucartambo y Urubamba*. Lima: La Opinión Nacional.

Heggarty, Paul, and David Beresford-Jones. 2010. "Agriculture and Language Dispersals: Limitations, Refinements, and an Andean Exception?" *Current Anthropology* 51 (2): 163–91.

Heggarty, Paul, and David G. Beresford-Jones. 2012. *Archaeology and Language in the Andes*. Oxford: Oxford University Press.

Heller, Monica, and Bonnie McElhinny. 2017. *Language, Capitalism, Colonialism: Toward a Critical History*. Toronto: University of Toronto Press.

Hemming, John. 1970. *The Conquest of the Incas*. New York: Harcourt.

Henrich, Joseph. 2000. "Does Culture Matter in Economic Behavior? Ultimatum Game Bargaining Among the Machiguenga of the Peruvian Amazon." *The American Economic Review* 90 (4): 973–79.

Hill, David. 2014. "Search for Inca 'Lost City' in Amazon May Endanger Indigenous People." *The Guardian*, April 7, 2014. https://www.theguardian.com/science/2014/apr/07/search-inca-lost-city-amazon-peru-paititi.

Hill, David. 2016. "Pioneer Gas Project in Latin America Fails Indigenous Peoples." *The Guardian*, June 3, 2016. https://www.theguardian.com/environment/andes-to-the-amazon/2016/jun/02/pioneer-gas-latin-america-indigenous-peoples.

Hill, Jane H. 1995. "The Voices of Don Gabriel." In *The Dialogic Emergence of Culture*, edited by Dennis Tedlock and Bruce Mannheim, 97–147. Urbana: University of Illinois Press.

Hill, Jane H. 2001. "Mock Spanish, Covert Racism, and the (Leaky) Boundary Between Public and Private Spheres." In *Languages and Publics: The Making of Authority*, edited by Susan Gal and Kathryn A. Woolard, 83–102. Manchester: St. Jerome Publishing.

Hirsch, Eric. 2018. "Remapping the Vertical Archipelago: Mobility, Migration, and the Everyday Labor of Andean Development." *The Journal of Latin American and Caribbean Anthropology* 23:189–208.

Hobsbawm, E. J. E. 1969. "A Case of Neo-Feudalism: La Convención, Peru." *Journal of Latin American Studies* 1 (1): 31–50.

Hoelle, Jeffrey. 2015. *Rainforest Cowboys: The Rise of Ranching and Cattle Culture in Western Amazonia.* Austin: University of Texas Press.

Hornborg, Alf, and Jonathan D. Hill. 2011. *Ethnicity in Ancient Amazonia: Reconstructing Past Identities from Archaeology, Linguistics, and Ethnohistory.* Boulder: University Press of Colorado.

Huayhua, Margarita. 2013. "Racism and Social Interaction in a Southern Peruvian Combi." *Ethnic and Racial Studies* 37 (13): 2399–417.

Hvalkof, Søren, and Hanne Veber. 2005. "Ashéninka del Gran Pajonal." In *Guía etnográfica de la Alta Amazonía*, vol. 5, edited by Fernando Santos and Federica Barclay, 75–279. Lima: Institut Français d'Études Andines, Smithsonian Tropical Research Institute.

Hymes, Dell H. 1968. "Linguistic Problems in Defining the Concept of 'Tribe.'" In *Essays on the Problem of Tribe*, edited by June Helm, 23–48. Seattle: University of Washington Press.

Hymes, Dell H. 1972. "On Communicative Competence." In *Sociolinguistics: Selected Readings*, edited by John Pride and Janet Holmes, 269–93. Harmondsworth: Penguin.

INEI (Instituto Nacional de Estadística e Informática). 1940. *Censo Nacional 1940: V Censo de Población.* Lima: INEI.

INEI (Instituto Nacional de Estadística e Informática). 1961. *Censos Nacionales 1961: VI Censo de Población y I de Vivienda.* Lima: INEI.

INEI (Instituto Nacional de Estadística e Informática). 1972. *Censos Nacionales 1972: VII Censo de Población y II de Vivienda.* Lima: INEI.

INEI (Instituto Nacional de Estadística e Informática). 1981. *Censos Nacionales 1981: VIII Censo de Población y III de Vivienda.* http://censos.inei.gob.pe/censos1981/redatam/.

INEI (Instituto Nacional de Estadística e Informática). 1993. *Censos Nacionales 1993: IX Censo de Población y IV de Vivienda.* http://censos.inei.gob.pe/censos1993/redatam/.

INEI (Instituto Nacional de Estadística e Informática). 2007. *Censos Nacionales 2007: XI Censo de Población y VI de Vivienda.* http://censos.inei.gob.pe/Censos2007/redatam/.

International Coffee Organization. 2015. *Coffee in China.* London: ICO. http://www.ico.org/documents/cy2014–15/icc-115–7e-study-china.pdf.

International Coffee Organization. 2018. "Total Exports by All Exporting Countries." International Coffee Organization (website). http://www.ico.org/historical/1990%20onwards/PDF/1e-exports.pdf.

IPBES (Intergovernmental Science-Policy Platform on Biodiversity and Ecosystem Services). 2019. *Global Assessment Report on Biodiversity and Ecosystem Services.* Bonn, Germany: IPBES.

Irvine, Judith T. 1989. "When Talk Isn't Cheap: Language and Political Economy." *American Ethnologist* 16 (2): 248–67.

Irvine, Judith T. 2006. "Speech and Language Community." In *Encyclopedia of Language and Linguistics*, edited by Keith Brown, 689–98. Oxford: Elsevier.

Irvine, Judith T., and Susan Gal. 2000. "Language Ideology and Linguistic Differentiation." In *Regimes of Language: Ideologies, Polities, and Identities*, edited by Paul Kroskrity, 35–83. Santa Fe: School of American Research Press.

Isbell, Billie Jean. 1978. *To Defend Ourselves*. Austin: University of Texas Press.

Izaguirre, Bernardino. 1922. *História de las misiones franciscanas y narraciones de los progresos de la geografía en el oriente del Peru*. Vol. 8. Lima: Talleres Tipográficos de la Penitenciaría.

Izquierdo, Carolina, and Allen W. Johnson. 2007. "Desire, Envy and Punishment: A Matsigenka Emotion Schema in Illness Narratives and Folk Stories." *Culture, Medicine and Psychiatry* 31 (4): 419–44.

Jackson, Jean E. 1995. "Culture, Genuine and Spurious: The Politics of Indianness in the Vaupés, Colombia." *American Ethnologist* 22 (1): 3–27.

Johnson, Allen W. 1983. "Machiguenga Gardens." In *Adaptive Responses of Native Amazonians*, edited by R. B. Hames and W. T. Vickers, 29–63. New York: Academic Press.

Johnson, Allen W. 2003. *Families of the Forest: The Matsigenka Indians of the Peruvian Amazon*. Berkeley: University of California Press.

Johnson, Orna. 1978. "Interpersonal Relations and Domestic Authority Among the Machiguenga of the Peruvian Amazon." PhD dissertation, Columbia University.

Julien, Catherine. 2000. "Inca Estates and the Encomienda: Hernando Pizarro's Holdings in Cusco." *Andean Past* 6 (1): 12.

Keane, Webb. 2008. "Market, Materiality and Moral Metalanguage." *Anthropological Theory* 8 (1): 27–42.

Kernaghan, Richard. 2009. *Coca's Gone: Of Might and Right in the Huallaga Post-boom*. Palo Alto: Stanford University Press.

Kharraki, Abdennour. 2001. "Moroccan Sex-Based Linguistic Difference in Bargaining." *Discourse and Society* 12 (5): 615–32.

Killick, Evan. 2007. "Autonomy and Leadership: Political Formations Among the Ashéninka of Peruvian Amazonia." *Ethnos* 72 (4): 461–82.

Killick, Evan. 2008a. "Creating Community: Land Titling, Education, and Settlement Formation Among the Ashéninka of Peruvian Amazonia." *Journal of Latin American and Caribbean Anthropology* 13 (1): 22–47.

Killick, Evan. 2008b. "Godparents and Trading Partners: Social and Economic Relations in Peruvian Amazonia." *Journal of Latin American Studies* 40 (2): 303–28.

Kindberg, Lee. 1980. *Diccionario Ashaninca*. Yarinacocha, Peru: Instituto Lingüístico de Verano.

Klee, Carol A., and Rocío Caravedo. 2006. "Andean Spanish and the Spanish of Lima: Linguistic Variation and Change in a Contact Situation." In *Globalization and Language in the Spanish-Speaking World: Macro and Micro Perspectives*, edited by Clare Mar-Molinero and Miranda Stewart, 94–113. Houndmills, Basingstoke: Springer.

Krasnoukhova, Olga Vladimirovna. 2012. "The Noun Phrase in the Languages of South America." PhD dissertation, Radboud Universiteit.

Kroskrity, Paul V. 1998. "Arizona Tewa Kiva Speech as a Manifestation of a Dominant Language Ideology." In *Language Ideologies: Practice and Theory*, edited by Bambi B. Schieffelin, Kathryn A. Woolard, and Paul V. Kroskrity, 103–22. Oxford: Oxford University Press.

Labov, William. 1966. *The Social Stratification of English in New York City*. Washington, D.C.: Center for Applied Linguistics.

Landes, Joan B. 1998. *Feminism, the Public and the Private*. London: Oxford University Press.

Leinaweaver, Jessaca B. 2008. "Improving Oneself: Young People Getting Ahead in the Peruvian Andes." *Latin American Perspectives* 35 (4): 60–78.

Leinaweaver, Jessaca B. 2010. "Outsourcing Care: How Peruvian Migrants Meet Transnational Family Obligations." *Latin American Perspectives* 37 (5): 67–87.

Leite, Ilka Boaventura. 2000. "Os quilombos no Brasil: Questões conceituais e normativas." *Etnográfica* 4 (2): 333–54.

Le Moine, Genevieve, and J. Scott Raymond. 1987. "Leishmaniasis and Inca Settlement in the Peruvian Jungle." *Journal of Historical Geography* 13 (2): 113–29.

Little, Paul E. 2001. *Amazonia: Territorial Struggles on Perennial Frontiers*. Center Books in Natural History. Baltimore: Johns Hopkins University Press.

Lloyd, Peter. 1980. *The "Young Towns" of Lima: Aspects of Urbanization in Peru*. Cambridge, UK: Cambridge University Press.

Lombardo, Umberto, Katherine Szabo, José M. Capriles, Jan-Hendrik May, Wulf Amelung, Rainer Hutterer, Eva Lehndorff, Anna Plotzki, and Heinz Veit. 2013. "Early and Middle Holocene Hunter-Gatherer Occupations in Western Amazonia: The Hidden Shell Middens." *PLOS ONE* 8 (8): e72746.

Loughlin, Nicholas J. D., William D. Gosling, Patricia Mothes, and Encarni Montoya. 2018. "Ecological Consequences of Post-Columbian Indigenous Depopulation in the Andean-Amazonian Corridor." *Nature Ecology & Evolution* 2 (8): 1233–36.

Lyon, Patricia J. 1981. "An Imaginary Frontier: Prehistoric Highland-Lowland Interchange in the Southern Peruvian Andes." In *Networks of the Past: Regional Interaction in Archaeology; Proceedings of the Twelfth Annual Conference, the Archaeological Association of the University of Calgary*, edited by Peter D. Francis, F. J. Kense, and P. G. Duke, 3–18. Calgary: University of Calgary Archaeological Association.

Lyon, Sarah. 2010. *Coffee and Community: Maya Farmers and Fair-Trade Markets*. Boulder: University Press of Colorado.

Mannheim, Bruce. 1991. *The Language of the Inka Since the European Invasion*. 1st ed. Austin: University of Texas Press.

Mannheim, Bruce. 2018a. "Preliminary Disciplines." *Signs and Society* 6 (1): 111–19.

Mannheim, Bruce. 2018b. "Three Axes of Variability in Quechua: Regional Diversification, Contact with Other Indigenous Languages, and Social Enregisterment." In *The Andean World*, edited by Linda J. Seligmann and Kathleen Fine-Dare, 507–23. Milton Park: Routledge.

Mannheim, Bruce. 2018c. "Xavier Albó's 'The Future of the Oppressed Languages of the Andes' in Retrospect." In *Indigenous Languages, Politics, and Authority in Latin*

America: Historical and Ethnographic Perspectives, edited by Alan Durston and Bruce Mannheim, 207–30. South Bend: Notre Dame Press.

Marcoy, Paul. 1875. *Travels in South America from the Pacific Ocean to the Atlantic Ocean.* Vol. 1. New York: Scribner, Amstrong, & Co.

Maretti, Claudio C., Juan Carlos Riveros, Robert Hofstede, Denise Oliveira, Sandra Charity, Tarsicio Granizo, Cecília Alvarez, Paula Valdujo, and Christian Thompson. 2014. *State of the Amazon: Ecological Representation in Protected Areas and Indigenous Territories.* Brasília and Quito: WWF Living Amazon (Global) Initiative.

Marr, Timothy Gordon. 1998. "The Language Left at Ticlio: Social and Cultural Perspectives on Quechua Loss in Lima, Peru." PhD dissertation, University of Liverpool.

Martínez, Elicerio. 1926. "Misión de Santo Domingo de Chirumbia: Descripción e historia." *Misiones Dominicanas del Perú* 8 (36): 698–709.

Marx, Karl. (1867) 1978. "The Fetishism of Commodities and the Secret Thereof." In *The Marx-Engels Reader*, 2nd edition, edited by Robert C. Tucker, 319–29. New York: W. W. Norton & Company.

Matos Mar, José. 1986. *Taquile en Lima: Siete familias cuentan.* Lima: Instituto de Estudios Peruanos.

Maúrtua, Victor Manuel, ed. 1906. *Juicio de límites entre el Perú y Bolivia.* Vol. 12. Barcelona: Henrich.

Maúrtua, Victor Manuel, ed. 1907. *Juicio de límites entre el Perú y Bolivia: Contestación al alegato de Bolivia.* Buenos Aires: Imp. Europea de M. A. Rosas.

Mayer, Enrique. 2009. *Ugly Stories of the Peruvian Agrarian Reform.* Durham, N.C.: Duke University Press.

McClintock, Cynthia. 1981. *Peasant Cooperatives and Political Change in Peru.* Princeton, N.J.: Princeton University Press.

Menéndez Rúa, Angel. 1948. *Paso a la civilización.* Quillabamba, Perú: Padres Dominicos.

Meseth, Enrique, Liang-Chi Wang, Su-Hwa Chen, Jason C. S. Yu, and Michael Buzinny. 2015. "Reconstructing Agriculture in Vitcos Inca Settlement, Peru." *Irrigation and Drainage* 64 (3): 340–52.

Michael, Lev. 2008. "Nanti Evidential Practice: Language, Knowledge, and Social Action in an Amazonian Society." PhD dissertation, University of Texas, Austin.

Michael, Lev. 2011. "La reconstrucción y clasificación interna de la rama Kampa de la familia Arawak." Paper presented at the Conference on Indigenous Languages of Latin America V (CILLA V), Center for Indigenous Languages of Latin America, University of Texas, Austin, October 6–8, 2011.

Michael, Lev, Will Chang, and Tammy Stark. 2014. "Exploring Phonological Areality in the Circum-Andean Region Using a Naive Bayes Classifier." *Language Dynamics and Change* 4 (1): 27–86.

Mihas, Elena. 2015. "Landscape Terms in Alto Perené Kampa (Arawak) of Peru." *Acta Linguistica Hafniensia* 47 (2): 101–35.

Miller, General. 1836. "Notice of a Journey to the Northward and Also to the Eastward of Cuzco, and Among the Chunchos Indians, in July, 1835." *Journal of the Royal Geographical Society of London* 6:174–86.

MINAGRI (Ministerio de Agricultura y Riego). 2019. "Situación actual del café en el país." Ministerio de Agricultura y Riego (website). Accessed September 5, 2019, http://minagri.gob.pe/portal/485-feria-scaa/10775-el-cafe-peruano.

MINAM (Ministerio del Ambiente). 2013. "Minería ilegal." Press release, October 25, 2013. http://www.minam.gob.pe/prensa/wp-content/uploads/sites/44/2013/12/dialogo-con-la-prensa-2_Minereia_ilegal.pdf.

Morgan, Marcyliena H. 2014. *Speech Communities*. Cambridge, UK: Cambridge University Press.

Mumford, Jeremy. 2012. *Vertical Empire: The General Resettlement of Indians in the Colonial Andes*. Durham, N.C.: Duke University Press.

Murra, John V. 1972. "El control vertical de un máximo de pisos ecológicos en la economía de las sociedades andinas." In *Visita de la provincia de León de Huánuco en 1562, tomo II*, edited by John V. Murra, 429–62. Huánuco, Peru: Universidad Nacional Hermilio Valdizán.

Murra, John V. 1984. "Andean Societies." *Annual Review of Anthropology* 13 (1): 119–41.

Myers, Fred R., and Donald Lawrence Brenneis. 1984. "Introduction: Language and Politics in the Pacific." In *Dangerous Words: Language and Politics in the Pacific*, edited by Donald Lawrence Brenneis and Fred R. Myers, 1–29. New York: New York University Press.

Myers, Sarah. 1973. *Language Shift Among Migrants to Lima, Peru*. Chicago: University of Chicago Press.

Narayanan, Sandhya Krittika. 2018. "Are We One? Quechua-Aymara Contact and the Challenges of Boundary Maintenance in Puno, Peru." *Language & Communication* 62 (part B): 145–55.

Nicolau, Thomás. 1907. "Solicitud del P. Nicolau para que se nombre un maestro de camp á fin de que proteja á los misioneros de las fronteras de Urubamba: Letter dated 19 January, 1801." In *Juicio de límites entre el Perú y Bolivia: Contestación al alegato de Bolivia*, edited by Victor Manuel Maúrtua, 33–36. Buenos Aires: Imp. Europea de M. A. Rosas.

Nobre, Carlos A., Gilvan Sampaio, Laura S. Borma, Juan Carlos Castilla-Rubio, José S. Silva, and Manoel Cardoso. 2016. "Land-Use and Climate Change Risks in the Amazon and the Need of a Novel Sustainable Development Paradigm." *Proceedings of the National Academy of Sciences* 113 (39): 10759–68.

Nuckolls, Janis B. 1996. *Sounds Like Life: Sound-Symbolic Grammar, Performance, and Cognition in Pastaza Quechua*. Oxford Studies in Anthropological Linguistics, vol. 2. New York: Oxford University Press.

Nuckolls, Janis B., Joseph A. Stanley, Elizabeth Nielsen, and Roseanna Hopper. 2016. "The Systematic Stretching and Contracting of Ideophonic Phonology in Pastaza Quichua." *International Journal of American Linguistics* 82 (1): 95–116.

Nugent, Stephen, and Mark Harris. 2004. *Some Other Amazonians: Perspectives on Modern Amazonians*. London: Institute for the Study of the Americas.

Nuñez del Prado, Oscar. 1969. "El hombre y la familia: Su matrimonio y organización social en Q'ero." *Allpanchis* 1:5–27.

Oberem, Udo. 1970. *Los quijos: Historia de la transculturación de un grupo indígena en el oriente ecuatoriano (1538–1956)*. Madrid: Departamento de Antropología y Etnología de América, Universidad de Madrid.

Ødegaard, Cecilie Vindal. 2010. *Mobility, Markets and Indigenous Socialities: Contemporary Migration in the Peruvian Andes*. Surrey: Ashgate Publishing.

Oricaín, Pablo José. (1790) 1906. "Compendio breve de discursos varios sobre diferentes materias y noticias geográficas comprehensivas á este Obispado del Cuzco." In *Juicio de límites entre el Perú y Bolivia*, vol. 11, edited by Victor Manuel Maúrtua, 321–77. Barcelona: Imprenta de Henrich y Comp.

Orlove, Benjamin S. 1993. "Putting Race in Its Place: Order in Colonial and Postcolonial Peruvian Geography." *Social Research* 60 (2): 301–36.

Orr, Winnie W. F. 2007. "The Bargaining Genre: A Study of Retail Encounters in Traditional Chinese Local Markets." *Language in Society* 36 (1): 73.

Ortner, Sherry B. 2016. "Dark Anthropology and its Others: Theory Since the Eighties." *HAU: Journal of Ethnographic Theory* 6 (1): 47–73.

Ovalle-Rivera, Oriana, Peter Läderach, Christian Bunn, Michael Obersteiner, and Götz Schroth. 2015. "Projected Shifts in *Coffea arabica* Suitability Among Major Global Producing Regions Due to Climate Change." *PLOS ONE* 10 (4): e0124155.

Paerregaard, Karsten. 1997. *Linking Separate Worlds: Urban Migrants and Rural Lives in Peru*. Oxford: Berg Publishers.

Parker, Gary J. 1963. "La clasificación genética de los dialectos quechuas." *Revista del Museo Nacional* 32:241–52.

Pärssinen, Martti. 1992. *Tawantinsuyu: The Inca State and Its Political Organization*. Helsinki: Societas Historica Finlandiae.

Payne, David L. 1991. "A Classification of Maipuran (Arawakan) Languages Based on Shared Lexical Retentions." In *Handbook of Amazonian Languages*, vol. 3, edited by D. Derbyshire and G. Pullum, 355–500. Berlin: Mouton de Gruyter.

Pearce, Adrian J., David Beresford-Jones, and Paul Heggarty, eds. Forthcoming. *Rethinking the Andes-Amazonia "Divide": A Cross-Disciplinary Exploration*. Oxford: Oxford University Press.

Peluso, Daniela M. 2015. "Circulating Between Rural and Urban Communities: Multisited Dwellings in Amazonian Frontiers." *The Journal of Latin American and Caribbean Anthropology* 20 (1): 57–79.

Perez, Carlos, Claire Nicklin, Olivier Dangles, Steven Vanek, Stephen Sherwood, Stephan Halloy, Karen Garrett, and Gregory Forbes. 2010. "Climate Change in the High Andes: Implications and Adaptation Strategies for Small-Scale Farmers." *The International Journal of Environmental, Cultural, Economic and Social Sustainability* 6:71–88.

Pérez Silva, Jorge Iván, Jorge Acurio Palma, and Raúl Bendezú Araujo. 2008. *Contra el prejuicio lingüístico de la motosidad: Un estudio de las vocales del castellano andino desde la fonética acústica*. Lima: Pontificia Universidad Católica del Perú, Instituto Riva-Agüero.

Pulgar Vidal, Javier. 1967. *Geografía del Perú: Las ocho regiones naturales del Perú*. Lima: Editorial Universo.

Radcliffe, Sarah A. 1986. "Gender Relations, Peasant Livelihood Strategies and Migration: A Case Study from Cuzco, Peru." *Bulletin of Latin American Research* 5 (2): 29–47.

Radcliffe, Sarah, and Sallie Westwood. 1996. *Remaking the Nation: Identity and Politics in Latin America*. New York: Routledge.

Rademaker, Kurt, Gregory Hodgins, Katherine Moore, Sonia Zarrillo, Christopher Miller, Gordon R. M. Bromley, Peter Leach, David A. Reid, Willy Yépez Álvarez, and Daniel H. Sandweiss. 2014. "Paleoindian Settlement of the High-Altitude Peruvian Andes." *Science* 346 (6208): 466–69.

Raento, Pauliina, and Cameron J. Watson. 2000. "Gernika, Guernica, *Guernica*? Contested Meanings of a Basque Place." *Political Geography* 19 (6): 707–36.

Raymond, J. Scott. 1985. "Quechuas y Chunchos: Ethnic Boundaries in Eastern Peru." In *Status, Structure, and Stratification: Current Archaeological Reconstructions; Proceedings of the Sixteenth Annual Conference*, edited by Marc Thompson, Maria Teresa Garcia and F. J. Kense. Calgary: University of Calgary Archaeological Association.

Regalado de Hurtado, Liliana. 1992. *Religión y evangelización en Vilcabamba 1572–1602*. Lima: Fondo Editorial PUCP.

Reichman, Daniel R. 2018. "Big Coffee in Brazil: Historical Origins and Implications for Anthropological Political Economy." *The Journal of Latin American and Caribbean Anthropology* 23 (2): 241–61.

Renard-Casevitz, France-Marie. 1981. "Las fronteras de las conquistas en el siglo XVI en la montaña meridional del Perú." *Bulletin de l'Institut Français d'Études Andines* 10 (3–4): 113–40.

Renard-Casevitz, France-Marie, and Olivier Dollfus. 1988. "Geografía de algunos mitos y creencias: Espacios simbólicos y realidades geográficas de los machiguenga del Alto-Urubamba." *Amazonía Peruana* 8 (16): 7–40.

Renard-Casevitz, France-Marie, Thierry Saignes, Anne-Christine Taylor. 1988. *Al este de los Andes: Relaciones entre las sociedades amazónicas y andinas entre los siglos XV y XVII, tomo I*. Quito: Ediciones Abya-Yala; Lima: Instituto Francés de Estudios Andinos.

Robbins, Joel. 2013. "Beyond the Suffering Subject: Toward an Anthropology of the Good." *Journal of the Royal Anthropological Institute* 19 (3): 447–62.

Rodríguez Figueroa, Diego. (ca. 1565) 1913. "Narrative of the Route and Journey Made by Diego Rodríguez from the City of Cuzco to the Land of War of Manco Inca." In *The War of Quito and Inca Documents*, edited by Pedro de Cieza de León, translated and edited by Clements R. Markham, 170–99. London: Hakluyt Society.

Rojas Zolezzi, Martha. 1998. "Mujer matsiguenga y percepción del mestizo." *Anthropológica* 16: 87–109.

Rosaldo, Michelle Zimbalist. 1974. "Woman, Culture, and Society: A Theoretical Overview." In *Woman, Culture, and Society*, edited by Michelle Zimbalist Rosaldo and Louise Lamphere, 17–42. Stanford: Stanford University Press.

Rosengren, Dan. 1987. *In the Eyes of the Beholder: Leadership and the Social Construction of Power and Dominance Among the Matsigenka of the Peruvian Amazon*. Göteborg: Göteborg Etnografiska Museum.

Rosengren, Dan. 2000. "The Delicacy of Community: On *Kisagantsi* in Matsigenka Narrative Discourse." In *The Anthropology of Love and Anger: The Aesthetics of Conviviality in Native Amazonia*, edited by Joanna Overing and Alan Passes, 221–34. London: Routledge.

Rosengren, Dan. 2003. "The Collective Self and the Ethnopolitical Movement: 'Rhizomes' and 'Taproots' in the Amazon." *Identities* 10 (2): 221–40.

Rosengren, Dan. 2004. "Los matsigenka." In *Guía etnográfica de la Alta Amazonía*, vol. 4, edited by Fernando Santos-Granero and Frederica Barclay, 1–157. Lima: Smithsonian Tropical Research Institute / IFEA.

Rosengren, Dan. 2006. "Transdimensional Relations: On Human-Spirit Interaction in the Amazon." *Journal of the Royal Anthropological Institute* 12 (4): 803–16.

Rosengren, Dan. 2017. "Marriage Matsigenka Style: Some Critical Reflections on Theories of Marriage Practices." In *The Anthropology of Marriage in Lowland South America: Bending and Breaking the Rules*, edited by Paul Valentine, Stephen Beckerman, and Catherine Alès, 15–35. Gainesville: University of Florida.

Rose-Redwood, Reuben, Derek Alderman, and Maoz Azaryahu. 2010. "Geographies of Toponymic Inscription: New Directions in Critical Place-Name Studies." *Progress in Human Geography* 34 (4): 453–70.

Rostworowski, María. 1963. "Dos manuscritos inéditos con datos sobre Manco II, tierras personales de los incas y mitimaes." *Nueva Corónica* 1:223–39.

RPP Noticias. 2014. "Poblado de Quellouno en situación crítica por desborde de río." RPP Noticias (website). January 2, 2014. https://rpp.pe/peru/actualidad/poblado-de-quellouno-en-situacion-critica-por-desborde-de-rio-noticia-658921.

Saignes, Thierry. 1985. *Historia de un olvido*. Cochabamba, Bolivia: Ediciones CERES.

Sala i Vila, Núria. 1998. "Cusco y su proyección en el oriente amazónico, 1800–1929." In *Fronteras, colonización y mano de obra indígena en la Amazonía Andina (Siglos XIX-XX)*, edited by Pilar García Jordán, 401–535. Lima: Pontificia Universidad Católica del Perú / Universitat de Barcelona.

Samanez Ocampo, José B. 1907. "Exploracion de los ríos Apurimac, Ene, Tambo, Urubamba y Ucayali, 1883–1884." In *Colección de leyes, decretos, resoluciones y otros documentos oficiales referentes al departamento de Loreto*, vol. 11, edited by Carlos Larrabure y Correa, 254–369. Lima: La Opinion Nacional.

Sánchez, Liliana. 2003. *Quechua-Spanish Bilingualism: Interference and Convergence in Functional Categories*. Amsterdam: John Benjamins Publishing Company.

Sánchez Vásquez, Melisa. 2009. "Cambios en los machiguenga del Alto Urubamba-Cusco: Estudio comparativo de la organización social en Koribeni y Matoriato." Bachelor's thesis, Universidad Nacional Federico Villarreal, Lima.

Santos-Granero, Fernando. 1985. "Crónica breve de un etnocidio o génesis del mito del 'gran vacío amazónico.'" *Amazonía Peruana* 6 (11): 9–38.

Santos-Granero, Fernando. 1991. *The Power of Love: The Moral Use of Knowledge Amongst the Amuesha of Central Peru*. London: Athlone Press.

Santos-Granero, Fernando. 1998. "Writing History into the Landscape: Space, Myth, and Ritual in Contemporary Amazonia." *American Ethnologist* 25 (2): 128–48.

Santos-Granero, Fernando. 2002. "Boundaries Are Made to be Crossed: The Magic and Politics of the Long-Lasting Amazonian/Andes Divide." *Identities: Global Studies in Culture and Power* 9:545–69.

Santos-Granero, Fernando. 2004. "Arawakan Sacred Landscapes: Emplaced Myths, Place Rituals, and the Production of Locality in Western Amazonia." In *Kultur, Raum, Landschaft: Zur Bedeutung des Raumes in Zeiten der Globalität*, edited by Ernst Halbmayer and Elke Mader, 93–122. Frankfurt: Brandes & Apsel Verlag.

Sawyer, Suzana. 2004. *Crude Chronicles: Indigenous Politics, Multinational Oil, and Neoliberalism in Ecuador*. Durham, N.C.: Duke University Press.

Schieffelin, Bambi B., Kathryn A. Woolard, and Paul Kroskrity, eds. 1998. *Language Ideologies: Practice and Theory*. Oxford: Oxford University Press.

Schuurman, Frans Johan. 1979. "Colonization Policy and Peasant Economy in the Amazon Basin." *Boletín de Estudios Latinoamericanos y del Caribe* 27:29–41.

Seligmann, Linda J. 1993. "Between Worlds of Exchange: Ethnicity Among Peruvian Market Women." *Cultural Anthropology* 8 (2): 187–213.

Seligmann, Linda J. 1995. *Between Reform and Revolution: Political Struggles in the Peruvian Andes, 1969–1991*. Stanford: Stanford University Press.

Shaver, Harold. 1996. *Diccionario nomatsiguenga-castellano castellano-nomatsiguenga*. Yarinacocha, Peru: Instituto Lingüístico de Verano.

Shepard, Glenn H. 2002. "Primates in Matsigenka Subsistence and World View." In *Primates Face to Face: Conservation Implications of Human-Nonhuman Primate Interconnections*, edited by Agustín Fuentes and Linda D. Wolfe, 101–36. Cambridge, UK: Cambridge University Press.

Shepard, Glenn H. 2012a. "Roadless (and Fishless) in Camisea: Insidious Impacts of a Gas Pipeline in Peru." *Notes from the Ethnoground* (blog), February 16, 2012. http://ethnoground.blogspot.com/2012/02/roadless-and-fishless-in-camisea_16.html.

Shepard, Glenn H. 2012b. "Shipwrecked: The Sorry State of Development in the Lower Urubamba." *Notes from the Ethnoground* (blog), November 26, 2012. http://ethnoground.blogspot.com/2012/11/shipwrecked-sorry-state-of-development.html.

Shepard, Glenn H., and Kirla Oyola. 2017. "Compensation to Native Communities of the Lower Urubamba by the Camisea Consortium: Impacts, Benefits and Failure." Unpublished manuscript, available online at https://www.academia.edu/36453472/Compensation_to_Native_Communities_of_the_Lower_Urubamba_by_the_Camisea_Consortium_Impacts_Benefits_and_Failures.

Shepard, Glenn H., Douglas W. Wu, Manuel Lizarralde, and Mateo Italiano. 2001. "Rain Forest Habitat Classification Among the Matsigenka of the Peruvian Amazon." *Journal of Ethnobiology* 21 (1): 1–38.

Shoemaker, Robin. 1981. *The Peasants of El Dorado: Conflict and Contradiction in a Peruvian Frontier Settlement*. Ithaca, N.Y.: Cornell University Press.

Shulist, Sarah. 2016. "'Graduated Authenticity': Multilingualism, Revitalization, and Identity in the Northwest Amazon." *Language & Communication* 47:112–23.

Shulist, Sarah. 2018. *Transforming Indigeneity: Urbanization and Language Revitalization in the Brazilian Amazon*. Toronto: University of Toronto Press.

Silverstein, Michael. 1979. "Language Structure and Linguistic Ideology." In *The Elements: A Parasession on Linguistic Units and Levels*, edited by Paul Clyne, William F. Hanks, and Carol L. Hofbauer, 193–247. Chicago: Chicago Linguistic Society.

Silverstein, Michael. 1993. "Metapragmatic Discourse and Metapragmatic Function." In *Reflexive Language: Reported Speech and Metapragmatics*, edited by John A. Lucy, 33–58. Cambridge, UK: Cambridge University Press.

Silverstein, Michael. 1998. "Contemporary Transformations of Local Linguistic Communities." *Annual Review of Anthropology* 27:401–26.

Silverstein, Michael. 2003. "Indexical Order and the Dialectics of Sociolinguistic Life." *Language and Communication* 23 (3–4): 193–229.

Silverstein, Michael. 2005. "Axes of Evals: Token Versus Type Interdiscursivity." *Journal of Linguistic Anthropology* 15 (1): 6–22.

Simons, Gary F., and Charles D. Fennig, eds. 2018. *Ethnologue: Languages of the World*. 21st ed. Dallas: SIL International. https://www.ethnologue.com.

Sims-Williams, Patrick. 2006. *Ancient Celtic Place-Names in Europe and Asia Minor*. Oxford, UK: Blackwell.

Skar, Sarah Lund. 1994. *Lives Together—Worlds Apart: Quechua Colonization in Jungle and City*. Oslo: Scandinavian University Press.

Skeldon, Ronald. 1977. "The Evolution of Migration Patterns During Urbanization in Peru." *Geographical Review* 67 (4): 394–411.

Smith, Richard Chase. 2005. "Can David and Goliath Have a Happy Marriage? The Machiguenga People and the Camisea Project in the Peruvian Amazon." In *Communities and Conservation: Histories and Politics of Community-Based Natural Resource Management*, edited by J. Peter Brosius, Ann Lowenhaupt Tsing, and Charles Zerner, 231–55. Walnut Creek, Calif.: Altamira Press.

Snell, Betty A. 2011. *Diccionario matsigenka-castellano*. Lima: Instituto Lingüístico de Verano.

Spitulnik, Debra. 1996. "The Social Circulation of Media Discourse and the Mediation of Communities." *Journal of Linguistic Anthropology* 6 (2): 161–87.

Starbucks Corporation. 2016. "Complete Recap of Starbucks 2016 Annual Meeting of Shareholders." Starbucks Stories and News (website), Starbucks Corporation, March 23, 2016. https://news.starbucks.com/news/starbucks-2016-annual-meeting-of-shareholders.

Steele, Diana. 2015. "Geographies of Difference: Place, Race, and Modernity in Amazonian Migrant Livelihoods in Cusco, Peru." PhD dissertation, Purdue University.

Steele, Diana. 2018. "Higher Education and Urban Migration for Community Resilience: Indigenous Amazonian Youth Promoting Place-Based Livelihoods and Identities in Peru." *Anthropology & Education Quarterly* 49 (1): 89–105.

Steele, Diana, and Laura Zanotti. 2014. "Contested Border Crossings: Territorialities in the Brazilian and Peruvian Amazon." In *Negotiating Territoriality: Spatial Dialogues between State and Tradition*, edited by Allan Charles Dawson, Laura Zanotti, and Ismael Vaccaro, 99–113. New York: Routledge.

Steward, Julian H. 1948. *Handbook of South American Indians*. Vol. 3, *The Andean Civilizations*. Washington, D.C.: Smithsonian Institution.

Steward, Julian H. 1955. *Theory of Culture Change*. Urbana: University of Illinois Press.

Survival International. 2019. "What Brazil's President, Jair Bolsonaro, Has Said About Brazil's Indigenous Peoples." Survival International (website). Accessed September 19, 2019, https://www.survivalinternational.org/articles/3540-Bolsonaro.

Swenson, Jennifer J., Catherine E. Carter, Jean-Christophe Domec, and Cesar I. Delgado. 2011. "Gold Mining in the Peruvian Amazon: Global Prices, Deforestation, and Mercury Imports." *PLOS ONE* 6 (4): e18875.

Taj, Mitra. 2013. "Peru Coffee Growers Clash with Police in Protests." Reuters, August 21, 2013. Accessed March 17, 2014, http://www.reuters.com/article/2013/08/21/us-peru -coffee-protests-idUSBRE97K13A20130821.

Taj, Mitra. 2019. "Coffee Farmers in Peru Abandon Crops to Grow Coca: Group." Reuters, February 25, 2019. https://www.reuters.com/article/us-peru-drugs/coffee -farmers-in-peru-abandon-crops-to-grow-coca-group-idUSKCN1QE2ON.

Tallman, Paula Skye. 2019. "Water Insecurity and Mental Health in the Amazon: Economic and Ecological Drivers of Distress." *Economic Anthropology* 6 (2): 304–16.

Taylor, Anne Christine. 1988. *Al este de los Andes: Relaciones entre las sociedades amazónicas y andinas entre los siglos XV y XVII, tomo II*. Quito: Ediciones Abya-Yala; Lima: Instituto Francés de Estudios Andinos.

Taylor, Anne Christine. 1999. "The Western Margins of Amazonia from the Early Sixteenth Century to the Early Nineteenth Century." In *The Cambridge History of the Native Peoples of the Americas*, vol. 3, *South America*, part 2, edited by Frank Salomon and Stuart B. Schwartz, 188–256. Cambridge, UK: Cambridge University Press.

Taylor, Charles Lewis, and Michael C. Hudson. 1972. *World Handbook of Political and Social Indicators*. New Haven: Yale University Press.

Tennant, Julian. 1958. *Quest for Paititi: A Journey into Unexplored Peru*. London: Max Parrish.

Tessmann, Günter. 1930. *Die Indianer Nordost-Perus*. Hamburg: Friedrichsen, de Gruyter & Co.

Thomson, Hugh. 2010. *The White Rock: An Exploration of the Inca Heartland*. London: Hachette UK.

Tollefson, Jeff. 2011. "The Roadless Warrior." *Nature* 480 (7375): 22–24.

Torero, Alfredo. 1964. "Los dialectos quechuas." *Anales Científicos* 2 (4): 446–78.

Tubbeh, Ramzi M., and Karl S. Zimmerer. 2019. "Unraveling the Ethnoterritorial Fix in the Peruvian Amazon: Indigenous Livelihoods and Resource Management After Communal Land Titling (1980s–2016)." *Journal of Latin American Geography* 18 (2): 33–59.

Tulet, Jean-Christian. 2010. "Peru as a New Major Actor in Latin American Coffee Production." *Latin American Perspectives* 37 (2): 133–41.

UNODC (United Nations Office on Drugs and Crime). 2018. *Perú: Monitoreo de cultivos de coca 2017*. Lima: UNODC Research.

Urban, Matthias. 2019. "Is There a Central Andean Linguistic Area? A View from the Perspective of the 'Minor' Languages." *Journal of Language Contact* 12 (2): 271–304.

Urrutia, Rocío, and Mathias Vuille. 2009. "Climate Change Projections for the Tropical Andes Using a Regional Climate Model: Temperature and Precipitation Simulations for the End of the 21st Century." *Journal of Geophysical Research: Atmospheres* 114 (D2): D02108.

Uzendoski, Michael A. 2004. "The Horizontal Archipelago: The Quijos / Upper Napo Regional System." *Ethnohistory* 51 (2): 317–57.

Vadjunec, Jacqueline M., Marianne Schmink, and Alyson L. Greiner. 2011. "New Amazonian Geographies: Emerging Identities and Landscapes." *Journal of Cultural Geography* 28 (1): 1–20.

Valadeau, Céline, Joaquina Albán Castillo, Michel Sauvain, Augusto Francis Lores, and Geneviève Bourdy. 2010. "The Rainbow Hurts my Skin: Medicinal Concepts and Plants Uses Among the Yanesha (Amuesha), an Amazonian Peruvian Ethnic Group." *Journal of Ethnopharmacology* 127 (1): 175–92.

Valdez y Palacios, J. M. 1971. *Viaje del Cuzco a Belén en el Gran Pará (por los ríos Vilcamayo, Ucayali y Amazonas [1844–1846]).* Lima: Biblioteca Nacional del Perú.

Valqui, Jairo, and Michaela ZieMendorff. 2016. "Vestigios de una lengua originaria en el territorio de la cultura chachapoya." *Letras* 87 (125): 5–32.

van Gijn, Rik. 2014. "The Andean Foothills and Adjacent Amazonian Fringe." In *The Native Languages of South America: Origins, Development, Typology*, edited by Loretta O'Connor and Pieter Muysken, 102–25. Cambridge, UK: Cambridge University Press.

van Gijn, Rik, and Pieter Muysken. Forthcoming. "Highland-Lowland Relations: A Linguistic View." In *Rethinking the Andes-Amazonia "Divide": A Cross-Disciplinary Exploration*, edited by Adrian J. Pearce, David Beresford-Jones, and Paul Heggarty. Oxford, UK: Oxford University Press.

Varese, Stefano. 1968. *La sal de los cerros.* Lima: Universidad Peruana de Ciencias y Tecnología.

Varese, Stefano. 2002. *Salt of the Mountain: Campa Asháninka History and Resistance in the Peruvian Jungle.* Norman: University of Oklahoma Press.

Vargas Pereira, Haroldo, and José Vargas Pereira. 2013. *Matsigenka Texts.* Unpublished manuscript, University of California, Berkeley. http://linguistics.berkeley.edu/~levmichael/pubs/mcb_text_collection_30jun2013_v1.pdf.

Veber, Hanne. 1998. "The Salt of the Montaña: Interpreting Indigenous Activism in the Rain Forest." *Cultural Anthropology* 13 (3): 382–413.

Viveiros de Castro, Eduardo. 1998. "Cosmological Deixis and Amerindian Perspectivism." *The Journal of the Royal Anthropological Institute* 4 (3): 469–88.

Viveiros de Castro, Eduardo. 2004. "Perspectival Anthropology and the Method of Controlled Equivocation." *Tipití: Journal of the Society for the Anthropology of Lowland South America* 2 (1): 3–22.

Wachtel, Nathan. 1977. *The Vision of the Vanquished.* Hassocks: Harvester Press.

Waller, Jim M., M. Bigger, and Rory Hillocks. 2007. *Coffee Pests, Diseases and Their Management.* Cambridge, Mass.: CAB International.

Warner, Michael. 1990. *The Letters of the Republic: Publication and the Public Sphere in Eighteenth-Century America*. Cambridge, Mass.: Harvard University Press.

Warner, Michael. 1992. "The Mass Public and the Mass Subject." In *Habermas and the Public Sphere*, edited by Craig J. Calhoun, 377–401. Cambridge, Mass.: MIT Press.

Warner, Michael. 2005. *Publics and Counterpublics*. New York: Zone Books.

Weinreich, Uriel, William Labov, and Marvin I. Herzog. 1968. "Empirical Foundations for a Theory of Language Change." In *Directions for Historical Linguistics*, edited by Winifred P. Lehmann and Yakov Malkiel, 97–188. Austin: University of Texas Press.

West, Paige. 2012. *From Modern Production to Imagined Primitive: The Social World of Coffee from Papua New Guinea*. Durham, N.C.: Duke University Press.

White, Richard. 1991. *The Middle Ground: Indians, Empires, and Republics in the Great Lakes Region, 1650–1815*. Cambridge, UK: Cambridge University Press.

Whitten, Norman E. 2011. "Ethnogenesis and Interculturality in the 'Forest of Canelos': The Wild and the Tame Revisited." In *Ethnicity in Ancient Amazonia: Reconstructing Past Identities from Archaeology, Linguistics, and Ethnohistory*, edited by Alf Hornborg and Jonathan D. Hill, 321–34. Boulder: University Press of Colorado.

Whitten, Norman E., and Dorothea Scott Whitten. 2008. *Puyo Runa: Imagery and Power in Modern Amazonia*. Urbana: University of Illinois Press.

Wilkinson, Darryl. 2013. "Politics, Infrastructure and Non-human Subjects: The Inka Occupation of the Amaybamba Cloud Forests." PhD dissertation, Columbia University.

Wilkinson, Darryl. 2018. "The Influence of Amazonia on State Formation in the Ancient Andes." *Antiquity* 92 (365): 1362–76.

Wilkinson, Darryl. 2019. "Infrastructure and Inequality: An Archaeology of the Inka Road Through the Amaybamba Cloud Forests." *Journal of Social Archaeology* 19 (1): 27–46.

Wise, Mary Ruth. 1976. "Apuntes sobre la influencia inca entre los amuesha: Factor que oscurece la clasificación de su idioma." *Revista del Museo Nacional* 42:355–66.

Wolf, Eric. 1982. *Europe and the People Without History*. Berkeley: University of California Press.

Woolard, Kathryn A. 1989. "Sentences in the Language Prison: The Rhetorical Structuring of an American Language Policy Debate." *American Ethnologist* 16 (2): 268–78.

Zubieta, Ramón. 1903. Report from the Prefectura de Santo Domingo del Urubamba. *Anales de la propagación de la fé en el oriente del Perú* 3 (3): 133–47.

Zubieta, Ramón. 1905. Report from the Prefectura de Santo Domingo del Urubamba. *Anales de la obra de la propagación de la fé en el oriente del Perú* 4 (1): 44–52.

Zuidema, R. Tom, and Deborah Poole. 1982. "Los límites de los cuatro suyus incaicos en el Cuzco." *Boletín del Institut Français d'Études Andines* 11 (1–2): 83–89.

Index

About the Author

Nicholas Q. Emlen is a postdoctoral researcher at the DFG Center for Advanced Studies "Words, Bones, Genes, Tools," University of Tübingen, and at Leiden University Centre for Linguistics.